Published for
OXFORD INTERNATIONAL
AQA EXAMINATIONS

T0352827

International GCSE
PHYSICS

Revision Guide

Helen Reynolds

Alom Shaha

Editor: Primrose Kitten

Elizabeth McCullough

OXFORD
UNIVERSITY PRESS

Contents 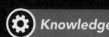 Knowledge Retrieval 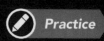 Practice

 Shade in each level of the circle as you feel more confident and ready for your exam.

How to use this book — iv

P1 Forces and interactions — 2
- Knowledge
- Retrieval
- Practice

P2 Forces and motion — 14
- Knowledge
- Retrieval
- Practice

P3 Momentum and safety — 26
- Knowledge
- Retrieval
- Practice

P4 Terminal velocity and moments — 38
- Knowledge
- Retrieval
- Practice

P5 Forces and energy — 48
- Knowledge
- Retrieval
- Practice

P6 Energy resources — 60
- Knowledge
- Retrieval
- Practice

P7 General properties of waves — 70
- Knowledge
- Retrieval
- Practice

P8 Electromagnetic waves — 80
- Knowledge
- Retrieval
- Practice

P9 Sound and ultrasound — 92
- Knowledge
- Retrieval
- Practice

P10 Reflection and refraction of light — 104
- Knowledge
- Retrieval
- Practice

P11 Lenses and the eye   **116**

⚙ *Knowledge*

⇄ *Retrieval*

✎ *Practice*

P12 Kinetic theory and energy transfer   **128**

⚙ *Knowledge*

⇄ *Retrieval*

✎ *Practice*

P13 Electric circuits   **140**

⚙ *Knowledge*

⇄ *Retrieval*

✎ *Practice*

P14 Magnetism and electromagnetism   **154**

⚙ *Knowledge*

⇄ *Retrieval*

✎ *Practice*

P15 Electricity   **166**

⚙ *Knowledge*

⇄ *Retrieval*

✎ *Practice*

P16 Household electricity and motors   **178**

⚙ *Knowledge*

⇄ *Retrieval*

✎ *Practice*

P17 Atomic structure   **190**

⚙ *Knowledge*

⇄ *Retrieval*

✎ *Practice*

P18 Nuclear physics   **202**

⚙ *Knowledge*

⇄ *Retrieval*

✎ *Practice*

P19 Space   **214**

⚙ *Knowledge*

⇄ *Retrieval*

✎ *Practice*

Physics equations   **226**

Answers

All of the **answers** are on the website at
www.oxfordsecondary.com/oxfordaqa-revision

How to use this book

This book uses a three-step approach to revision: **Knowledge**, **Retrieval**, and **Practice**.
It is important that you do all three; they work together to make your revision effective.

1 Knowledge

Knowledge comes first. Each chapter starts with a **Knowledge Organiser**. These are clear, easy-to-understand, concise summaries of the content that you need to know for your exam. The information is organised to show how one idea flows into the next so you can learn how all the science is tied together, rather than lots of disconnected facts.

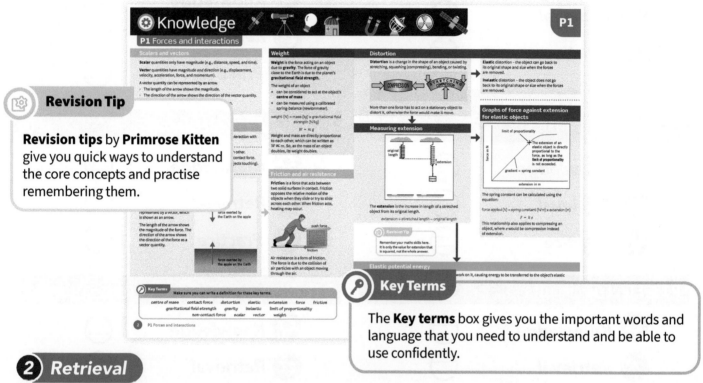

Revision Tip

Revision tips by **Primrose Kitten** give you quick ways to understand the core concepts and practise remembering them.

Key Terms

The **Key terms** box gives you the important words and language that you need to understand and be able to use confidently.

2 Retrieval

The **Retrieval questions** help you learn and quickly recall the information you've acquired. These are short questions and answers about the content in the Knowledge Organiser. Cover up the answers with some paper; write down as many answers as you can from memory. Check back to the Knowledge Organiser for any you got wrong, then cover the answers and attempt *all* the questions again until you can answer all the questions correctly.

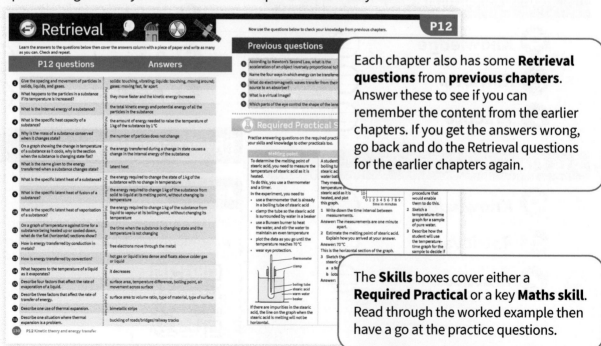

Each chapter also has some **Retrieval questions** from **previous chapters**. Answer these to see if you can remember the content from the earlier chapters. If you get the answers wrong, go back and do the Retrieval questions for the earlier chapters again.

The **Skills** boxes cover either a **Required Practical** or a key **Maths skill**. Read through the worked example then have a go at the practice questions.

Make sure you revisit the Retrieval questions on different days to help them stick in your memory. You need to write down the answers each time, or say them out loud, otherwise it won't work.

 Practice

Once you think you know the Knowledge Organiser and Retrieval answers really well, you can move on to the final stage: **Practice**.

Each chapter has lots of **exam-style questions**, including some questions from previous chapters, to help you apply all the knowledge you have learnt and can retrieve.

Each question has a difficulty icon that shows the level of challenge.

 These questions build your confidence.

These questions consolidate your knowledge.

These questions stretch your understanding.

Make sure you attempt all of the questions no matter what grade you are aiming for.

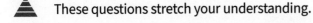

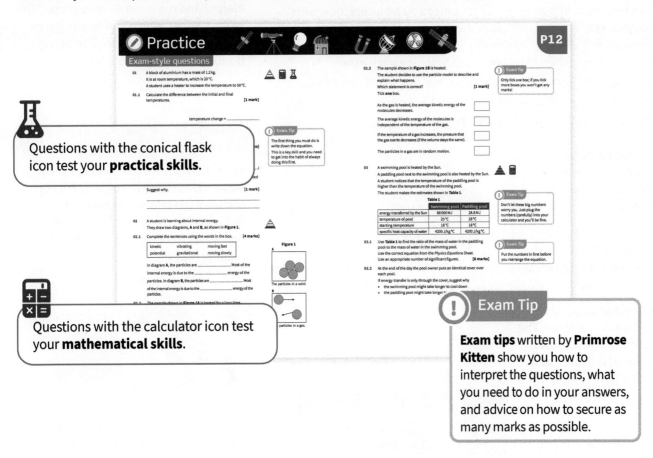

Questions with the conical flask icon test your **practical skills**.

Questions with the calculator icon test your **mathematical skills**.

Exam tips written by **Primrose Kitten** show you how to interpret the questions, what you need to do in your answers, and advice on how to secure as many marks as possible.

⚙ Knowledge

P1 Forces and interactions

Scalars and vectors

Scalar quantities only have magnitude (e.g., distance, speed, and time).

Vector quantities have magnitude *and* direction (e.g., displacement, velocity, acceleration, force, and momentum).

A vector quantity can be represented by an arrow.

- The length of the arrow shows the magnitude.
- The direction of the arrow shows the direction of the vector quantity.

Displacement is the distance travelled in a given direction.

Velocity is speed with a direction.

Forces

A **force** can be a push or pull on an object caused by an interaction with another object. Forces are vector quantities.

Contact forces occur when two objects are touching each other. For example, friction, air resistance, tension, and normal contact force.
Non-contact forces act at a distance (without the two objects touching). For example, gravity, electrostatics, and magnetism.

When an object exerts a force on another object, it will experience an *equal and opposite* force.

This means that forces always occur in pairs. Each force can be represented by a vector, which is shown as an arrow.

The length of the arrow shows the magnitude of the force. The direction of the arrow shows the direction of the force as a vector quantity.

force exerted by the Earth on the apple

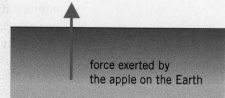
force exerted by the apple on the Earth

Weight

Weight is the force acting on an object due to **gravity**. The force of gravity close to the Earth is due to the planet's **gravitational field strength**.

The weight of an object:

- can be considered to act at the object's **centre of mass**
- can be measured using a calibrated spring-balance (newtonmeter).

weight (N) = mass (kg) × gravitational field strength (N/kg)

$$W = m\,g$$

Weight and mass are directly proportional to each other, which can be written as $W \propto m$. So, as the mass of an object doubles, its weight doubles.

Friction and air resistance

Friction is a force that acts between two solid surfaces in contact. Friction opposes the relative motion of the objects when they slide or try to slide across each other. When friction acts, heating may occur.

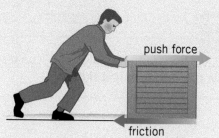
push force

friction

Air resistance is a form of friction. The force is due to the collision of air particles with an object moving through the air.

 **Key Terms**

Make sure you can write a definition for these key terms.

centre of mass   contact force   distortion   elastic   extension   force   friction

gravitational field strength   gravity   inelastic   limit of proportionality

non-contact force   scalar   vector   weight

Distortion

Distortion is a change in the shape of an object caused by stretching, squashing (compressing), bending, or twisting.

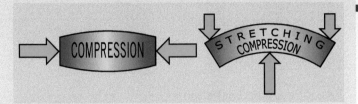

More than one force has to act on a stationary object to distort it, otherwise the force would make it move.

Measuring extension

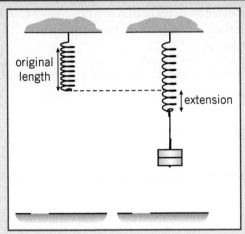

The **extension** is the increase in length of a stretched object from its original length.

extension = stretched length – original length

Revision Tip

Remember your maths skills here. It is only the value for extension that is squared, not the whole answer.

Elastic distortion – the object can go back to its original shape and size when the forces are removed.

Inelastic distortion – the object does not go back to its original shape or size when the forces are removed.

Graphs of force against extension for elastic objects

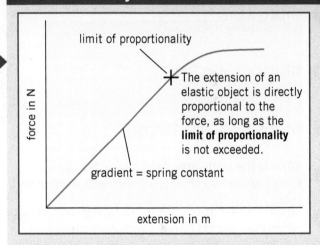

The extension of an elastic object is directly proportional to the force, as long as the **limit of proportionality** is not exceeded.

The spring constant can be calculated using the equation:

force applied (N) = spring constant (N/m) × extension (m)

$$F = k\,e$$

This relationship also applies to compressing an object, where e would be compression instead of extension.

Elastic potential energy

A force that stretches or compresses an object does work on it, causing energy to be transferred to the object's elastic potential energy.

The elastic potential energy in an elastically stretched or compressed spring can be calculated using:

elastic potential energy (J) = $\frac{1}{2}$ × spring constant (N/m) × (extension)^2 (m^2)

$$E_e = \frac{1}{2}\,k\,e^2$$

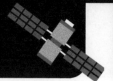
Learn the answers to the questions below then cover the answers column with a piece of paper and write as many as you can. Check and repeat.

P1 questions

Answers

1 What is a scalar quantity?

only has size (magnitude)

2 Name three scalar quantities.

distance, speed, time

3 What is a vector quantity?

has both size and direction

4 Name three vector quantities.

three from: displacement, velocity, acceleration, force, momentum

5 What is a force?

a push or pull that acts on an object due to the interaction with another object

6 What is a contact force?

a force between objects that are physically touching (e.g., friction, air resistance, tension, normal contact force)

7 What is a non-contact force?

a force between objects that are physically separated (e.g., gravitational, electrostatic, magnetic)

8 What is the same about the interaction pair of forces when two objects interact with each other?

the forces are the same size

9 What is different about the interaction pair of forces when two objects interact with each other?

forces are in opposite directions

10 What is the name for the force acting on an object due to gravity?

weight

11 What instrument can be used to measure the weight of an object?

calibrated spring-balance (newtonmeter)

12 What two quantities do you need to calculate the weight of an object?

mass and gravitational field strength

13 What is elastic distortion?

an object can go back to its original shape and size when distorting forces are removed

14 What is inelastic distortion?

an object does not go back to its original shape and size when distorting forces are removed

15 How do you find the spring constant from a force–extension graph of a spring?

find the gradient of the straight-line section

16 On a force–extension graph, where is the limit of proportionality?

where the straight line starts to curve

17 What type of energy is stored in a spring?

elastic potential energy

18 What does the energy stored in a spring depend on?

spring constant and extension

Put paper here

Required Practical Skills

Practise answering questions on the required practicals using the example below. You need to be able to apply your skills and knowledge to other practicals too.

Extension of a spring	Worked example	Practice

Extension of a spring

In this practical you measure the extension of a spring as different forces are applied to it.

To be accurate and precise you need to:

- measure extension using a pointer directed at the same position on the spring each time

- ensure the ruler is positioned so that it is parallel to the spring

- make measurements by looking in a direction perpendicular to the ruler

- convert mass to weight (force), if necessary

- use a measurement of zero force = zero extension

- use the equation
$$\text{gradient} = \frac{1}{\text{spring constant}}$$
for a graph of force against extension.

Worked example

A student records the following measurements for a spring.

Force in N						
Mass in kg	0	0.1	0.2	0.3	0.4	0.5
Length in cm	5.0	9.2	13.1	17.4	21	25
Extension in cm						

1 Calculate the spring extensions and forces.

weight (= force) = mass × gravitational field strength (= 10 N/kg)

extension = length – 5 (original length of spring)

Force in N	0	1	2	3	4	5
Extension in cm	0	4.2	8.1	12.4	16	20

2 Plot a graph of the results. Calculate the spring constant from your graph and give the unit.

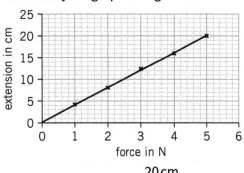

$$\text{gradient} = \frac{20\,\text{cm}}{5\,\text{N}} = 4$$

$$\text{gradient} = \frac{1}{\text{spring constant}}$$

so spring constant $= \dfrac{1}{\text{gradient}} = \dfrac{1}{4} = 0.25\,\text{N/cm or 25 N/m}$

Practice

1 A student measures an extension of 24 mm when they hang a 40 g mass on a spring. Calculate the spring constant in N/m. Show your working.

2 Compare the meaning of the gradient of a graph of force against extension with the meaning of the gradient of a graph of extension against force.

Exam-style questions

01 Force is a vector.

01.1 Select the correct definition of a vector. **[1 mark]**
Tick **one** box.

A vector has magnitude only. ☐

A vector has direction only. ☐

A vector has magnitude and direction. ☐

> **! Exam Tip**
>
> Tick only one box here. Ticking two boxes (or all the boxes) will mean you won't get any marks, even if you pick the correct answer.

01.2 Some forces are contact forces and some are non-contact forces.
Here are some forces.
Circle the non-contact forces. **[2 marks]**

| weight | air resistance | friction | magnetism |

> **! Exam Tip**
>
> Look at the number of marks given here. This is a two mark question so you need to circle two things.

01.3 Name a contact force that is not listed in **01.2**. **[1 mark]**

_____

02 Sometimes people confuse 'weight' and 'mass'.

02.1 Match the words on the left to their descriptions on the right.
You should draw **two** lines for each word. **[4 marks]**

| Mass |

| Weight |

is measured in kilograms.

is a measure of the force of gravity on an object.

is measured in newtons.

is a measure of the amount of material in an object or its reluctance to move when you apply a force.

02.2 Write down the name of the region around the Earth where the force of gravity acts on objects. **[1 mark]**

_____

02.3 Complete the sentences using the words in the box below. You may use each word once, more than once, or not at all. **[4 marks]**

weight	mass	N/kg	N	kg

To calculate the weight of an object, you need to know the

_____ and gravitational field strength.

Gravitational field strength is measured in _____.

The weight of an object can be considered to act at a point, which

we call the centre of _____.

You measure _____ with a newtonmeter.

03 A student investigates the extension of a spring.

03.1 Give the name of the pieces of equipment that they could use to measure force and extension. **[2 marks]**

! Exam Tip

The units for force and extension might give you a clue.

03.2 Describe how they can use this equipment to make the measurements. **[4 marks]**

03.3 Explain why the student should take repeat measurements. **[1 mark]**

03.4 Suggest what the student should do if they see a result that does not fit with the pattern of their other results. **[1 mark]**

! Exam Tip

If you only get one result, how do you know that it is the correct result?

03.5 Describe the type of graph the student should plot.
Give reasons for your answer. **[2 marks]**

04 A student watches a video about forces.
The video shows a piece of wood floating in a tank of water.

04.1 Write down the name of the non-contact force acting on the wood and the name of the contact force acting on the wood. **[2 marks]**

04.2 Write down whether the forces in **04.1** are scalar or vector. **[1 mark]**

04.3 In the video the presenter shows that a piece of wood from an ironwood tree will sink rather than float. The presenter shows this by placing the ironwood on the surface of the water. It moves down through the water until it reaches the bottom of the tank.
Give the name of **one** other force that is acting on the wood as it moves through the water.
Write down whether it is a contact or a non-contact force. **[2 marks]**

! Exam Tip

This question has two parts – make sure you answer both.

05 A student investigates the deflection of a ruler. To do this, they put a ruler between two supports. They tie a piece of string in a loop and hang it in the centre of the ruler. They add weights to the loop, and the centre of the ruler is deflected.

05.1 Suggest a problem the student might find when measuring the deflection of the ruler. **[1 mark]**

05.2 **Table 1** shows the measurements taken by the student.

Table 1

Weight in N	Deflection in mm			Mean deflection in mm
	Repeat 1	Repeat 2	Repeat 3	
0	0	0	0	0
2	3	2	2	2
4	4	5	6	5
6	10	12	17	
8	14	15	15	15
10	17	18	17	17
12	17	18	18	18

Calculate the mean deflection for the weight of 6 N. **[1 mark]**

05.3 Using the axes in **Figure 1**, plot a graph of the data in **Table 1**. Include a line of best fit. **[4 marks]**

Figure 1

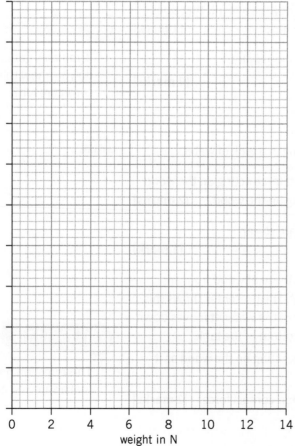

weight in N

05.4 Determine whether the deflection is proportional to the force. Explain your answer. **[2 marks]**

06 A student is investigating material to make a newtonmeter. They collect data on the stretching of a sample of material. The results are shown in **Table 2**.

Table 2

Weight in g	Length in cm			Average length in cm
	Repeat 1	Repeat 2	Repeat 3	
100	3.7	3.5	3.5	3.6
200	4.7	4.8	4.1	4.5
300	5.0	5.4	5.2	5.2
400	6.8	7.1	6.8	6.9
500	8.5	9.0	9.2	8.9

06.1 Describe the error the student has made in the first column in **Table 2**. Suggest how to correct it. **[2 marks]**

Exam Tip

The name of the equipment should give you a clue to the units needed.

06.2 Using the axes in **Figure 2**, plot a graph of weight against average length. Gravitational field strength = 10 N/kg. **[4 marks]**

Exam Tip

The question has given you the value for gravitational field strength. This should give you a clue that you need to do a calculation.

Figure 2

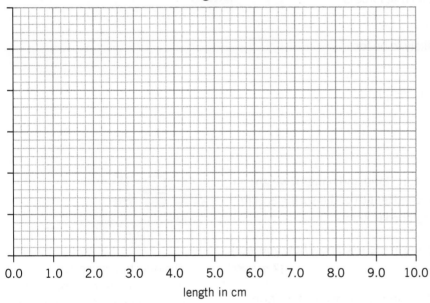

length in cm

06.3 Estimate the original length of the sample. Describe your method. **[2 marks]**

Exam Tip

You'll need to draw on the graph for this!

06.4 Use the shape of the graph to explain how the stiffness of the material changes as the force increases. **[1 mark]**

06.5 The student wants to use the material to make a newtonmeter. Explain why the material would or would not be suitable. **[2 marks]**

07 A student is carrying heavy books in a plastic bag. This has caused the handles of the bag to stretch. Changing the shape of an object by stretching requires two forces. One of these forces is the force of the books on the bag.

07.1 Name the other force involved in stretching the bag. **[1 mark]**

07.2 When the student takes the books out of the bag there is inelastic distortion of the handles. Define 'inelastic distortion'. **[1 mark]**

07.3 The student cuts the plastic bag into sections then applies different forces to the plastic sections and measures the extension. The student then repeats the experiment with a spring. They plot graphs of their data. One of the graphs is a curved line. The other graph is a straight line. **[2 marks]**

Tick the **two** correct statements.

The graph for the plastic bag shows a non-linear relationship between force and extension. ☐

The graph for the plastic bag shows that force is proportional to extension. ☐

A graph that is a straight line is likely to be for a spring. ☐

The material that produced a linear graph has been inelastically distorted. ☐

Exam Tip

Definitions of key words are easy marks in exams – learn them!

Exam Tip

If you tick more than two boxes, you won't get full marks even if you pick both the correct answers.
Only tick **two** statements.

08 A student attaches a spring to a retort stand and hangs a weight on the end of the spring. The unstretched length of the spring is 2 cm. The length of the spring when stretched is 3 cm.

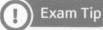

08.1 Calculate the extension of the spring in metres. Show how you work out your answer. **[2 marks]**

08.2 Write down the equation which links force, extension, and spring constant. **[1 mark]**

08.3 The student used a weight of 2 N. Show that the spring constant of the spring is 200 N/m. **[2 marks]**

08.4 Calculate the energy stored in the spring. Use the correct equation from the *Physics Equation Sheet*. **[2 marks]**

08.5 The spring is not distorted inelastically. Write down the work done on the spring. Justify your answer. **[2 marks]**

Exam Tip

The question gives you numbers in centimetres, but the answer wants the number in metres. Be careful with your conversions here.

Exam Tip

'Show' questions are amazing! You can just keep playing with the numbers until you get the correct answer.

09 A student stretched two springs using different forces, and measured the extension. **Figure 3** shows the graph of the results.

Figure 3

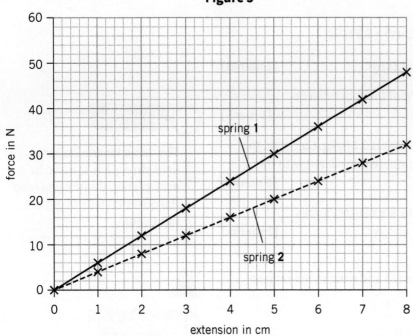

09.1 Show that the force required to stretch spring **1** by 5 cm is 1.5 times bigger than the force required to stretch spring **2** by 5 cm. **[2 marks]**

09.2 The student stretched each spring by pulling on both ends. Suggest the difference between the two springs in terms of their stiffness. Explain your answer. **[2 marks]**

09.3 Write the equation that links the spring constant, the extension, and the force applied to a spring. **[1 mark]**

09.4 Calculate the spring constant for both springs. **[6 marks]**

10 A climber is descending a cliff. For safety, they are attached using a piece of rope.

10.1 Write down the equation that links force, the spring constant, and the extension for a material below its limit of proportionality. **[1 mark]**

10.2 The original length of the rope was 20.00 m. The final length of the rope was 20.14 m. Calculate the extension of the rope. **[1 mark]**

10.3 The climber has a mass of 80 kg. The gravitational field strength is 9.8 N/kg. Calculate the spring constant of the rope. Use an appropriate number of significant figures. **[5 marks]**

10.4 The climber changes the length of the rope to 30 m. A longer rope will have a greater extension. Suggest what happens to the spring constant of the rope.

Explain your answer. **[2 marks]**

> **! Exam Tip**
>
> Draw lines on the graph to help you work out which numbers you need to do the calculations with.

> **! Exam Tip**
>
> You need to do two sets of calculations for **09.4**. Make sure you label them clearly so the examiner knows which number goes with which spring.

> **! Exam Tip**
>
> Significant figures is a measure of resolution.
>
> Your answer can't have a higher resolution than the numbers given in the question, so giving too many significant figures would be inappropriate.

11 Scientists attach scientific instruments to robots, which travel to Mars and land on the planet. Here is some data relating to a robot which is sent to Mars:

- mass of robot = 140 kg
- gravitational field strength on Earth = 9.8 N/kg

11.1 Calculate the weight of the robot on Earth. **[2 marks]**

11.2 Name the point at which the weight of the robot can be considered to act. **[1 mark]**

11.3 The gravitational field strength on Mars is 3.8 N/kg. Calculate the weight of the robot on Mars and compare this weight with the weight of the robot on Earth. **[5 marks]**

11.4 Identify whether gravitational forces are contact forces or non-contact forces. Justify your answer. **[2 marks]**

12 A student takes measurements of mass and weight of a range of different objects.

Table 3 shows their data.

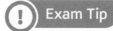
Table 3

Mass	Weight			Mean weight
	Repeat 1	Repeat 2	Repeat 3	
0.3	2.8	3.0	3.3	3.0
1.2	11	12	13	12
1.5	14	15	17	15
2.1	20	21	23	

12.1 Write down one thing that the student forgot to do when they drew the table. **[1 mark]**

12.2 Calculate the missing mean weight in the table. Show your working. Use the correct number of significant figures. **[2 marks]**

The student plots the graph shown in **Figure 4**.

Figure 4

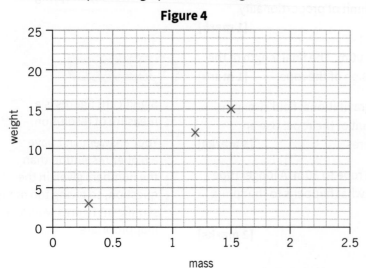

12.3 Complete the graph by adding units to the axes and plotting the final values from the table. **[2 marks]**

12.4 Draw a line of best fit. **[1 mark]**

12.5 Describe the relationship between weight and mass. **[1 mark]**

13 A student stretches three types of material. They add weights to a sample of the material, and measure the extension. **Figure 5** shows the graphs of their data.

Figure 5

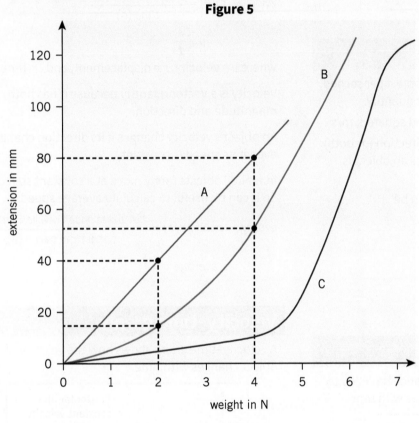

13.1 Use data from the graph to explain why the extension of A is proportional to the force applied. **[2 marks]**

13.2 Suggest what material A might be. **[1 mark]**

13.3 Use data from the graph to explain why the extension of B is *not* proportional to the force applied. **[2 marks]**

13.4 Suggest what material B might be. **[1 mark]**

13.5 Imagine pulling material A, then pulling material C. Use the graphs to describe a difference that you would notice. **[1 mark]**

⚙ Knowledge

P2 Forces and motion

Distance and displacement

Distance is how far an object moves. It is a scalar quantity, so does not have direction.

Displacement is a vector and includes the *distance* and *direction* of a straight line from an object's starting point to its finish point.

Acceleration

Acceleration is the change in velocity of an object per second, or the rate of change of velocity. It is a vector quantity.

The unit of acceleration is metres per second squared, m/s^2.

An object is accelerating if its speed or its direction (or both) are changing. A negative acceleration means an object is slowing down, and is called **deceleration**.

The average acceleration, a, of an object can be calculated using:

$$acceleration \ (m/s^2) = \frac{change\ in\ velocity\ (m/s)}{time\ taken\ (s)}$$

$$a = \frac{\Delta v}{t}$$

Velocity and average speed

The **velocity** of an object is its **speed** in a given direction.

Velocity can be calculated using:

$$velocity \ (m/s) = \frac{displacement\ (m)}{time\ (s)}$$

$$v = \frac{s}{t}$$

where v = velocity, s = displacement, and t = time.

Velocity is a vector quantity because it has both magnitude and direction.

An object's velocity changes if its direction changes, even if its speed is constant.

In reality, objects rarely move at a constant speed. So it can be useful to calculate average speed:

$$average\ speed \ (m/s) = \frac{total\ distance\ travelled\ (m)}{total\ time\ taken\ (s)}$$

$$average \ v = \frac{s}{t}$$

Distance–time graphs

A distance–time graph shows how the distance travelled by an object travelling in a straight line changes with time.

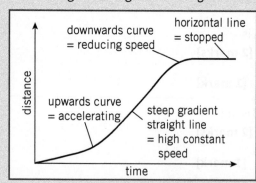

The gradient of the line in a distance–time graph is equal to the object's speed.

If the object is accelerating, the speed at any time can be found by calculating the gradient of a tangent to the curved line at that time.

Velocity–time graphs

A velocity–time graph shows how the velocity of an object changes with time.

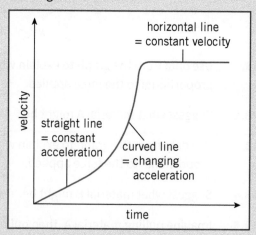

The gradient of the line in a velocity–time graph is equal to the object's acceleration.

The area under the line on a velocity–time graph represents the distance travelled (or displacement).

🔑 Key Terms

Make sure you can write a definition for these key terms.

acceleration	balanced	deceleration	displacement
resultant force	speed	unbalanced	velocity

Equal and opposite forces

Newton's Third Law states that whenever two objects interact with each other, they exert *equal and opposite* forces on each other.

This means that forces always occur in pairs.

The forces in a pair:

- act on separate objects
- are the same size as each other
- act in opposite directions along the same line
- are of the same type, for example, two gravitational forces or two electrostatic forces.

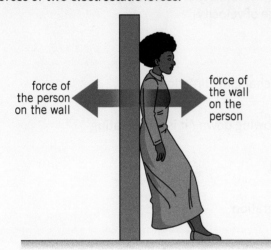

force of the person on the wall

force of the wall on the person

Force, mass, and acceleration

Newton's Second Law says that the acceleration a of an object:

- is proportional to the resultant force on the object

$$a \propto F$$

- is inversely proportional to the mass of the object

$$a \propto \frac{1}{m}$$

This means that $a = \dfrac{F}{m}$. Resultant force, mass, and acceleration are linked by the equation:

resultant force (N) = mass (kg) × acceleration (m/s²)

$$F = ma$$

Resultant forces

Parallel forces

If two or more forces act on an object along the same line, their effect is the same as if they were replaced with a single **resultant force**. The resultant force is:

- the sum of the magnitudes of the forces if they act in the same direction
- the difference between the magnitudes of the forces if they act in opposite directions.

Forces at an angle

If the forces do not act along the same line, the resultant of two forces can be found by making a scale drawing using a ruler and a protractor.

Scale drawings

Scale drawings can be used to find the resultant of two forces which are not acting along the same line.

The forces are drawn end to end. The resultant can then be drawn between the two ends, forming a triangle:

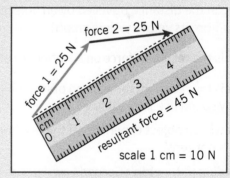

force 2 = 25 N

force 1 = 25 N

resultant force = 45 N

scale 1 cm = 10 N

The effect of resultant forces

If the resultant force on an object is zero, the forces are said to be **balanced**, and:

- a moving object will continue to move at the same velocity
- a stationary object will remain at rest.

This is **Newton's First Law**.

If the resultant force on an object is not zero, the forces are said to be **unbalanced**, and an object will accelerate (change its speed or direction of motion) in the direction of the resultant force.

This is **Newton's Second Law**.

Retrieval

Learn the answers to the questions below then cover the answers column with a piece of paper and write as many as you can. Check and repeat.

	P2 questions	Answers
1	What is the difference between distance and displacement?	distance is a scalar quantity and only has magnitude (size); displacement is a vector quantity and has both magnitude and direction
2	What is the difference between speed and velocity?	speed is a scalar quantity and only has magnitude (size); velocity is a vector quantity and has both magnitude and direction
3	What is acceleration?	change in velocity of an object per second / the rate of change of velocity
4	What is the unit of acceleration?	m/s^2
5	How can an object be accelerating even if it is travelling at a steady speed?	if it is changing direction
6	What is happening to an object if it has a negative acceleration?	it is slowing down / it is decelerating
7	What information does the gradient of the line in a distance–time graph provide?	speed
8	What information does the gradient of the line in a velocity–time graph provide?	acceleration
9	How can the distance travelled by an object be found from its velocity–time graph?	calculate the area under the graph
10	What is the resultant force on a stationary object?	zero
11	What is the resultant force on an object moving at a steady speed in a straight line?	zero
12	What will an object experience if the resultant force on it is not zero?	acceleration / change in velocity
13	According to Newton's Second Law, what is the acceleration of an object proportional to?	the force acting on it
14	According to Newton's Second Law, what is the acceleration of an object inversely proportional to?	mass
15	What does Newton's Third Law say?	when two objects interact, they exert equal and opposite forces on each other
16	Starting to move, stopping moving, speeding up, slowing down, and changing direction are all examples of which type of motion?	acceleration / changing velocity

Put paper here

Now use the questions below to check your knowledge from previous chapters.

P2

Previous questions

Answers

1	What instrument can be used to measure the weight of an object?	calibrated spring-balance (newtonmeter)
2	What is a scalar quantity?	only has magnitude (size)
3	What is a vector quantity?	has both magnitude and direction
4	What is elastic distortion?	an object can go back to its original shape and size when distorting forces are removed
5	How do you find the spring constant from a force–extension graph of a spring?	find the gradient of the straight-line section

Put paper here (repeated)

Maths Skills

Practise your maths skills using the worked example and practice questions below.

Area of graphs	Worked example	Practice

Area of graphs

The area between the line of a graph and the x-axis sometimes represents a useful quantity.

To find the area under a graph made up of straight lines, split the shape under the line into rectangles and triangles, and add their individual values together.

If the graph has curved sections, estimate the area under the curve by following these steps:

1 Calculate the area of a single small square on the graph.

2 Count the whole and half squares under the curved part of the line.

3 Multiply the number of squares by the area per square.

Worked example

The graph shows how the velocity of an object changes with time. How far does the object travel during 24 seconds?

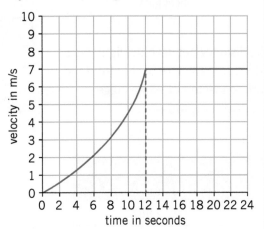

Calculate the area of the rectangular section: $7\,\text{m/s} \times (24 - 12)\,\text{s} = 7 \times 12 = 84\,\text{m}$

Calculate the area a single square represents: $1\,\text{m/s} \times 2\,\text{s} = 2\,\text{m}$

Count the number of whole squares under the curved part of the line (adding any half squares together): 15

Multiply the number of squares under the curved line by the area one square represents: $15 \times 2\,\text{m} = 30\,\text{m}$

Add the area under the curved section to the area of the rectangular section:

$$84\,\text{m} + 30\,\text{m} = 114\,\text{m}$$

Practice

The graph below shows a velocity–time graph for a cyclist:

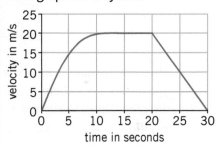

1 Describe the cyclist's motion in the time between 10 and 20 seconds.

2 Calculate the acceleration of the cyclist at 8 seconds.

3 Calculate the total distance travelled by the cyclist in the first 20 seconds.

Exam-style questions

01 A student sets up some equipment to measure the acceleration due to gravity as shown in **Figure 1**.

Figure 1

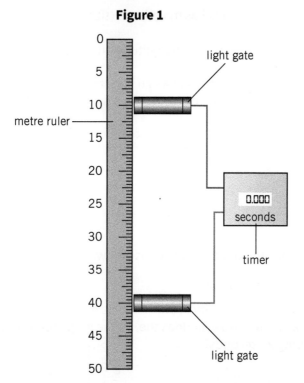

They use the ruler to measure the distance between the light gates. The distance is 30.0 cm. The student drops a piece of card from the top of the ruler. The light gates are connected to a data logger.

The student records the measurements in **Table 1**.

Table 1

Attempt	Velocity at light gate 1 in m/s	Velocity at light gate 2 in m/s
1	1.376	2.987
2	0.254	2.664
3	1.769	3.187

01.1 Describe how they should use the ruler to get an accurate measurement of the distance between the light gates. **[2 marks]**

_____

_____

_____

01.2 Suggest why the velocities of the card at light gate 1 are different. **[1 mark]**

_____

_____

01.3 Explain why there are more significant figures in the velocities recorded in **Table 1** than in the distance measurements.   **[3 marks]**

_____

_____

_____

_____

_____

01.4 The time between the measurements for attempt 1 is 0.17 s. Calculate the acceleration due to gravity using the measurements for attempt 1. Use the correct equation from the *Physics Equations Sheet*.

Give your answer to an appropriate number of significant figures.   **[3 marks]**

acceleration = _____ m/s^2

01.5 Suggest **one** reason why the measured value of the acceleration due to gravity is different from the agreed value.   **[1 mark]**

_____

_____

02 Two students are travelling to school. Student **A** is walking at 1.5 m/s. Student **B** is cycling at 6 m/s.

02.1 Write down the equation that links distance travelled, speed, and time.   **[1 mark]**

_____

02.2 Both students travel 1.5 km.

They leave their houses at the same time.

Calculate the difference in the times that they take to reach the school. Give your answer in minutes.   **[6 marks]**

difference in time = _____ minutes

02.3 Student **B** monitors their speed. They see that their fastest speed is much faster than their average speed.

Explain why. **[2 marks]**

_____

_____

_____

03 **Table 2** shows the data for a student in a race on sports day.

Table 2

Time in s	Distance in m
0	0
2	2
4	5
6	8
8	14
10	20
12	22

03.1 Plot the data on **Figure 2**. **[2 marks]**

Figure 2

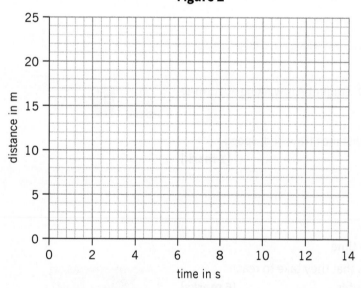

> **! Exam Tip**
>
> Always plot points using crosses and use a pencil in case you go wrong.

03.2 Calculate the speed of the student at a time of 4 seconds. **[3 marks]**

03.3 Describe the motion of the student between 6 seconds and 12 seconds. **[2 marks]**

> **! Exam Tip**
>
> You should show your working on the graph.

04   A group of students collect data for journeys by three different cars. The journeys are shown as lines on the graph in **Figure 3**.

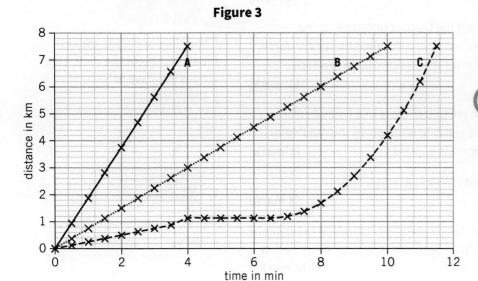

Figure 3

04.1   Identify which car travelled at the highest steady speed. Give reasons for your answer.   **[2 marks]**

04.2   Identify which car or cars stopped at some point during the journey. Give reasons for your answer.   **[2 marks]**

04.3   Identify which car or cars accelerated. Give reasons for your answer.
                                                              [2 marks]

04.4   All three cars travelled the same overall distance. Which car has the highest average speed? Give reasons for your answer.   **[2 marks]**

04.5   Use the graph to calculate the highest average speed.   **[4 marks]**

05   A teacher demonstrates how changing the force applied to an object changes its acceleration. **Figure 4** shows a graph of the results.

Figure 4

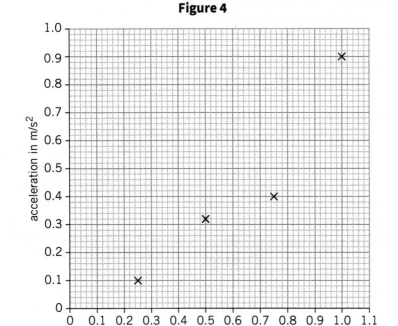

05.1 On **Figure 4** circle the measurement that is an outlier. **[1 mark]**

05.2 On **Figure 4** draw a line of best fit. **[1 mark]**

Exam Tip

Your line of best fit should best represent the data. This does not have to include all the points.

05.3 After the data has been plotted the teacher realises that the newtonmeter they used does not read zero when there is no force applied. Identify the type of error that this problem produces. **[1 mark]**

05.4 Give the reason why you can tell that there is this type of error by looking at the graph. Use the graph to write down the reading on the newtonmeter when no force is applied. **[1 mark]**

05.5 Write down the equation that links force, mass, and acceleration. **[1 mark]**

Exam Tip

Draw on your graph to ensure you use the correct values.

05.6 Use one of the points on your line of best fit to calculate the mass of the object. Explain how you have dealt with the error described in **05.3** and **05.4**. **[4 marks]**

06 A person needs to travel 20 miles to work. They have a choice of three different methods of transport to use – car, bicycle, and train. Typical speeds are: car – 30 m/s , bicycle – 6 m/s, train – 50 m/s.

06.1 Compare the time it would take, on average, to travel 20 miles by these methods. Choose suitable units for your calculations. There are 1609 m in 1 mile. **[3 marks]**

Exam Tip

Look out for mixtures of units and convert between them if you need to.

06.2 Write down any assumptions you made for your calculations in **06.1**. Suggest the effect on your answers if you do not make these assumptions. **[3 marks]**

07 Many drivers use satellite navigation (satnav) devices when driving to a destination. The satnav communicates with a global positioning system (GPS) satellite. A GPS satellite is at a distance of 20 200 km above the surface of the Earth. The signals from the satnav device to the satellite travel at a speed of 3×10^8 m/s.

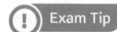

07.1 Show that the time it takes the signal to travel from the car to the satellite and back is about 0.1 s. **[3 marks]**

Exam Tip

In a 'show' question, you've already been given the answer. If you're not exactly sure what to do, work backwards from the numbers given, using the correct equations. Once you've got it, make sure your final answer is clear to the examiner.

07.2 A car is travelling at 55 mph. Calculate the distance the car would have moved in the time it takes the signal to travel to the satellite and back. There are 1609 m in 1 mile. There are 3600 s in 1 hour. **[3 marks]**

07.3 To pinpoint the position of the car, the satnav device communicates with at least three satellites. This reduces the error in the position to about 30 cm. Suggest whether the error is a systematic or a random error. Explain your answer. **[2 marks]**

07.4 Suggest how the satnav device calculates the speed of the car. **[3 marks]**

07.5 The GPS satellite is orbiting the Earth at a constant speed. Explain how it can be accelerating at the same time as it is moving with a constant speed. **[2 marks]**

08 A dance teacher wants to hang a large mirror in a studio using two lengths of wire. They use two different arrangements as shown in **Figure 5**.

Figure 5

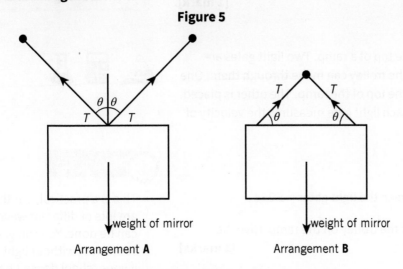

weight of mirror   weight of mirror

Arrangement **A**   Arrangement **B**

In arrangement **A** the tension in each string = 100 N. The angle θ = 40°. The mirror is hanging and is stationary.

08.1 Use a scale diagram to calculate the weight of the mirror in arrangement **A**. **[3 marks]**

08.2 Suggest what happens to the tension in the strings when the angle increases in arrangement **A**. Give reasons for your answer. **[2 marks]**

08.3 Another teacher suggests that the force in the string would be less if the mirror was fixed using arrangement **B**. Compare the tensions in the strings in the two arrangements. Assume that the angles are the same. **[4 marks]**

> **! Exam Tip**
>
> You may be more used to using these skills in maths, but don't be surprised when they turn up in physics.

09 A student collects data by stretching a spring and measuring the extension. They plot the graph shown in **Figure 6**.

Figure 6

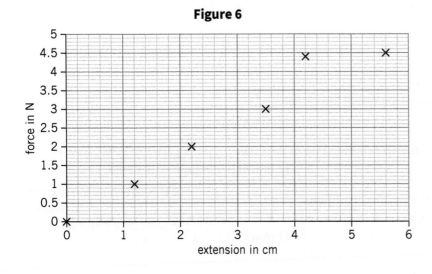

09.1 Suggest which reading is an outlier. **[1 mark]**

09.2 Write the equation that links force, spring constant, and extension.
[1 mark]

09.3 Use the graph to find the spring constant of the spring. **[4 marks]**

09.4 Describe the shape of the graph if the limit of proportionality is exceeded. **[1 mark]**

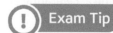

Exam Tip

You need to draw a line of best fit first. Make sure you do not include the outlier from **09.1** when drawing this line.

10 A student puts a trolley at the top of a ramp. Two light gates are placed on the ramp so that the trolley can move through them. One light gate is placed close to the top of the ramp. The other is placed at the bottom of the ramp. Each light gate measures the velocity of the trolley as it passes:

- initial velocity = 1.12 m/s
- final velocity = 7.12 m/s
- time taken to travel between the light gates = 1.25 s

10.1 Calculate the acceleration of the trolley on the ramp. Give the correct unit with your answer. **[3 marks]**

10.2 Compare this acceleration with the acceleration due to gravity. Give your answer as a ratio. **[2 marks]**

Exam Tip

This is a practical, but there are lots of different ways this can be done. You can get the same data without light gates if your school doesn't have them.

10.3 The trolley leaves the ramp with the final velocity and moves on a rough section of the floor. The trolley takes 5 seconds to stop. The data logger plots a velocity–time graph for the trolley when it is both accelerating and decelerating. Sketch the graph the data logger makes. Assume that the acceleration and deceleration are constant. Explain the shape of the graph. **[5 marks]**

Exam Tip

A sketched graph just shows the overall shape of the line. You do not need to plot any points or add any values.

11 A student has learnt about scalars and vectors.

11.1 They know that two of the quantities they learnt about are vectors, and two are scalars.

Choose **one** answer. **[1 mark]**

Speed and velocity are vectors.

Displacement and velocity are scalars.

Distance and speed are vectors.

Distance and speed are scalars.

11.2 A cyclist starts from home and travels 10 km north, then 20 km south. Calculate the final displacement of the cyclist from home. **[2 marks]**

11.3 Explain why the total distance travelled is not the same as the final displacement. **[2 marks]**

11.4 The cyclist says: '*I travelled at 6 km/h north, then 10 km/h south.*' Is the cyclist describing their speed or velocity? Give reasons for your answer. **[2 marks]**

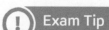

Exam Tip

For this question you will need to be clear on the difference between speed and velocity.

12 A student wants to investigate the relationship between the mass of an object and its acceleration.

12.1 Name the independent and dependent variables. **[2 marks]**

12.2 Describe an experiment that would enable the student to collect data to plot a graph of acceleration against mass. **[5 marks]**

12.3 Write down Newton's Second Law. **[1 mark]**

12.4 The student plots their data on **Figure 7**. The student notices that a 0.2 kg mass does not have an acceleration of 20 m/s².

Figure 7

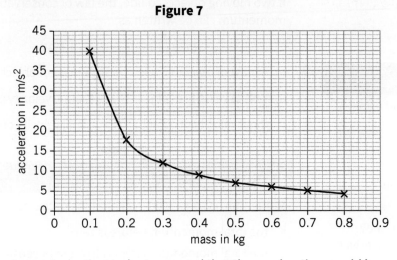

Suggest why the student expected that the acceleration would be 20 m/s².

Justify your answer. **[2 marks]**

12.5 Another student suggests that increasing the mass may have increased friction, which would have affected the acceleration.

Do you agree with this student? Explain your answer. **[3 marks]**

13 A helicopter is collecting an object from a remote location. A rope, hanging down from the helicopter, is attached to the object. The object has a mass of 110 kg. The helicopter accelerates upwards with an acceleration of 2.0 m/s². Gravitational field strength = 9.8 N/kg.

13.1 Calculate the weight of the object. **[3 marks]**

13.2 Calculate the force needed to accelerate the object at 2.0 m/s². **[3 marks]**

13.3 Show that the total force that the helicopter must exert on the object is about 1300 N. **[2 marks]**

13.4 Describe what happens to the object if the helicopter exerts a force of 1078 N. Give reasons for your answer. **[3 marks]**

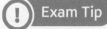

P3 Momentum and safety

Momentum

Momentum is a property of all moving objects. It is a vector quantity.

Momentum depends on the mass and velocity of an object and is defined by the equation:

momentum (kg m/s) = mass (kg) × velocity (m/s)

$$p = mv$$

Deceleration

The **deceleration** of a vehicle can be found using:

braking force (N) = mass (kg) × acceleration (m/s^2)

$$F = ma$$

The greater the braking force, the larger the deceleration.

If the braking force is very large, the brakes may overheat or the vehicle may skid, causing the driver to lose control.

Changes in momentum

If an object is moving or is able to move, an unbalanced force acting on it will change its momentum.

Since $F = ma$ and $a = \dfrac{\Delta v}{t}$, we can write:

$$F = \frac{m\Delta v}{t}$$

or

$$F = \frac{\Delta p}{t}$$

where Δp is the change in momentum of an object.

The greater the time taken for the change in momentum of an object:

- the smaller the rate of change of momentum
- the smaller the force the object experiences.

This means the force acting on an object is equal to the rate of change of momentum of the object.

Safety features increase the time taken for the change in momentum, for example:

- air bags, seat belts, and crumple zones in cars
- cycling helmets
- crash mats used for gymnastics.

Law of Conservation of Momentum

The Law of Conservation of Momentum says that:

In a closed system, the total momentum before an event (a collision or an explosion) is *equal* to the total momentum after the event.

If two moving objects collide, the law of conservation of momentum can be written as:

$$m_1u_1 + m_2u_2 = m_1v_1 + m_2v_2$$

m_1 = mass of object 1 m_2 = mass of object 2

u_1 = initial velocity of object 1 u_2 = initial velocity of object 2

v_1 = final velocity of object 1 v_2 = final velocity of object 2

Explosions

Momentum is conserved in explosions because:

- the total momentum before is zero
- the total momentum after is also zero because the different parts of the object travel in different directions and so the momentum of each part will cancel out with the momentum of another part.

If two moving objects **recoil** from each other, they start off with a total momentum of zero and end up moving away from each other with velocities v_1 and v_2. In this case, the law of conservation of momentum can be written as:

$$m_1v_1 + m_2v_2 = 0$$

Steady speed

Newton's First Law says that the velocity, speed, and/or direction of an object *will only change if a resultant force is acting on the object*.

This means that:

- If the resultant force on a stationary object is zero, the object will remain stationary.
- If the resultant force on a moving object is zero, it will continue moving at the same velocity, in a straight line.
- If the resultant force on an object is not zero, its velocity *will* change.

When a car is travelling at a steady speed, the resistive forces (e.g., friction and air resistance) must be balanced with the driving forces. This is why you have to keep your foot on the accelerator when driving, otherwise you'll slow down because the driving force will be less than the resistive forces.

 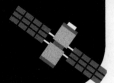
Thinking distance, braking distance, and stopping distance

Speed is one of the factors that affects the distance it takes to stop a car.

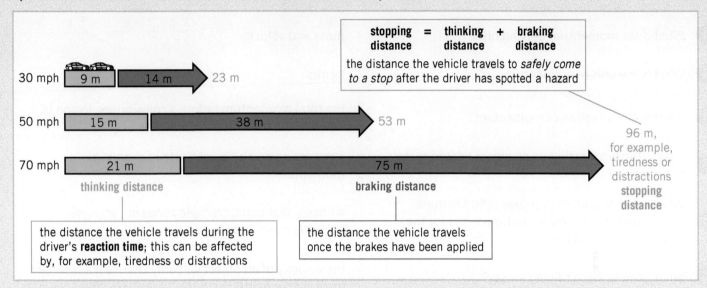

stopping distance = thinking distance + braking distance
the distance the vehicle travels to *safely come to a stop* after the driver has spotted a hazard

30 mph | 9 m | 14 m | 23 m

50 mph | 15 m | 38 m | 53 m

70 mph | 21 m | 75 m | 96 m, for example, tiredness or distractions **stopping distance**

thinking distance

braking distance

the distance the vehicle travels during the driver's **reaction time**; this can be affected by, for example, tiredness or distractions

the distance the vehicle travels once the brakes have been applied

Speed has a bigger effect on braking distance than on thinking distance.

A graph of distance against speed for a vehicle shows that:

- thinking distance is proportional to the speed of the vehicle (straight line)
- braking distance is not proportional to speed but is proportional to the speed squared.

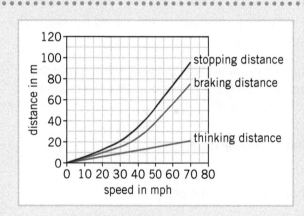

Factors affecting braking distance

The braking distance of a vehicle can be affected by:

- the speed of the vehicle
- road conditions
- the condition of brakes and tyres.

Any condition that reduces friction between the tyres and the road can lead to skidding, which increases the braking distance.

When the brakes of a vehicle are applied, a frictional force is applied to its wheel.

Work done by the frictional force between the brakes and wheel transfers energy from the kinetic energy of the car to the thermal energy of the brakes. This increases the temperature of the brakes.

The braking force, braking distance, and energy transferred are related by the equation:

energy transfer (J) = braking force (N) × distance (m)
$$W = Fs$$

 **Key Terms**

Make sure you can write a definition for these key terms.

| braking distance | deceleration | momentum | reaction time |
| recoil | stopping distance | thinking distance | |

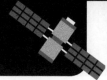

Learn the answers to the questions below then cover the answers column with a piece of paper and write as many as you can. Check and repeat.

	P3 questions		Answers
1	What does momentum depend on?	Put paper here	mass and velocity
2	What is the unit of momentum?		kg m/s
3	What is conservation of momentum?		the total momentum before a collision/explosion is equal to the total momentum after
4	How is the force acting on an object related to its momentum?	Put paper here	force acting on an object = rate of change of momentum
5	What are examples of everyday safety features which work by increasing the time taken for the change in momentum?		air bags, seat belts, crumple zones in cars, cycle helmets, crash mats in gyms
6	What does Newton's First Law say?	Put paper here	the velocity of an object will only change if a resultant force is acting on it
7	What forces are balanced when an object travels at a steady speed?		resistive forces = driving forces
8	What is the name given to the distance a vehicle travels to safely come to a stop after the driver has spotted a hazard?	Put paper here	stopping distance
9	What is thinking distance?		the distance a vehicle travels during the driver's reaction time
10	What is braking distance?	Put paper here	the distance a vehicle travels once the brakes have been applied
11	What is the relationship between stopping distance, thinking distance, and braking distance?		stopping distance = thinking distance + braking distance
12	Does the speed of a vehicle have a bigger effect on braking distance or thinking distance?		braking distance
13	Which distance is proportional to the speed of the vehicle?	Put paper here	thinking distance
14	Which distance increases by an increasing amount as speed increases?		braking distance
15	What are three factors that can affect the braking distance of a vehicle?	Put paper here	speed, road conditions, condition of tyres and brakes
16	Why does the temperature of a vehicle's brakes increase when the brakes are applied?		work done by the frictional force between the brakes and the wheels transfers energy from the kinetic energy of the car to the thermal energy of the brakes
17	What can happen if the braking force used to stop a vehicle is very large?		brakes may overheat / the vehicle may skid

Now use the questions below to check your knowledge from previous chapters.

P3

Previous questions / Answers

#	Previous questions	Answers
1	What two quantities do you need to calculate the weight of an object?	mass and gravitational field strength
2	On a force–extension graph, where is the limit of proportionality?	where the straight line starts to curve
3	What is the difference between speed and velocity?	speed is a scalar quantity and only has a magnitude (size); velocity is a vector quantity and has both magnitude and direction
4	What information does the gradient of the line in a distance–time graph provide?	speed
5	Starting to move, stopping moving, speeding up, slowing down, and changing direction are all examples of which type of motion?	acceleration / change in velocity

Put paper here

Maths Skills

Practise your maths skills using the worked example and practice questions below.

Graphs	Worked example	Practice

Graphs

Once you have plotted a graph, you often need to find the gradient of the graph. The gradient is another word for slope.

The gradient of a straight-line graph can be calculated using:

$$\text{gradient} = \frac{\text{change in } y}{\text{change in } x}$$

When a graph is curved, you can find the gradient of the curve at a specific point. You do this by drawing a straight-line tangent at that point and then calculating the gradient of the straight line.

Worked example

Calculate the deceleration of the car at 200 s.

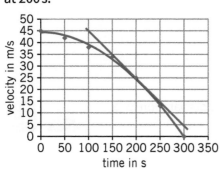

Step 1 Draw a straight-line tangent at the curve.

Step 2: Pick two points on the tangent and calculate the gradient of the tangent using:

$$\text{gradient} = \frac{\text{change in } y}{\text{change in } x}$$

$$= \frac{5\,\text{m/s} - 45\,\text{m/s}}{300\,\text{s} - 100\,\text{s}}$$

$$= -0.2\,\text{m/s}^2$$

Practice

1 Use the distance–time graph to determine the speed of the car.

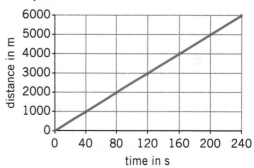

2 The distance–time graph shows a car as it approaches a sign.

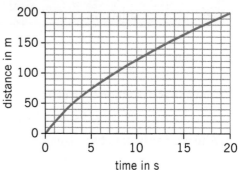

Determine the speed of the car at 10 seconds.

Practice

Exam-style questions

01 **Table 1** lists some factors that affect the thinking distance and braking distance of a car.

Table 1

Factor	Affects thinking distance	Affects braking distance
road conditions		
distractions in the car		
speed		

01.1 Tick **all** the correct boxes in the table. **[2 marks]**

01.2 Suggest **one** other factor that affects thinking distance.
Explain the effect of this factor on the thinking distance. **[3 marks]**

_____

_____

01.3 Describe **one** type of road condition that can affect the stopping distance of a car.
Explain how and why the stopping distance is affected. **[3 marks]**

_____

_____

_____

_____

! Exam Tip

Don't use factors that are mentioned in **01.1**. You are asked for another factor, so you won't gain a mark for repeating one.

02 A student is learning about stopping distances in preparation for a driving test.

They produce **Table 2** in which to record stopping distances for different speeds.

Table 2

Speed in mph	Braking distance in m	Thinking distance in m	Stopping distance in m
30	13.9		
50			53.0

02.1 A driver has a reaction time of 0.67 s.
Calculate their thinking distance for a speed of 30 mph (13.4 m/s).
Write your answer to **two** significant figures. **[2 marks]**

! Exam Tip

If you do not give your answer to two significant figures, you won't get full marks on this question.

_____ m

02.2 Calculate the stopping distance for 30 mph.
Write your answer to **two** significant figures. **[2 marks]**

———————————— m

02.3 The thinking distance for a speed of 50 mph can be calculated using the formula:

thinking distance at 50 mph = thinking distance at 30 mph $\times \dfrac{50}{30}$

Calculate the thinking distance at 50 mph.

Use the idea of proportion to justify the use of this calculation. **[3 marks]**

_____

_____

_____

_____

02.4 Calculate the braking distance at 50 mph. **[2 marks]**

———————————— m

03 A student models the effect of road conditions on stopping distance using a trolley, a ramp, and different floor coverings (carpet, tiles, etc.).

03.1 Identify the independent variable, the dependent variable, and two control variables in this investigation. **[4 marks]**

03.2 Write an experimental method to obtain sufficient data to plot a graph. **[5 marks]**

03.3 Identify a source of error in the experiment. Suggest an improvement to reduce its effect. **[2 marks]**

03.4 Evaluate to what extent this is a good model of the effect of surface on the stopping distance of a car. Use ideas about work and friction in your answer. **[3 marks]**

03.5 Suggest a limitation of this model. Give a reason for your answer. **[2 marks]**

04 A teacher is explaining thinking distance to a physics class. In pairs, the students measure their reaction time by grabbing a falling ruler. In each pair, student **A** holds a ruler just above student **B**'s hand. Student **A** then drops the ruler and student **B** grabs it. They record the distance the ruler has fallen. **Figure 1** shows the relationship between the distance fallen and reaction time.

Figure 1

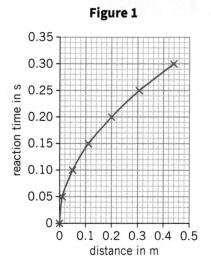

Exam Tip

You may be familiar with this from biology required practicals, but you need to think about it in a physics context. Don't let the change in context put you off.

04.1 Explain the relationship between reaction time and distance shown in **Figure 1**. **[2 marks]**

04.2 One student measures a distance on the ruler of 25 cm. Use **Figure 1** to work out the reaction time of the student. **[1 mark]**

04.3 Explain whether the reaction time of the student falls within the range of normal reaction times. **[2 marks]**

04.4 Suggest **one** source of error in doing this experiment. Explain the possible effect of this error on the measurement of reaction time. **[3 marks]**

05 A medical journal published an article on injuries due to falling coconuts. Here is a summary of the study as reported in the journal.

A 4-year review of trauma admissions to the Provincial Hospital, Alotau, Papua New Guinea, reveals that 2.5% of such admissions were due to being struck by falling coconuts.

Since mature coconut palms may have a height of up to 35 metres and an unhusked coconut may have a mass of up to 4 kg, blows to the head of a force exceeding 1 metric tonne, or 1000 kg, are possible.

Exam Tip

Sort out which information is useful and what is just a distraction by crossing out information that will not help you answer the question. For example, the fact that this happened in the Provincial Hospital, Alotau, Papua New Guinea is not helpful for the physics. This can be crossed out. However, the height that the coconuts fall is useful for the physics.

05.1 Suggest why the statement *a force exceeding 1 metric tonne* is incorrect. **[1 mark]**

05.2 Write down the equation that links gravitational field strength, mass, and weight. **[1 mark]**

05.3 Calculate the force exerted by a mass of 1000 kg. Gravitational field strength = 9.8 N/kg. **[2 marks]**

05.4 Suggest why the authors chose to describe the force in this way in the summary. **[1 mark]**

05.5 A coconut of mass 2.5 kg falls from a tree in 2.5 seconds. Calculate the momentum of the coconut just before it hits the ground. **[4 marks]**

06 Two people are on an ice rink. They are wearing ice skates. Person **A** is stationary. Person **B** is skating towards person **A** with a speed of 5.0 m/s to the right. They collide. The mass of person **B** is 65 kg.

06.1 Calculate the momentum of person **B** before the collision. Give the unit with your answer. **[3 marks]**

06.2 When they collide, the people link arms and move off together without stopping. Explain why the velocity of the skaters is different after the collision. Write down an assumption that you have made in your answer. **[4 marks]**

06.3 The mass of person **A** is 85 kg. Calculate the velocity of the two skaters after the collision. **[3 marks]**

06.4 At the end of the session the two skaters skate to the edge of the rink, collide gently with the barrier, and stop. Explain why momentum is not conserved in this situation. **[2 marks]**

07 A driver is travelling along the road at 70 mph.

07.1 Convert 70 mph to m/s. There are 1609 m in 1 mile. **[3 marks]**

07.2 The driver sees a sign that says:
'*Keep two chevrons apart*'.
Chevrons are large '⋀' shapes painted on the road. Each driver should be able to see two chevrons between themselves and the driver in front of them. Suggest what this system is designed to do. **[2 marks]**

07.3 The stopping distance for a car travelling at 70 mph is 96 m. The braking distance is 75 m. Calculate the reaction time of the driver. **[4 marks]**

07.4 A student calculates that the distance between the chevrons should be 48 m. Suggest how the student worked out this number. **[1 mark]**

07.5 The chevrons are actually 40 m apart. Suggest a reason why the actual distance is smaller than the value in **07.4**. **[2 marks]**

08 It is very important to be able to stop a road vehicle quickly in an emergency. **Figure 2** shows a graph of braking distance against speed for a car in normal conditions and in an emergency.

Figure 2

08.1 Write down which curve on **Figure 2**, **A** or **B**, relates to an emergency stop. Use the words force and acceleration to explain your answer. **[4 marks]**

08.2 Suggest **one** harmful effect of having to do an emergency stop. **[1 mark]**

08.3 **Figure 2** does not include the thinking distance. Compare the thinking distance when stopping in normal conditions and when doing an emergency stop. **[2 marks]**

Exam Tip

The question tells you some key words to use so make sure that you do use them.

09 **Figure 3** shows the effect that using a mobile phone has on reaction times.

Figure 3

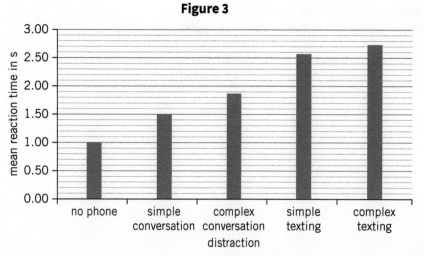

Exam Tip

Use a ruler to draw a line from the top of the bars to the axis. This will help you read off the data accurately.

09.1 Many countries have now banned the use of mobile phones by the drivers of cars. Use **Figure 3** to suggest why. Explain your reasoning. **[3 marks]**

Exam Tip

Use data from the graph and compare the different uses of mobile phones to the no phone column.

09.2 A car is travelling at 30 mph (13.4 m/s). Calculate the difference in thinking distance between a driver holding a complex conversation and a driver with no phone. **[3 marks]**

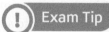

09.3 Calculate the speed that the person with no phone would need to travel at to have the same thinking distance as the person having the complex conversation at 30 mph. Use ratios to convert the speed to miles per hour.

Comment on your answer. **[5 marks]**

10 A company is writing an advice leaflet to go with the baby bouncer that they sell. The leaflet will give parents a guide to the height off the floor to fix the bouncer for babies of different weights.

Figure 4

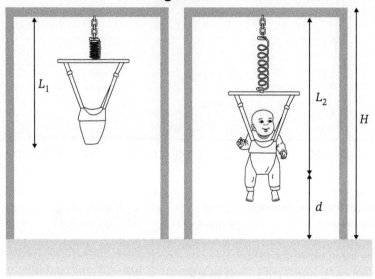

For safety, the distance d as shown in **Figure 4** should be no less than 50 cm. The length of the chain, spring, and harness $L_1 = 1.00$ m. When the baby is put in the harness, the length $L_2 = 1.25$ m.

The weight of the baby is 100 N.

10.1 Write down the equation that links force, spring constant, and extension. **[1 mark]**

10.2 Calculate the spring constant of the spring holding the harness. **[4 marks]**

10.3 Calculate the height, H, from the floor that you need to fix the baby bouncer so the baby can be safe. **[2 marks]**

11 A company has been experimenting with airbags. They have used a forcemeter connected to a data logger to monitor the force on a model person in a car. The car collides with a barrier. In one test there is no air bag attached to the model. In the second test, the air bag inflates.

The graph of force on the model person against time for both collisions is shown in **Figure 5**.

Exam Tip

Label these lines 'first test' and 'second test'. This might make things clearer for you.

Figure 5

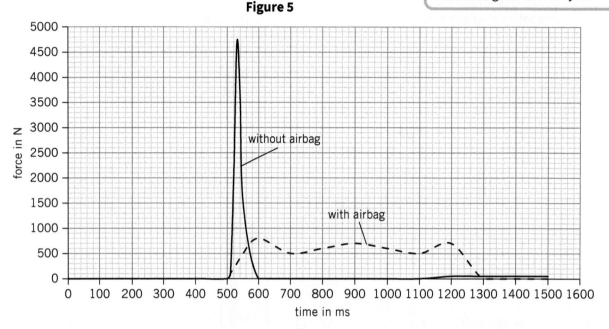

11.1 Use **Figure 5** to compare the maximum force experienced by the model person with and without an airbag. **[3 marks]**

11.2 Use **Figure 5** to estimate the average force exerted by the airbag while it was bringing the model person to a stop. **[1 mark]**

11.3 Calculate the initial velocity of the model person when an airbag is used. Assume that the time the airbag took to inflate was 750 ms. Assume that the mass of the model person is 60 kg. Use the equation momentum = mass × velocity and an equation from the *Physics Equation Sheet*. **[5 marks]**

11.4 Explain why airbags result in less injury to the human body involved in a car accident. **[2 marks]**

Exam Tip

Draw lines across from the top of the impact line to the *y*-axis to help you read off the maximum force values.

Exam Tip

Here, you have to merge the equation you have been given with one from the *Physics Equation Sheet*.

12 The acceleration of a rocket is often used as an example of Newton's Third Law.

12.1 Write down Newton's Third Law. **[1 mark]**

12.2 When a rocket's engines fire, exhaust gases move downwards out of the rocket and the rocket accelerates upwards. Explain why there is an upwards force on the rocket. **[2 marks]**

12.3 Before the rocket launches, it is stationary on the launch pad. A student says: '*The forces acting on the rocket are equal and opposite. This is an example of Newton's Third Law.*' Do you agree? Explain your answer. **[2 marks]**

13 A car accelerates from 0 to 40 mph.

13.1 Convert 40 mph to m/s. There are 1609 m in 1 mile. There are 3600 s in an hour. **[3 marks]**

13.2 Write down what further information you need in order to state the velocity of the car. **[1 mark]**

13.3 Compare this speed to that of a typical cyclist. **[1 mark]**

13.4 The car accelerates over a time of 3.5 s. Calculate the acceleration of the car. **[2 marks]**

13.5 The car travels at a constant speed for another 3.5 s. Sketch the velocity–time graph for this journey. **[3 marks]**

14 A local group wants to reduce the number of injuries due to cars striking pedestrians. The group wants to change the speed limit from 30 mph (13.4 m/s) to 25 mph (11.2 m/s) in all built-up areas. To persuade the public to accept the new speed limit, the group plans to use calculations to show why it is important.

A car travelling at 25 mph comes to a complete stop after a distance of 9.4 m.

14.1 The mass of the car is 1500 kg. Calculate the kinetic energy of the car as it comes to a complete stop when travelling at 30 mph. Give your answer in standard form. **[3 marks]**

14.2 Using your answer from **14.1**, calculate the difference in the distance the car travels to come to a complete stop when travelling at 30 mph compared to when travelling at 25 mph. The braking force of a car is 10 kN. **[5 marks]**

14.3 A car travelling at 30 mph with an acceleration of −6.7 m/s^2 will still be moving after travelling 9.4 m. Use ideas about work and energy to show that the car has about 40 000 J of energy when it has travelled this distance. **[5 marks]**

14.4 Show that the car will be travelling at about 7 m/s when it gets to 9.4 m. This is about 15 mph. **[2 marks]**

! Exam Tip

Always show all of your working in a maths question. You can pick up some marks even if you don't get the final answer correct.

! Exam Tip

With any calculation, the first thing you should write down is the equation you are going to use.

! Exam Tip

When sketching this graph make sure you label 3.5 s and 7.0 s.

! Exam Tip

Write down which equation you will use to answer **14.1**. Selecting the correct equation is an important skill that you need to show in the exams.

! Exam Tip

There are lots of different units in **14.3**. Make sure you don't mix them up.

P4 Terminal velocity and moments

Drag forces

When an object moves through a fluid (liquid or gas) a frictional force drags on it.

These drag forces:

- always act in the opposite direction to an object's movement
- increase with the object's speed – the greater the speed, the greater the frictional force
- depend on the shape and size of the object.

The frictional drag force in air is called **air resistance**.

Streamlining an object reduces the drag it experiences. For example:

- some animals, such as sharks, have adapted to become more streamlined
- some cars are designed to be more streamlined.

Terminal velocity

For an object falling through a fluid:

- there are two forces acting – its weight due to gravity and the drag force
- the weight remains constant
- the drag force is small at the beginning, but gets bigger as the object speeds up
- the resultant force gets smaller as the drag force increases
- the acceleration decreases as the object falls
- if the object falls for a long enough time, it will reach a final steady speed.

Terminal velocity is the constant velocity a falling object reaches when the frictional force acting on it is equal to its weight.

Parachutes are designed to increase the drag force on a parachutist so that the terminal velocity is reduced.

Graph of terminal velocity

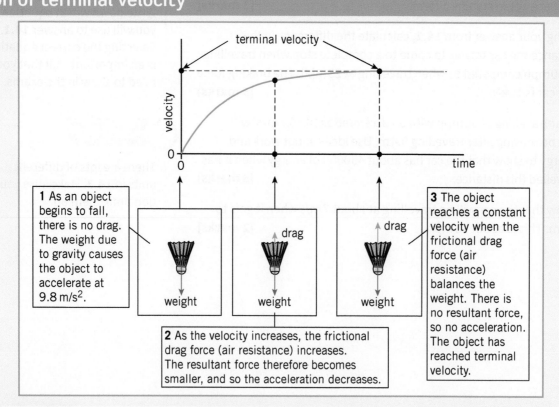

1 As an object begins to fall, there is no drag. The weight due to gravity causes the object to accelerate at 9.8 m/s².

2 As the velocity increases, the frictional drag force (air resistance) increases. The resultant force therefore becomes smaller, and so the acceleration decreases.

3 The object reaches a constant velocity when the frictional drag force (air resistance) balances the weight. There is no resultant force, so no acceleration. The object has reached terminal velocity.

 Key Terms

Make sure you can write a definition for these key terms.

air resistance   centre of mass   force multiplier   lever   moment

streamlining   terminal velocity

Centre of mass

The **centre of mass** of an object is the point at which the mass of the object may be thought to be concentrated.

For some regularly shaped objects with uniform density, the centre of mass is in the centre of the object.

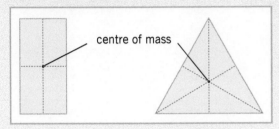
centre of mass

The centre of mass of a symmetrical object will always be somewhere along the line of symmetry. The position of the centre of mass affects the stability of objects.

Finding the centre of mass

For irregular flat shapes, you can find the centre of mass using a plumbline. This method uses the fact that when an object is suspended, its centre of mass will always be directly below the point of suspension.

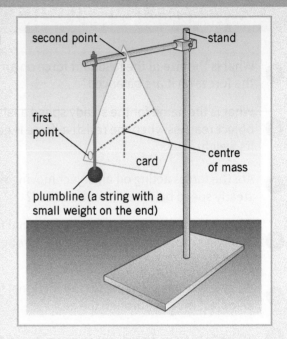

Moments

A force or system of forces can cause an object to rotate.

The turning effect of a force is called the **moment** of the force, and its size can be calculated using the equation:

moment of a force (Nm) = force (N) × distance (m)

$$M = F d$$

If an object is balanced, the sum of the clockwise moments equals the sum of the anticlockwise moments.

Levers

Levers can be used to increase the moment of a force, making it easier to lift or rotate an object.

A lever allows a large moment of force to be produced by allowing force to be applied further from the pivot.

A lever is a **force multiplier**.

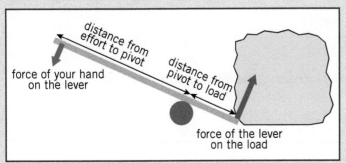

Stability and centre of mass

If the line of action of the weight of an object lies outside the base of the object, there will be a resultant moment and the body will topple.

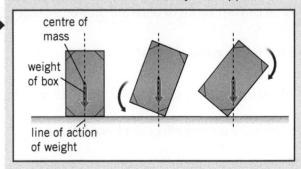

If the centre of mass is high, it will only require a small force to move the centre of mass past a pivot point. It will be less stable than an object with a lower centre of mass. This means:

- tall vehicles can be unstable in high winds
- some balancing toys are designed so the centre of mass is always over the pivot point.

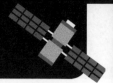
Learn the answers to the questions below then cover the answers column with a piece of paper and write as many as you can. Check and repeat.

P4 questions | Answers

#	Question	Answer
1	What is the size of the resultant force on an object if the forces on it are balanced?	zero
2	What is the name for the steady speed a falling object reaches when the resistive force is equal to its weight?	terminal velocity
3	Are the forces acting on an object moving with a steady speed balanced or unbalanced?	balanced
4	What is the general name for the frictional forces an object experiences when moving through a fluid (liquid or gas)?	drag
5	What is the general name for the frictional force on an object moving through the air?	air resistance
6	Which is bigger: air resistance or water resistance?	water resistance
7	In which direction does the drag on an object always act?	in the direction opposite to which it is moving
8	What happens to the drag on an object as its speed increases?	the drag increases
9	What can be done to reduce the drag on an object?	streamlining
10	What is the centre of mass?	the point through which the weight of an object can be considered to act
11	Where is the centre of mass of a symmetrical object?	along the line of symmetry
12	What is the turning effect of a force called?	a moment
13	What two quantities do you need to calculate a moment?	force and distance from a pivot
14	What can you say about clockwise and anticlockwise moments on a balanced object?	sum of all the clockwise moments about any point = sum of all the anticlockwise moments about that point
15	Are objects with a high centre of mass easier to topple or less easy to topple than objects with a low centre of mass?	easier
16	How does a lever reduce the amount of force needed to create a particular sized moment?	by increasing the distance from the pivot

Put paper here

Now use the questions below to check your knowledge from previous chapters.

P4

Previous questions | Answers

	Previous questions	Answers
1	What is inelastic distortion?	an object does not go back to its original shape and size when distorting forces are removed
2	What is the difference between speed and velocity?	speed is a scalar quantity and only has magnitude (size); velocity is a vector quantity and has both magnitude and direction
3	What information does the gradient of the line in a velocity–time graph provide?	acceleration
4	What is conservation of momentum?	the total momentum before a collision/explosion is equal to the total momentum after
5	What is the relationship between stopping distance, thinking distance, and braking distance?	stopping distance = thinking distance + braking distance

Put paper here

 ## Maths Skills

Practise your maths skills using the worked examples and practice questions below.

Significant figures	Worked examples	Practice
The significant figures of a value are the ones which are meaningful based on what the number represents. We also use significant figures to make sure we are not introducing error by giving a false level of accuracy. Significant figures (s.f.) follow these rules: • non-zero digits are always significant • zeros between non-zero digits are significant • leading zeros are not significant • trailing zeros are not significant if there is no decimal point • trailing zeros are significant if there is a decimal point in the number. When answering questions, you use the same number of s.f. as the data with the fewest s.f. in the question. When giving a value to a specific number of s.f. you need to check if the value should be rounded. You use the next number after the desired s.f. to determine whether to round the value up or down.	1 How many significant figures are there in 2.5070? **Answer:** 5 s.f. as there are 3 non-zero numbers, 1 zero between these, and 1 trailing zero after the decimal point. 2 Round 0.0037094 to 3 s.f. **Answer:** Counting from the first s.f. to the number required gives you 0.00370 as leading zeros are not significant, but the zero between non zero-digits is significant. The next number (9) tells you to round up the last s.f. 0.0037094 = 0.00371 to 3 s.f.	1 How many significant figures are there in 1.2708? 2 How many significant figures are there in 0.0035008? 3 Round 35.073 to 3 s.f. 4 Round 67812 to 2 s.f.

Practice

Exam-style questions

01 **Figure 1** shows a seesaw.

Figure 1

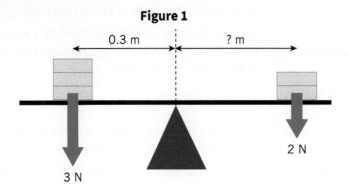

0.3 m   ? m

3 N

2 N

> ### Exam Tip
>
> Annotate the diagram with the forces and distances (F_1, d_1, F_2) that you are going to use for the calculation in part **01.3**. this will make interpreting the diagram easier.

01.1 Define the moment of a force. **[1 mark]**

_____

_____

01.2 Use the idea of moments to describe the condition for a seesaw to be balanced. **[1 mark]**

_____

_____

01.3 Using **Figure 1**, deduce the distance from the pivot at which you would need to place the 2 N weight for the seesaw to be balanced. Show your working. **[3 marks]**

distance = _____ m

02 A student is investigating how objects topple over.

They manage to balance this stool on its leg **(Figure 2)**.

Figure 2

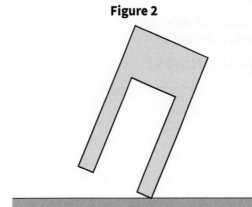

02.1 Suggest how they could find the position of the centre of mass of an object that is this shape. **[4 marks]**

_____

_____

_____

_____

_____

They decide to investigate the effect of the height of the water in a bottle on the angle at which it topples **(Figure 3)**.

Figure 3

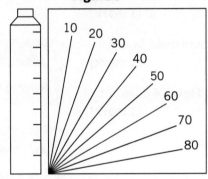

02.2 Write down the independent variable. **[1 mark]**

_____

02.3 Write down the dependent variable. **[1 mark]**

_____

02.4 Suggest what happens to the angle at which the bottle topples as the volume of water in the bottle increases. Explain your answer. **[2 marks]**

_____

_____

_____

02.5 Suggest **one** situation where having a low centre of mass is beneficial. **[1 mark]**

_____

_____

03 Sailing boats, such as boat **A** in **Figure 4**, can be very unstable. Heavy weights, called 'ballast', are placed in the bottom of boats to make them more stable.

Figure 4

Boat A   Boat B

03.1 Explain in terms of centre of mass why the ballast makes the boat more stable. **[1 mark]**

03.2 Suggest **one** other way that the boat designer could make boat **A** in **Figure 4** more stable. **[1 mark]**

Exam Tip

Refer to the shape of the boats.

03.3 Explain in terms of centre of mass why boat **B** in **Figure 4** does not require ballast to be stable. **[1 mark]**

03.4 A student makes a model of boat **A**, and writes this investigation title.

'How does the mass of ballast affect the angle at which the boat topples?'

Name a control variable in this investigation. **[1 mark]**

Exam Tip

Use a highlighter when reading the title of the investigation to help you identify the variables.

04 A teacher shows the class a spinning paper helicopter. They drop the helicopter and use a data logger to record how the velocity changes over time. **Figure 5** shows the velocity–time graph for the helicopter.

Figure 5

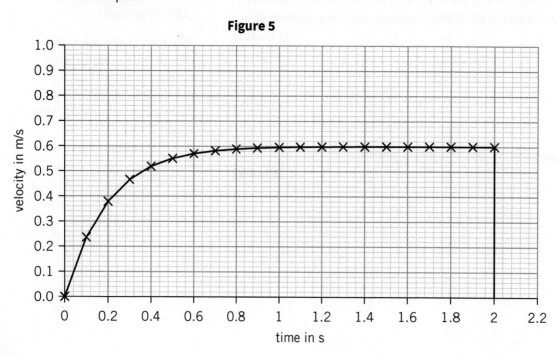

04.1 Write down the terminal velocity of the helicopter. **[1 mark]**

04.2 Use **Figure 5** to estimate the distance travelled by the helicopter. Describe your method. **[3 marks]**

04.3 The teacher adds paper clips to the body of the helicopter and drops the helicopter again from the same height. On **Figure 5**, sketch the graph for the helicopter with additional paper clips. Assume that the helicopter reaches terminal velocity. Explain the shape of the line that you have drawn. **[6 marks]**

04.4 Suggest **one** reason why the acceleration of the helicopter is not constant. **[1 mark]**

05 An ice hockey puck is moving along the ice at a steady speed.

05.1 Student **A** says: '*If the speed is steady, there are no forces acting on the puck*'.
Do you agree with student **A**? Justify your answer. **[2 marks]**

05.2 Student **B** says: '*The puck will only stop when the force it is carrying runs out*'.
Do you agree with student **B**? Justify your answer. **[2 marks]**

05.3 One of the players hits the puck with a hockey stick and the puck moves in the opposite direction.
Student **C** says: '*While the stick is in contact with the puck, the stick exerts a bigger force on the puck than the puck exerts on the stick*'.
Do you agree with student **C**? Justify your answer. **[2 marks]**

05.4 Determine whether the puck experienced an acceleration while in contact with the stick. Give reasons for your answer. **[2 marks]**

06 A student sees a large crane moving a load. There are counterbalance weights on the other side of a pivot. The load exerts a force of 1000 N. The student estimates that the load is 8 m from the pivot.

06.1 Calculate the moment of the force exerted by the load. **[2 marks]**

06.2 The crane pauses. The counterbalance weights are 4 m away from the pivot. The crane is balanced. Calculate the force exerted by the counterbalance weights. Explain how you worked out your answer. **[4 marks]**

06.3 The crane uses a motor to lift the load. The motor uses gears. Use the words **high** or **low** to complete this sentence. **[1 mark]**
The gears provide a **high / low** speed and a **high / low** turning effect.

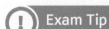

Exam Tip

You're asked to sketch a graph, which means you have to add a drawing to get full marks, but you don't need to add on grid lines or points. A sketched graph only needs labelled axes and a line of best fit.

Exam Tip

Thinking about Newton's Laws will help with this question. Try writing them all down for reference.

Exam Tip

Don't confuse moment and momentum; they are different things and have different equations.

Exam Tip

It is a good idea to sketch out a quick diagram to help with this calculation. Add on arrows to show the direction of the forces.

07	A student investigates terminal velocity by dropping balls of modelling clay in a liquid. The student measures the velocity just before the ball enters the liquid and again after a certain distance.

07.1	Identify suitable equipment that the student can use to measure the velocity of the ball.	**[1 mark]**

07.2	For a particular ball, they make the following measurements:
- initial velocity = 3.5 cm/s
- final velocity = 1.3 cm/s
- time over which the velocity changes = 12 seconds

Use the correct equation from the *Physics Equations Sheet* to calculate the average acceleration in cm/s². Justify the sign of the acceleration.	**[4 marks]**

> **(!)** Exam Tip
>
> Acceleration can be positive or negative. A negative acceleration is often called deceleration.

07.3	The student wonders if the modelling clay reaches terminal velocity. Suggest how the student could take measurements to check whether terminal velocity has been reached.	**[2 marks]**

07.4	The student repeats the experiment with fluids of different densities. They measure the distance over which the velocity changes from 3.5 m/s to 1.3 m/s.

Suggest how and why the distance depends on the density.

[3 marks]

08	Some animals can accelerate very quickly. **Table 1** shows the acceleration and top speed of a leafhopper (an insect) and a cheetah.

Table 1

Animal	Acceleration in m/s²	Top speed in m/s	Mass of animal
leafhopper	1000	4	2 mg
cheetah	5	30	50 kg

08.1	Show that the force generated by the cheetah is 125 000 times greater than the force generated by the leafhopper.	**[6 marks]**

08.2	Use **Table 1** to suggest whether the acceleration of the animal and the top speed of the animal are directly proportional. Justify your answer with calculations.	**[4 marks]**

08.3	A company makes an acceleration suit for a human. The suit allows the wearer to have the same level of acceleration as a leafhopper. A human tries on the suit. They have a mass of 70 kg. Calculate the force produced by the suit. Compare your answer with the forces produced by vehicles in everyday road transport. Forces produced by cars are about 40 kN.	**[4 marks]**

> **(!)** Exam Tip
>
> In a show question, you know what the answer should be. So if you don't get that answer when you're doing your working out then you can try again until you get there. Just be careful of the amount of time you have in an exam.

09 A student wants to model how avalanches start. They put a tub with sand in it on an adjustable ramp. **Figure 6** shows the tub of sand when the ramp is flat on the workbench (left) and when it is raised (right).

Figure 6

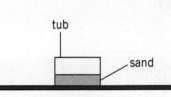
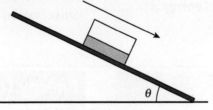

09.1 The student raises the ramp as shown and writes down the angle (θ) when the tub just starts to move. When the ramp is raised further, the tub accelerates down the ramp. Explain why there is a resultant force on the tub when the ramp is raised. Use ideas about components of forces and friction in your answer. **[3 marks]**

09.2 The student repeats the experiment with different masses of sand in the tub. The results show that the angle of the ramp needed to start the tub moving is independent of the mass of sand. Sketch a graph of angle against mass of sand. **[2 marks]**

09.3 Suggest a reason for the shape of the graph. **[1 mark]**

> **!** **Exam Tip**
>
> 'Sketch' means you just need the shape and axis labels. Numbers and plotted points are not needed.

10 A student drops two types of ball that are the same size, and uses a motion sensor to plot the speed against time for each ball (see **Figure 7**).

Figure 7

10.1 Use data from the graph to calculate the acceleration of the rubber ball. **[3 marks]**

10.2 Use the graph to write down the terminal velocity of the plastic ball. **[1 mark]**

10.3 Explain how you found the terminal velocity from the graph. **[2 marks]**

10.4 Explain why the line for the plastic ball is below the line for the rubber ball. **[1 mark]**

10.5 State and explain where the acceleration of the balls is nearly the same. **[1 mark]**

P5 Forces and energy

Systems and conservation of energy

A **system** is an object or group of objects.

Whenever anything changes in a system, energy is transferred to the surroundings.

Energy can be transferred usefully, stored or dissipated, but cannot be created or destroyed. This is the **conservation of energy**.

Energy types

kinetic	energy an object has because it is moving
gravitational potential	energy an object has because of its height above the ground
elastic potential	energy an elastic object has when it is stretched or compressed
thermal (or internal)	energy an object has because of its temperature (the total kinetic and potential energy of the particles)
chemical	energy that can be transferred by chemical reactions involving foods, fuels, and the chemicals in batteries
nuclear	energy stored in the nucleus of an atom
magnetic	energy a magnetic object has when it is near a magnet or in a magnetic field
electrostatic	energy a charged object has when near another charged object

Energy transfers

Energy can be transferred by:

Heating
Energy is transferred from one object to another object with a lower temperature.

Waves
Waves (e.g., light and sound waves) can transfer energy by radiation.

Electricity
When an electric current flows it can transfer energy.

Forces (mechanical work)
Energy is transferred when a force moves or changes the shape of an object.

The pendulum

When a pendulum swings, forces continuously transfer energy between kinetic energy and gravitational potential energy.

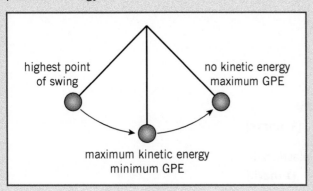

highest point of swing

no kinetic energy maximum GPE

maximum kinetic energy minimum GPE

Work

Work is done when a force moves an object through a distance that is in the direction of the force.

Work done by a force can be calculated using:

work done (J) = force (N) × distance (m)

$$W = F \times d$$

Energy is transferred by the force when work is done.

- If the force is in the *same* direction, energy is transferred *to* the object.
- If the force is in the *opposite* direction, energy is transferred *from* the object.

When an object slows down due to friction, energy is transferred by heating, and the object gets hotter.

Gravity can do work on an object to both slow it down and speed it up.

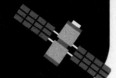

Energy equations

When you lift an object, you do work against the gravitational force. Gravitational potential energy is calculated using:

gravitational potential energy (J) = mass (kg) × gravitational field strength (N/kg) × height (m)

$$E_p = m\,g\,h$$

The kinetic energy of an object can be calculated using:

kinetic energy (J) = 0.5 × mass (kg) × (speed)^2 (m/s)

$$E_k = \frac{1}{2} m\,v^2$$

Power is how much work is done (or how much energy is transferred) per second. Work done means the same thing as energy transferred. The unit of power is the watt (W).

1 watt = 1 joule of energy transferred per second

$$\text{power (W)} = \frac{\text{energy transferred (J)}}{\text{time (s)}}$$

$$P = \frac{E}{t}$$

or

$$\text{power (W)} = \frac{\text{work done (J)}}{\text{time (s)}}$$

$$P = \frac{W}{t}$$

The elastic potential energy of a stretched spring can be calculated using:

elastic potential energy (J) = 0.5 × spring constant (N/m) × (extension)^2 (m)

$$E_e = \frac{1}{2} k\,e^2$$

assuming the limit of proportionality has not been exceeded.

Useful and dissipated energy

Dissipated energy is often described as being wasted. The energy flow in a system can be shown using a **Sankey diagram**.

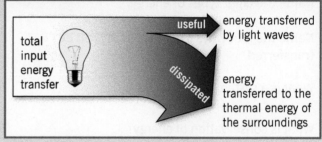

Energy is never entirely transferred usefully – some energy is always dissipated, meaning it is transferred to less useful types.

All energy eventually ends up transferred to the thermal energy store of the surroundings.

In machines, work done against the force of friction usually causes energy to be wasted because energy is transferred to the thermal energy of the machine and its surroundings.

Lubrication is a way of reducing unwanted energy transfer due to friction.

Streamlining is a way of reducing energy wasted due to air resistance or drag in water.

Efficiency is a measure of how much energy is transferred usefully. The equation to calculate efficiency as a *decimal* is:

$$\text{efficiency} = \frac{\text{useful energy out (J)}}{\text{total energy in (J)}}$$

or

$$\text{efficiency} = \frac{\text{useful power out (W)}}{\text{total power in (W)}}$$

To give efficiency as a *percentage*, just multiply the result from the above calculation by 100 and add the % sign to the answer.

🔑 **Key Terms**

Make sure you can write a definition for these key terms.

chemical	conservation of energy	dissipated	efficiency	elastic potential
electrostatic	gravitational potential	kinetic	magnetic	nuclear power
Sankey diagram	system	thermal	work done	

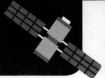
Learn the answers to the questions below then cover the answers column with a piece of paper and write as many as you can. Check and repeat.

	P5 questions	Answers
1	Name the eight types of energy.	kinetic, gravitational potential, elastic potential, thermal, chemical, nuclear, magnetic, electrostatic
2	Name the four ways in which energy can be transferred.	heating, waves, electric current, mechanically (by forces)
3	What is a system?	an object or group of objects
4	What is conservation of energy?	energy cannot be created or destroyed, only transferred or dissipated
5	What is work done?	energy transferred when a force moves an object
6	What is the unit for energy?	joule (J)
7	What is one joule of work?	the work done when a force of 1 N causes an object to move 1 m in the direction of the force
8	Describe the energy transfer when a moving car slows down.	energy is transferred from the kinetic energy of the car to the thermal energy in its brakes – some energy is dissipated to the thermal energy of the surroundings
9	Describe the energy transfer when an electric kettle is used to heat water.	the electric current in a kettle transfers energy to the heating element's thermal energy – energy is then transferred by heating to the thermal energy of the water
10	Describe the energy transfer when a ball is fired using an elastic band.	energy is transferred from the elastic energy of the elastic band to the kinetic energy of the band and the ball – some energy is dissipated to the thermal energy of the surroundings
11	Describe the energy transfer when a battery powered toy car is used.	energy is transferred from the chemical energy of the battery to the kinetic energy of the toy car – some energy is dissipated to the thermal energy of the surroundings
12	Describe the energy transfer when a falling apple hits the ground.	energy is transferred from the kinetic energy of the apple and dissipated to the thermal energy of the surroundings by sound waves
13	Name the unit that represents one joule transferred per second.	watt (W)
14	Describe the energy changes in a pendulum.	energy oscillates between kinetic energy and gravitational potential energy

Put paper here

Now use the questions below to check your knowledge from previous chapters.

P5

Previous questions

Answers

1 What is a non-contact force?

a force between objects that are physically separated (e.g., gravitational, electrostatic, magnetic)

2 What is the resultant force on a stationary object?

zero

3 What is thinking distance?

the distance a vehicle travels during the driver's reaction time

4 What is the centre of mass?

the point through which the weight of an object can be considered to act

5 What is the name for the steady speed a falling object reaches when the resistive force is equal to its weight?

terminal velocity

Put paper here

Put paper here

 Maths Skills

Practise your maths skills using the worked example and practice questions below.

Rearranging equations	Worked example	Practice
You need to be able to rearrange and apply many equations in physics, for example, the equation for power. Power is the rate at which energy is transferred or the rate at which work is done. It can be calculated using: $$\text{power (W)} = \frac{\text{energy transferred (J)}}{\text{time taken (s)}}$$ Remember: • a power of 1 W means a rate of energy transfer of 1 J per second • the shorter the time taken for an energy transfer, the greater the power • if the time taken to transfer energy is given in minutes or hours, you must convert it to seconds before calculating the power.	A microwave is marked as having a power of 900 W. How long does it take to transfer 13 500 J of energy? **Step 1:** write down the equation. $$\text{power (W)} = \frac{\text{energy transferred (J)}}{\text{time taken (s)}}$$ **Step 2:** work out which information in the question relates to the variables in the equation. power = 900 W, energy transferred = 13 500 J **Step 3:** put the numbers into the equation. $$900 = \frac{13\,500}{\text{time}}$$ **Step 4:** rearrange the equation. Multiply both sides of the equation by time: $$900 \times \text{time} = 13\,500$$ Then divide both sides of the equation by 900: $$\text{time} = \frac{13\,500}{900} = 15\,\text{s}$$ *Alternatively:* **Step 3:** rearrange the equation first. $$\text{time} = \frac{\text{energy}}{\text{power}}$$ **Step 4:** put the numbers into the equation. $$\text{time} = \frac{13\,500}{900} = 15\,\text{s}$$	**1** An LED lamp transfers 360 J of energy in 30 seconds. Calculate its power. **2** An electric cooker transfers 3 MJ of energy in 5 minutes. Calculate its power. **3** An electric kettle has a power of 3000 W. How much energy does it transfer in 45 seconds? **4** Rearrange the equation linking efficiency, useful power out, and total power in to calculate the total power out of a system.

Exam-style questions

01 A student is playing with a slinky spring.
They hold one end and pull the other end of the spring.

01.1 Energy is stored in the spring.
Identify where this energy has come from. **[1 mark]**
Tick **one** box.

Chemical energy in the student's muscles ☐

Chemical energy in a battery ☐

Light energy ☐

Sound energy ☐

01.2 Identify how the energy has been transferred to the spring. **[1 mark]**
Tick **one** box.

By an electric current ☐

By light ☐

By force ☐

By sound ☐

01.3 The spring has a spring constant of 20 N/m.
When the student pulls the spring it extends by 0.2 m.
Calculate the energy stored in the spring. Use the correct equation from the *Physics Equations Sheet*. **[2 marks]**

> **! Exam Tip**
>
> Always start your calculations by writing down the equation you're going to use!

energy stored = _____ J

02 This question is about conservation of energy.

02.1 Complete the statement of the law of conservation of energy. **[1 mark]**

Energy cannot be _____

_____ only transferred, stored, or dissipated.

02.2 When energy is dissipated it is stored in less useful ways.
Select **two** definitions of 'dissipated energy'. **[2 marks]**
Tick **two** boxes.

Useful energy that we can use ☐

Any energy created by a device ☐

Energy transferred to the surroundings that we cannot use ☐

Energy that is wasted ☐

> **! Exam Tip**
>
> Key definitions are really important to learn as they are easy marks in the exam.

02.3 **Figure 1** shows a pendulum.

Write the letter **K** in the box or boxes where the kinetic energy of the pendulum bob is at a maximum. **[1 mark]**

Figure 1

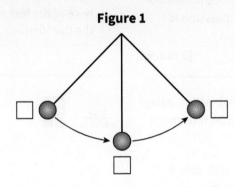

02.4 The pendulum swings backwards and forwards. The pendulum gradually stops swinging.

Explain why. **[1 mark]**

_____

_____

03 A student investigates the energy transfers of a tennis ball when it is dropped onto the classroom floor.

The student wants to calculate the energy transferred to the floor and surroundings when the ball first bounces.

03.1 Describe the measurements that the student needs to make.

Suggest measuring instruments that they could use to do this. **[5 marks]**

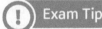
Exam Tip

There are two parts to this question. For everything you want to measure, you also have to say how you are going to measure it.

03.2 Suggest a problem that the student may have with making the measurements and how it might be overcome. **[2 marks]**

03.3 Describe in detail how they can use the measurements to calculate the energy transferred to the floor/surroundings. **[5 marks]**

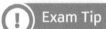
Exam Tip

The majority of the time, problems in practicals can be overcome by using technology.

03.4 Suggest whether you can or cannot use the term *efficiency* when describing what happens when the ball bounces.

Justify your answer. **[2 marks]**

04 A gymnast runs and lands on a springboard. Springs store energy when they are stretched or compressed. You can use the same equation to calculate energy in a stretched or compressed spring. You use compression instead of extension in your equation.

04.1 The gymnast is travelling at 10 m/s when they land on the springboard. The springboard contains a large spring that compresses when the gymnast lands on it. The mass of the gymnast is 40 kg.

Calculate the kinetic energy of the gymnast. **[2 marks]**

04.2 The spring constant of the spring is 20 000 N/m. Assume that all of the gymnast's kinetic energy is transferred to the elastic potential energy of the spring when the gymnast lands. Calculate the compression of the spring. **[3 marks]**

04.3 A manufacturer tests the spring in a springboard. The manufacturer finds that the spring does not compress by the distance predicted by the calculation. Suggest whether the actual compression is bigger or smaller than the predicted compression.
Explain your answer. **[3 marks]**

 Exam Tip

If you're confused, go back and re-read the text at the start of the question.

05 An Olympic archer can shoot an arrow at a target that is 80 m away. The archer draws back the string of a bow and releases it to shoot the arrow.

05.1 Describe the energy changes between the moment just before the archer releases the arrow and the moment when the arrow no longer has contact with the string. Write down the method by which the energy is transferred. **[3 marks]**

05.2 The archer decides to calculate the energy stored in the string. They make the following estimates:

- the spring constant of the string is 10^5 N/kg

- the extension of the string is 5 cm.

Use the correct equation from the *Physics Equations Sheet* to calculate the energy stored in the string. **[2 marks]**

 Exam Tip

Don't worry about the big numbers in this calculation. If you're not sure how to put 10^5 into your calculator, now is a great chance to practise.

05.3 The archer wants to find the speed of the arrow when it leaves the bow by direct measurement. Suggest a technique for finding the speed of the arrow. **[1 mark]**

05.4 Suggest **one** reason why the speed of the arrow determined by this technique might be lower than the values from **05.2** suggest. **[1 mark]**

05.5 The arrow hits the target and stops. Name the type of energy which has increased as a result of this process. **[1 mark]**

06 The high-speed train in **Figure 2** travels at a top speed of 200 mph (90 m/s).

Figure 2

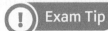

06.1 Suggest in terms of energy why the front of the train has the shape shown in **Figure 2**. **[1 mark]**

06.2 Calculate the kinetic energy of the train when it is travelling at top speed. Write your answer in kJ. Give your answer to **three** significant figures. The mass of the train is 700 000 kg. **[4 marks]**

 Exam Tip

Be careful with this equation; it's just the speed that is squared not the whole right-hand side.

06.3 Write down the work done by the brakes to bring the train to a complete stop. **[1 mark]**

07 An astronaut on the Moon is holding a hammer. They let it go and it hits the ground.

07.1 Describe the energy changes from the moment when the astronaut drops the hammer to the moment before the hammer hits the ground. **[2 marks]**

07.2 Give the method of energy transfer that is producing the change. **[1 mark]**

Exam Tip

The energy at the start and the end will be different. Be sure to use the correct terms to describe the energy changes.

07.3 Compare the speed of the hammer when it hits the ground on the Moon with the speed at which it would hit the ground if they were on Earth.
- Assume the mass of the hammer is the same.
- The gravitational field strength of the Moon is less than that of Earth.
- The hammer is dropped from the same height.

Explain your answer. You do not need to do any calculations. **[5 marks]**

Exam Tip

The question has given you three bullet points to discuss – make sure you cover all of them in your answer.

08 A tall hotel building has a lift designed to carry guests and their luggage.

08.1 A family, the lift, and their luggage have a total mass of 1220 kg. Calculate the change in the gravitational potential energy when the family moves up four floors. Each floor is 3.0 m high. Gravitational field strength is 9.8 N/kg. **[2 marks]**

Exam Tip

Don't forget to calculate the total height first!

08.2 The motor transfers a total energy of 280 kJ. Calculate the efficiency of the lift motor as a percentage. **[3 marks]**

08.3 There is also a lift designed to carry trolleys of cleaning supplies and laundry. The power of this lift is 10 kW. Suggest measurements that you could make to work out which lift motor is more efficient. Explain how you would use the measurements to calculate the efficiency. **[6 marks]**

Exam Tip

Students often forget to convert the decimal to a percentage or forget the % sign after the answer; both of these mistakes will cost you marks.

09 In a factory, a forklift truck does work lifting a box onto a shelf.

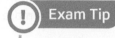

09.1 Write down the equation that links power, energy transferred, and time. **[1 mark]**

09.2 To lift the box onto the shelf, the motor of the forklift truck transfers 30 000 J of energy. The power of the truck motor is 15 000 W. Show that it takes 2 seconds for the truck to lift the box onto the shelf. **[3 marks]**

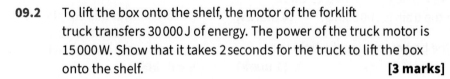
Exam Tip

'Show' questions are amazing – you already know what the answer is; you just need to do the working. The great thing is, if you don't get the right answer, you can just try again!

09.3 A second truck lifts an identical box onto the same shelf. The second truck takes longer to move the box onto the shelf. Compare the power of the two trucks. **[1 mark]**

10 A teacher set the students a challenge to check their understanding of energy. The teacher puts a piece of track on the desk and raises one end. A marble rolls down the track and moves horizontally off the desk, as shown in **Figure 3**.

Figure 3

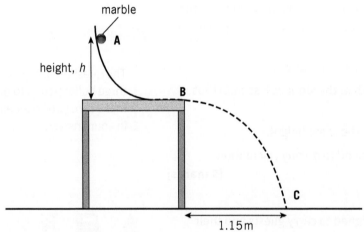

Exam Tip

Try labelling the diagram at each point with the types of energy; it will help with later questions.

10.1 Describe the changes in energy between points **A** and **B**. **[2 marks]**

10.2 The ball is travelling at a horizontal speed of 1.3 m/s when it leaves the table.

Suggest the equipment that the students could use to measure the speed of the ball at the end of the track. **[1 mark]**

10.3 There is a target at point **C** on the floor that the students are aiming to hit. The horizontal distance of **C** from the edge of the table is 1.15 m. It takes 820 ms for the marble to move from **B** to **C**. Calculate the distance travelled by the ball.

Write down **one** assumption that you made. Write down whether or not the marble will hit the target. **[5 marks]**

Exam Tip

There are three different parts to this question; make sure you include all of them in your answer.

10.4 Suggest how the students should adjust the equipment to make the ball hit the target. Explain your answer in terms of energy. **[4 marks]**

11 A student researches the efficiency of different electric motors used in cars. In all system changes, energy is wasted.

11.1 Describe what is meant by wasted energy. **[1 mark]**

11.2 The student knows that car **A** requires a total energy input of 20 J to move across the floor. It has useful energy output of 12 J. Draw a Sankey diagram to show this transfer. **[2 marks]**

11.3 Calculate the efficiency of car **A** as a decimal. **[2 marks]**

11.4 The efficiency of car **B** is 50%. Write down which car wastes more energy. Explain your answer. **[2 marks]**

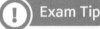

> ! **Exam Tip**
>
> This question has asked for the answer as a decimal, so don't multiply by 100.

12 A student investigates how the height of a ramp affects the speed of a trolley. The student puts the trolley at the top of a ramp. They release the trolley and measure the speed of the trolley at the bottom of the ramp.

12.1 Explain why the student cannot use a ruler and stopclock to measure the speed at the bottom of the ramp.

Suggest the equipment that the student should use instead.
[2 marks]

12.2 The student measures the height of the ramp. It is 0.12 m. Gravitational field strength is 9.8 N/kg. The mass of the trolley is 0.25 kg. Calculate the gravitational potential energy of the trolley at the top of the ramp. **[2 marks]**

> ! **Exam Tip**
>
> You'll always be given the value for gravitational field strength, so you don't need to remember it.

12.3 The student measures the kinetic energy of the trolley at the bottom of the ramp. They discover that the kinetic energy of the trolley is less than the gravitational potential energy.

The student says: '*There is a mistake in the data. The answers should be the same.*'

Do you agree? Give reasons for your answer. **[2 marks]**

13 A student is watching a video about car safety. In the video, cars with robot drivers hit a barrier. The student notices that:

- some cars stop after colliding with the barrier
- some cars bounce off the barrier.

13.1 The barrier compresses on impact but does not return to its original shape.

Explain why you cannot use the equation for elastic potential energy in energy transfer calculations in this case. **[1 mark]**

13.2 Data about two cars colliding with the same barrier is shown in **Table 1**.

Table 1

Car	Mass in kg	Speed before hitting the barrier in m/s	Speed after hitting the barrier in m/s	Energy transferred during collision in J
A	1000	50	0	1.25×10^6
B	1000	50	25	

Calculate the energy transferred by car **B** during the collision.

Give your answer in standard form and to an appropriate number of significant figures. **[7 marks]**

Exam Tip

Don't use more significant figures than the question asks for.

13.3 Identify which car transfers less energy to the surroundings. Explain why. **[2 marks]**

Exam Tip

You need to give the why to get the second mark in this question.

13.4 Another student looks at the data and sees that the speed of car **B** has been reduced by 50% compared with car **A** after the collision. Car **A**'s speed has been reduced by 100% after the collision. The student expected the energy transferred by car **B** would be half the energy transferred by car **A**.

Suggest why this is **not** the case. **[2 marks]**

Exam Tip

There are lots of other energy types involved in this situation – try to think of as many as you can.

14 A motorcycle company produces data that shows how the efficiency of a motorcycle compares with that of a car over a range of speeds. Graphs of efficiency against speed for the motorcycle and car are shown in **Figure 4**.

Figure 4

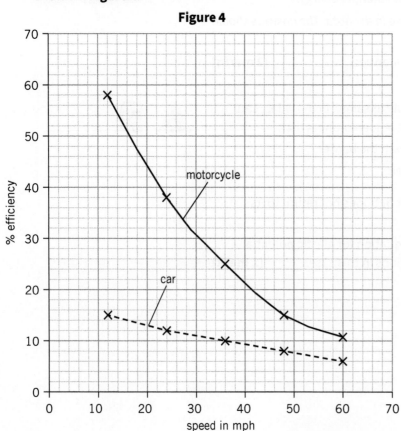

14.1 Suggest what the company used as the source of input energy.

[1 mark]

14.2 Write down the type of energy into which this energy was usefully transferred.

[1 mark]

14.3 Suggest a process that transfers energy in a way that is **not** useful.

[2 marks]

14.4 Describe how the efficiency of each vehicle varies with speed.

[4 marks]

14.5 Calculate the rate of change of efficiency with speed for the motorcycle at 30 mph.

The units are % per mph.

[3 marks]

> **! Exam Tip**
>
> The units give you a big clue to the equation. % per mph is a bit like saying % divided by mph.

15 A student makes a track for marbles to roll down (**Figure 5**). They let the marble go from point A.

Figure 5

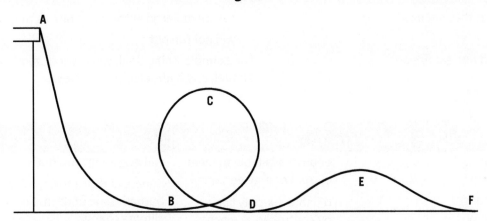

15.1 At which point A, B, C, D, E, or F does the marble have the *most* gravitational potential energy?

[1 mark]

15.2 At which points A, B, C, D, E, or F does the marble have *no* gravitational potential energy?

[1 mark]

15.3 At which point or points A, B, C, D, E, or F does the marble have the *most* kinetic energy?

[1 mark]

15.4 Describe and explain what would happen if point C was *higher* than point A.

[2 marks]

15.5 When it reaches point F, the marble does not have the same amount of energy that it had at the start. Suggest and explain where the energy has gone.

[2 marks]

P6 Energy resources

Energy resources

The main ways in which we use the Earth's energy resources are:
- generating electricity
- heating
- transport.

Most of our energy currently comes from **fossil fuels** – coal, oil, and natural gas.

Fuels are useful stores of energy. The choice of fuel depends on factors such as ease of storage, energy content, and safety.

Reliability, efficiency, environmental impact

Some energy resources are more reliable and efficient than others.
- **Reliable** energy resources are ones that are available all the time (or at predictable times) and in sufficient quantities.
- **Efficient** energy resources do not transfer a lot of energy to the surroundings when they are used.

Both **renewable** and **non-renewable** energy resources have some kind of **environmental impact** when we use them.

Non-renewable energy resources

- not replaced as quickly as they are used
- will eventually run out

For example, fossil fuels and nuclear fission.

Renewable energy resources

- can be replaced at the same rate as they are used
- will not run out

For example, solar, tidal, wave, wind, geothermal, biofuel, and hydroelectric energies.

Resource	Main uses	Source	Advantages	Disadvantages
coal	generating electricity	extracted from underground	enough available to meet current energy demands	will eventually run out
oil	generating electricity, transport, heating	extracted from underground	reliable – supply can be controlled to meet demand; relatively cheap to extract and use	release carbon dioxide when burned – one of the main causes of climate change; release other polluting gases, such as sulfur dioxide (from coal and oil), which causes acid rain; oil spills in the oceans kill marine life
natural gas	generating electricity, heating	extracted from underground		
nuclear fission	generating electricity	mining naturally occurring elements, such as uranium and plutonium	no polluting gases or greenhouse gases produced; large amount of energy transferred per kg of fuel; reliable – supply can be controlled to meet demand	produces nuclear waste, which is: • dangerous • difficult and expensive to dispose of • stored for centuries before it is safe to dispose of nuclear power plants are expensive to: • build and run • shut down

(Table row label, left side: Non-renewable energy resources)

Key Terms

Make sure you can write a definition for these key terms.

carbon neutral   efficient   environmental impact   fossil fuel
non-renewable   reliable   renewable

Resource	Main uses	Source	Advantages	Disadvantages
solar energy	generating electricity	sunlight transfers energy to solar cells	can be used in remote places very cheap to run once installed no pollution/greenhouse gases produced	supply depends on weather expensive to buy and install cannot supply large-scale demand
	heating	sunlight transfers energy to solar heating panels		
hydroelectric energy	generating electricity	water flowing downhill turns generators	low running cost no fuel costs reliable supply can be controlled to meet demand	expensive to build hydroelectric dams flood a large area behind the dam, destroying habitats and resulting in greenhouse gas production from rotting vegetation
tidal energy	generating electricity	turbines on tidal barrages turned by water as the tide comes in and goes out	predictable supply as there are always tides can produce large amounts of electricity no fuel costs no pollution/greenhouse gases produced	tidal barrages: • change marine habitats and can harm animals • restrict access and can be dangerous for boats • are expensive to build and maintain • cannot control supply • supply varies depending on time of month
wave energy	generating electricity	floating generators powered by waves moving up and down	low running cost no fuel costs no pollution/greenhouse gases produced	floating generators • change marine habitats and can harm animals • restrict access and can be dangerous for boats • are expensive to build, install, and maintain • are dependent on weather • cannot supply large-scale demand
wind energy	generating electricity	turbines turned by the wind	low running cost no fuel costs no pollution/greenhouse gases produced	supply depends on weather large amounts of land needed to generate enough electricity for large-scale demand can produce noise pollution for nearby residents
geothermal energy	generating electricity heating	radioactive substances deep within the Earth transfer heat energy to the surface	low running cost no fuel costs no pollution/greenhouse gases produced	expensive to set up only possible in a few suitable locations around the world
biofuels	generating electricity transport	fuel produced from living or recently living organisms, for example, plants and animal waste	can be **carbon neutral** – the amount of carbon dioxide released when the fuel is burnt is equal to the amount of carbon dioxide absorbed when the fuel is grown reliable and supply can be controlled to meet demand	expensive to produce biofuels growing biofuels requires a lot of land and water that could be used for food production can lead to deforestation – forests are cleared for growing biofuel crops

Renewable energy resources

Retrieval

Learn the answers to the questions below then cover the answers column with a piece of paper and write as many as you can. Check and repeat.

	P6 questions	Answers
1	What is a fuel?	a useful store of energy
2	What factors affect the choice of fuel?	energy content, ease of use, safety
3	Why is a fuel not 100% efficient?	some energy is transferred to the surroundings
4	What is a non-renewable energy resource?	will eventually run out; is not replaced at the same rate it is being used
5	What is a renewable energy resource?	will not run out; it is being (or can be) replaced at the same rate as it is used
6	What are the main renewable and non-renewable resources available on Earth?	renewable: solar, tidal, wave, wind, geothermal, biofuel, hydroelectric non-renewable: coal, oil, gas, nuclear
7	What are the main advantages of using coal as an energy resource?	enough available to meet current demand, reliable, can control supply to match demand, cheap to extract and use
8	What are the main disadvantages of using coal as an energy resource?	will eventually run out, releases CO_2 which contributes to climate change, releases sulfur dioxide which causes acid rain
9	What are the main advantages of using solar energy?	can be used in remote places, no polluting gases, no waste products, very low running cost
10	What are the main disadvantages of using solar energy?	unreliable, cannot control supply, initial set up expensive, cannot be used on a large scale
11	What are the main advantages of using wave turbines?	no polluting gases produced, no waste products, low running cost, no fuel costs
12	What are the main disadvantages of using wave turbines?	unreliable, dependent on weather, cannot control supply, initial set up expensive, can harm marine habitats, hazard for boats, cannot be used on a large scale
13	What are the main advantages of using wind turbines?	low running cost, no fuel costs, no pollution/greenhouse gases produced
14	What are the main disadvantages of using wind turbines?	unreliable, dependent on weather, cannot control supply, take up a lot of space, can produce noise pollution
15	What are the advantages and the disadvantages of using geothermal energy?	advantages: no polluting gases, low running cost disadvantages: initial set up expensive, available in few locations
16	What are the main advantages and disadvantages of using biofuels?	advantages: can be 'carbon neutral', reliable disadvantages: expensive to produce, use land/water that might be needed to grow food
17	What are the main advantages and disadvantages of using hydroelectric power?	advantages: no polluting gases, no waste products, low running cost, no fuel cost, reliable, can be controlled to meet demand disadvantages: initial set up expensive, dams can harm/destroy marine habitats

Now use the questions below to check your knowledge from previous chapters.

P6

Previous questions

Answers

1	According to Newton's Second Law, what is the acceleration of an object proportional to?	the force acting on it
2	What two quantities do you need to calculate a moment?	force and distance from a pivot
3	Why does the temperature of a vehicle's brakes increase when the brakes are applied?	work done by the frictional force between the brakes and the wheels transfers kinetic energy to thermal energy
4	What is the unit for energy?	joule (J)
5	Describe the energy transfers when a battery-powered toy car is used.	energy is transferred from the chemical energy of the battery to the kinetic energy of the toy car – some energy is dissipated to the thermal energy of the surroundings

Put paper here

 # Maths Skills

Practise your maths skills using the worked example and practice questions below.

Converting units	Worked example	Practice
You need to use standard units in calculations. If the numbers that you are given are not in standard units, you should convert them. Remember, standard units of: • energy = joules, J • power = watts, W • time = seconds, s Small and large numbers are sometimes shown with prefixes. Remember: • kilo, k = 1000 • Mega, M = 1 000 000 • milli, m = 0.001, or $\frac{1}{1000}$ In terms of time: • there are 60 seconds in a minute • there are 60 minutes in an hour When doing calculations of energy: energy transferred (J) = work done (J) power (W) = $\frac{\text{energy transferred (J)}}{\text{time taken (s)}}$	A shower has a power of 10 kW. Calculate the energy transferred per week if the shower is used for one hour every day. **Step 1:** convert power to watts. 1 kW = 1000 W 10 kW = 10 000 W **Step 2:** convert time to seconds. 1 hour = 60 s/min × 60 min/hr = 3600 s **Step 3:** rearrange the equation. energy (J) = power (W) × time (s) **Step 4:** calculate the energy per hour. energy = 10 000 W × 3600 s = 36 000 000 J **Step 5:** calculate the energy transferred per week. energy = 36 000 000 J × 7 (hours used per week) = 252 000 000 J	1 A power station produces 7800 MW of power. Calculate the energy it transfers in a day. 2 An LED lamp has a power of 12 mW. Calculate the energy it transfers in one minute. 3 Calculate the time it takes a 52 kW motor to transfer 120 000 J.

Practice

Exam-style questions

01 A student finds some data about electricity production and how it has changed over time.

They plot the data on a bar chart, as shown in **Figure 1**.

Figure 1

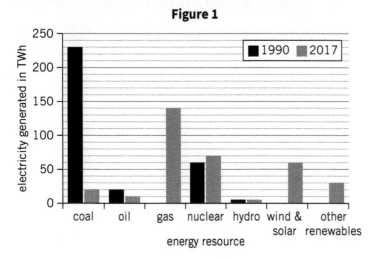

 Exam Tip

Draw lines from the tops of the bars across to the axis to help you read off data.

01.1 Explain why the student plotted the data as a bar chart and not as a line graph. **[2 marks]**

_____

_____

01.2 Compare the amount of electricity generated using renewable resources in 1990 with the equivalent figure in 2017. **[2 marks]**

Exam Tip

Use data from the graph.

_____

_____

_____

01.3 Estimate the change in the use of fossil fuels between the two years in terawatt hours (TWh). **[3 marks]**

Exam Tip

Don't worry if you've never heard of TWh before. Just use them as the unit for this question, treating them the same as you would any other unit.

_____

_____

_____

_____

01.4 There was a large decrease in the use of one non-renewable resource for generating electricity between 1990 and 2017.

Identify this resource.

Suggest why use of this resource in power stations has decreased since 1990. **[2 marks]**

_____

_____

_____

02 A student investigates friction. The student ties string around a wooden block and applies a force. They measure the frictional force when the block just begins to move. They increase the weight on the block and repeat the experiment. They repeat the experiment with a brick.

The data is plotted in **Figure 2**.

Figure 2

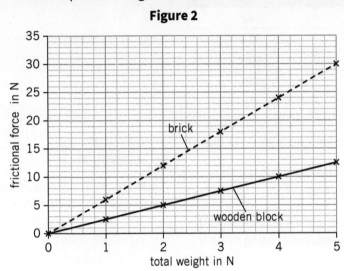

02.1 Write down the frictional force on a brick with a weight of 2.5 N when the brick just begins to move. **[1 mark]**

_____

02.2 Write down the equation that links weight, mass, and gravitational field strength. **[1 mark]**

_____

02.3 A wooden block has a weight of 1.4 N. Calculate the mass of the block. Gravitational field strength = 9.8 N/kg. **[3 marks]**

mass = _____ kg

02.4 A student applies a force of 5 N to the wooden block. Calculate the expected acceleration of the block. **[6 marks]**

acceleration = _____ m/s^2

02.5 The actual acceleration is found to be larger than the value calculated in **02.4**. Suggest a reason why. **[1 mark]**

_____

03 A student finds data relating to the cost of generating electricity and the grams of CO_2 produced. A unit is a measure of electricity generation. The CO_2 produced included emissions while the power station or equipment was being built and while it is in use. **Table 1** shows the data found by the student.

Table 1

Resource	Cost per unit	CO_2 produced per unit in g
solar (the Sun)	40.0	48
nuclear fuel	3.0	12
coal	1.5	820
natural gas	5.0	490
biofuel	2.0	230

03.1 Suggest why the cost per unit for solar power is so high. **[1 mark]**

03.2 Suggest why the cheapest method in the table may cause environmental problems. Explain your answer. **[3 marks]**

03.3 **Table 1** shows that nuclear fuel is a relatively low-cost option, with the lowest emissions. Suggest **two** disadvantages of using nuclear power stations to generate electricity. **[2 marks]**

03.4 The student thinks about how biofuel is produced. They suggest that the impact of biofuel in terms of CO_2 emissions is actually lower than that shown in **Table 1**. Suggest why. **[3 marks]**

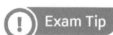
While the Sun is free, it's not free to harvest that energy.

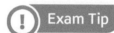
Think about safety and renewability.

04 A student is investigating how wind turbines work. The student measures the power output of a wind turbine for different wind speeds.

The data for wind speed and power is shown in **Table 2**.

04.1 Using the axes in **Figure 3**, plot the data in **Table 2**. **[5 marks]**

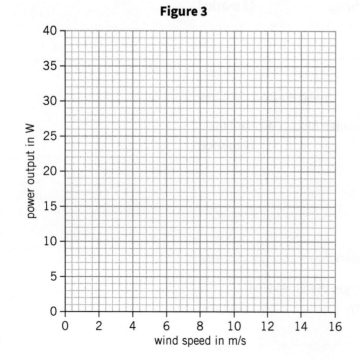

Figure 3

Table 2

Wind speed in m/s	Power output in W
0	0.0
2	0.0
4	0.1
6	1.2
8	2.4
10	3.6
12	3.6
14	3.6

04.2 Describe the relationship between wind speed and power output.

[3 marks]

04.3 Wind generators can be used to produce electricity used in homes. Suggest **one** advantage and **one** disadvantage of generating electricity using the wind.

[2 marks]

05 A student collects data from a solar cell. They use a lamp to represent the Sun, and model the effect of clouds by putting sheets of transparent film on top of the solar cell. Then they calculate the energy per second produced by the solar cell. Their results are shown in **Table 3**.

Table 3

Number of sheets of transparent film	Energy per second		Mean energy per second
	Test 1	Test 2	
0	5.24	5.15	5.2
1	4.12	4.32	4.22
2	3.65	2.11	2.88
3	3.21	3.32	3.27
4	2.5	2.4	2.45
5	1.7	1.6	1.65

05.1 Write down the independent and dependent variables. **[2 marks]**

05.2 List **three** control variables. **[3 marks]**

05.3 Another student looked at the results in **Table 3**. They gave the following feedback.

Statement 1: 'For two sheets, 2.11 is an outlier.'

Statement 2: 'The columns are not labelled correctly.'

Statement 3: 'The significant figures of the measurements are inconsistent.'

Read each of the statements. Write down what action, if any, should be taken as a result. **[3 marks]**

05.4 Calculate the uncertainty in the measurement of energy when one sheet was used. **[2 marks]**

06 There are different methods of generating electricity. Some of the resources used to generate electricity are also used for transportation. Some are only used to generate electricity. Some are renewable and some are non-renewable.

06.1 Describe the difference between a renewable and a non-renewable resource. **[1 mark]**

> 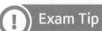 **Exam Tip**
>
> Independent variables are the ones that you change.

> 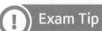 **Exam Tip**
>
> In your answer make it clear which statements you're referring to. Don't make it hard to mark your work by not laying it out in a neat manner.

06.2 Tick **all** the correct boxes in **Table 4**. There will be a minimum of two ticks in each column. **[3 marks]**

Exam Tip

The question tells you a lot here. There will be at least two ticks in each column, and that should help you work out the answer.

Table 4

Resource	Used to generate electricity	Used as a fuel in cars	Is a renewable resource
coal			
biofuel			
oil			
wind			

06.3 Some non-renewable resources cause environmental problems, such as pollution. Describe **one** reason why, despite this fact, they are used to generate electricity. **[1 mark]**

07 The way in which electricity has been generated has changed over time. **Figure 4** shows the changes in the primary sources of energy in the UK between 1990 and 2015.

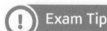

Figure 4

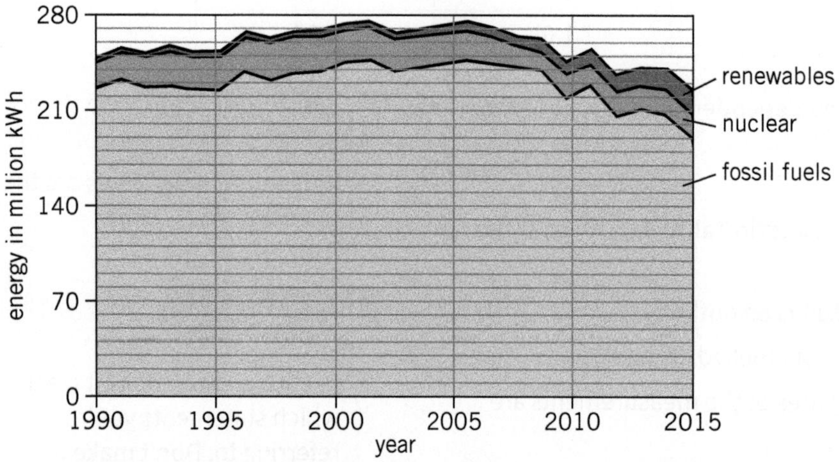

07.1 Name **one** renewable source of energy. **[1 mark]**

07.2 Use data from **Figure 4** to compare the percentage energy use from fossil fuels in 1990 with the percentage use in 2015. Show calculations to justify your answer. **[5 marks]**

Exam Tip

Use data from the graph and clearly link it to the statements you make.

07.3 Estimate the rate of decrease of energy use between 2010 and 2015. Use your estimate to determine the number of years it will take for the energy use in the UK to become half of the value in 2015. **[4 marks]**

07.4 Suggest **one** reason why the total energy use might halve in this time and **one** reason why the total energy use might **not** halve in this time. **[2 marks]**

08 A village has a wind turbine installed. The output of the turbine varies between zero and 60 kW. The people in the village are considering increasing their use of renewables using either wind turbines or biofuel generators.

They collect the following data:

- annual energy requirement of village = 7000 MWh
- cost of wind turbine = £1 million
- cost per kWh generated with biofuel (installation and running) = £0.50

08.1 Calculate the annual energy requirement of the village in joules (J). **[2 marks]**

08.2 The mean power output of a wind turbine is 33 kW. Calculate how many wind turbines are needed to produce the annual energy requirements of the village. **[4 marks]**

08.3 Calculate which renewable resource would be cheaper to produce the annual energy requirements of the village. **[4 marks]**

08.4 Evaluate the use of each renewable resource in terms of its effect on the environment. **[6 marks]**

09 A student is comparing fossil fuels with energy resources that involve water.

09.1 Name **two** fossil fuels. **[2 marks]**

09.2 The student learns that electricity can be generated using the motion of waves at sea. Name another resource that uses water to generate electricity. Describe how electricity is generated using that resource. **[3 marks]**

09.3 One benefit of using fossil fuels is that they are a reliable resource. Compare the reliability of the resource you described in **09.2** with that of fossil fuels. **[2 marks]**

09.4 Fossil fuels produce carbon dioxide when they burn. Explain why this is an environmental issue. **[2 marks]**

09.5 Describe **one** environmental issue with the resource you described in **09.2**. **[1 mark]**

10 A bungee jumper is standing on a platform attached to a 3.2 m bungee cord. They jump off the platform and touch some water 10 m below. **Figure 5** shows the platform.

The mass of the bungee jumper is 60 kg. Gravitational field strength is 9.8 N/kg.

10.1 Write down the equation that links gravitational potential energy, mass, gravitational field strength, and height. **[1 mark]**

10.2 Calculate the gravitational potential energy of the bungee jumper before they jump. **[2 marks]**

10.3 Calculate the spring constant of the bungee cord. Use the correct equation from the *Physics Equations Sheet*. Assume that no energy is wasted during energy transfer. Give your answer to **two** significant figures. **[5 marks]**

Figure 5

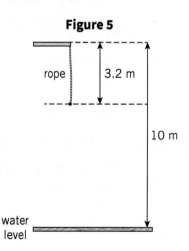

rope | 3.2 m

10 m

water level

P7 General properties of waves

Waves in air, fluids, and solids

Waves are disturbances produced by oscillating sources that transfer energy or information from one place to another without transferring matter. Waves may be **transverse** or **longitudinal**.

For waves in water and air, it is the wave and not the substance that moves.

- When a light object is dropped into still water, it produces ripples (waves) on the water which spread out, but neither the object nor the water moves with the ripples.
- When you speak, your voice box vibrates, making sound waves travel through the air. The air itself does not travel away from your throat, otherwise a vacuum would be created.

Mechanical waves

Mechanical waves require a substance (a medium) to travel through.

Mechanical waves can be longitudinal or transverse. Examples of mechanical waves include sound waves, water waves, waves on springs and ropes, and seismic waves produced by earthquakes.

When waves travel through a substance, the particles in the substance **oscillate** (vibrate) and pass energy on to neighbouring particles.

Transverse waves

The oscillations of a transverse wave are *perpendicular* (at right angles) to the direction in which the waves transfer energy.

Ripples on the surface of water and electromagnetic waves are examples of transverse waves.

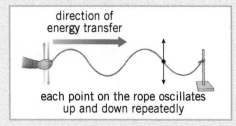

direction of energy transfer

each point on the rope oscillates up and down repeatedly

Longitudinal waves

The oscillations of a longitudinal wave are *parallel* to the direction in which the waves transfer energy.

Longitudinal waves cause particles in a substance to be squashed closer together and pulled further apart, producing areas of **compression** and **rarefaction** in the substance.

Sound waves in air are an example of longitudinal waves.

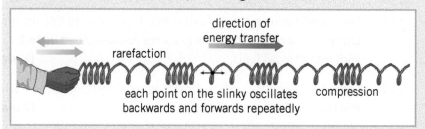

direction of energy transfer

rarefaction

each point on the slinky oscillates backwards and forwards repeatedly

compression

Describing waves

Wave motion is described by a number of properties.

Property	Description	Unit
amplitude A	maximum displacement of a point on a wave from its undisturbed position	metre (m)
frequency f	number of waves passing a fixed point per second	hertz (Hz)
period T	time taken for one complete wave to pass a fixed point	second (s)
wavelength λ	distance from one point on a wave to the equivalent point on the next wave	metre (m)
wave speed v	distance travelled by each wave per second, and the speed at which energy is transferred by the wave	metres per second (m/s)

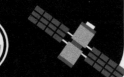

P7

Properties of waves

Frequency and period are related by the equation:

$$\text{period (s)} = \frac{1}{\text{frequency (Hz)}} \qquad T = \frac{1}{f}$$

All waves obey the wave equation:

$$\text{wave speed (m/s)} = \text{frequency (Hz)} \times \text{wavelength (m)}$$

$$v = f\lambda$$

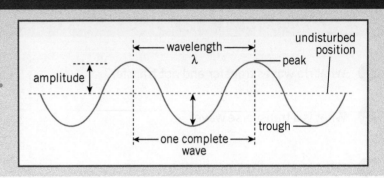

When waves travel from one medium to another, their speed and wavelength may change but the frequency always stays the same.

The speed of ripples on water can be slow enough to measure using a stopwatch and ruler, and applying the equation:

$$\text{speed (m/s)} = \frac{\text{distance (m)}}{\text{time (s)}}$$

The speed of sound in air can be measured by using a stopwatch to measure the time taken for a sound to travel a known distance, and applying the same equation.

Waves at boundaries

When waves arrive at the boundary between two different substances, one or more of the following things can happen:

Absorption – the energy of the waves is transferred to the energy of the substance they travel into (for example, when food is heated in a microwave)

Diffraction – waves spread out when they go through a gap

Reflection – the waves bounce back

Refraction – the waves change speed and direction (velocity) as they cross the boundary

Transmission – the waves carry on moving once they've crossed the boundary, but may be refracted

Applications and effects of diffraction and refraction

- Radio waves are diffracted around hills.

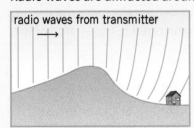

- Telescope images can be blurred because of diffraction.
- Refraction of ultrasound waves in medical scanning can result in double images.

Diffraction

Waves diffract (spread out) when they go through a gap or move past an obstacle. If the size of the gap and wavelength of the wave are about the same, the waves are diffracted a lot.

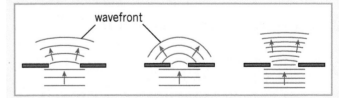

 **Key Terms**

Make sure you can write a definition for these key terms.

| absorption | amplitude | compression | diffraction | frequency | longitudinal | mechanical wave | oscillate |
| period | rarefaction | reflection | refraction | transmission | transverse | wavelength | wave speed |

   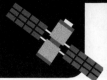

Learn the answers to the questions below then cover the answers column with a piece of paper and write as many as you can. Check and repeat.

P7 questions	Answers
1 What do waves transfer and not transfer?	transfer energy and information; do not transfer matter
2 What is a transverse wave?	oscillations/vibrations are perpendicular (at right angles) to the direction of energy transfer
3 What is a longitudinal wave?	oscillations/vibrations are parallel to the direction of energy transfer
4 Give an example of a transverse wave.	electromagnetic waves; waves on the surface of water
5 Give an example of a longitudinal wave.	sound waves
6 What is a compression?	area in longitudinal waves where the particles are squashed closer together
7 What is a rarefaction?	area in longitudinal waves where the particles are pulled further apart
8 What is the amplitude of a wave?	maximum displacement of a point on the wave from its undisturbed position
9 What is the wavelength of a wave?	distance from a point on one wave to the equivalent point on the adjacent wave
10 What is the frequency of a wave?	number of waves passing a fixed point per second
11 What unit is frequency measured in?	hertz (Hz)
12 What is the period of a wave?	the time for one wave to pass a fixed point
13 What happens when waves are absorbed by a substance?	energy of the wave is transferred to the energy of the substance
14 What is the equation for wave speed?	wave speed = frequency × wavelength
15 What three things can happen to a wave that hits a boundary between two media?	it can be reflected, transmitted, or absorbed
16 What happens to a wave when it is diffracted?	it spreads out
17 When is diffraction more noticeable?	when the wavelength is about the same size as the gap

Put paper here

Now use the questions below to check your knowledge from previous chapters.

P7

Previous questions

Answers

	Previous questions	Answers
1	How do you find the spring constant from a force–extension graph of a spring?	find the gradient of the straight-line section
2	How is the force acting on an object related to its momentum?	force acting on an object = rate of change of momentum
3	What is a non-renewable energy resource?	a resource that will eventually run out; it is not replaced at the same rate it is being used
4	What is conservation of energy?	energy cannot be created or destroyed, only transferred or dissipated
5	What is a system?	an object or group of objects

Put paper here *Put paper here*

 ## Maths Skills

Practise your maths skills using the worked example and practice questions below.

Rearranging equations	Worked example	Practice
You need to be able to rearrange and apply many equations in physics, for example, the equation for wave speed.	A doctor uses a source of gamma rays in a hospital. The wavelength of the gamma rays is 1.2×10^{-15} m. Calculate the frequency of the gamma rays if they travel at 3×10^{8} m/s.	1 A microwave oven produces microwaves with a wavelength of 2.5 cm. Calculate the frequency if they travel at 3×10^{8} m/s.

Wave speed is the distance travelled by each wave per second, and the speed at which energy is transferred by the wave. It can be calculated using:

$$\text{speed (m/s)} = \text{frequency (Hz)} \times \text{wavelength (m)}$$

The numbers involved in this calculation can be very long when written down, so it is usually better to rearrange the equation before doing the calculation.

For electromagnetic waves, you can check your calculation. Put your calculated number back into the equation to calculate the wave speed. It should equal 3×10^{8} m/s. All electromagnetic waves travel at this speed through space or in a vacuum.

Step 1: write down the equation.

speed (m/s) = frequency (Hz) × wavelength (m)

Step 2: rearrange the equation.

$$\text{frequency (Hz)} = \frac{\text{speed (m/s)}}{\text{wavelength (m)}}$$

Step 3: put the numbers into the equation.

$$\text{frequency} = \frac{3\times10^{8}\,\text{m/s}}{1.2\times10^{-15}\,\text{m}} = 2.5\times10^{23}\,\text{Hz}$$

Step 4: check your calculation is correct.

speed (m/s) = frequency (Hz) × wavelength (m)

$$= 2.5\times10^{23}\,\text{Hz} \times 1.2\times10^{-15}\,\text{m}$$

$$= 3\times10^{8}\,\text{m/s}$$

This is the speed at which gamma rays (electromagnetic waves) travel.

2 An X-ray machine produces X-rays of wavelength 1.5×10^{-10} m. Calculate the frequency if they travel at 3×10^{8} m/s.

3 The human eye detects waves with a frequency of 4×10^{14} Hz as 'red'. Calculate the wavelength of red light if it travels at 3×10^{8} m/s.

01 A student makes a wave on a long thin spring.

The spring is attached to the wall.

The wave is shown in **Figure 1**.

Figure 1

hand motion

01.1 Write down the type of wave that the student produces. **[1 mark]**

_____

01.2 On **Figure 1** draw an arrow to show the wavelength of the wave.

[1 mark]

01.3 Describe what the student should do to produce waves with a smaller amplitude.

Explain your answer. **[2 marks]**

_____

_____

_____

02 One of the highest measured ocean waves was measured at a height of 34 metres from peak to trough.

The period of the wave was 14.8 s.

The wavelength was calculated to be 342 m.

02.1 Calculate the amplitude of the wave. **[2 marks]**

amplitude = _____ m

02.2 Calculate the speed of the wave.

Use an equation from the *Physics Equations Sheet*.

Show your working. **[4 marks]**

speed = _____ m/s

02.3 A student compares this wave with the waves seen in a ripple tank. A ripple tank is a tray of water on four legs.

Estimate the amplitude of waves in a ripple tank. **[1 mark]**

_____

02.4 The speed of waves in a ripple tank is found to be 50 cm/s. Suggest whether the speed of a wave is proportional to its amplitude.

[3 marks]

_____
_____
_____
_____

03 A child is throwing stones into a pond. The ripples move across the surface of the water.

03.1 Compare the motion of the surface of the water with the motion of the wave. **[1 mark]**

03.2 The stone makes a sound when it hits the water. The sound wave and the ripple move towards the child. Describe the difference between the motion of the particles on the surface of the water and the motion of the air particles in the sound wave. **[2 marks]**

03.3 Write down the equation that links wave speed, frequency, and wavelength. **[1 mark]**

03.4 The frequency of the sound that the stone makes is 400 Hz. The speed of sound in air is 340 m/s. Calculate the wavelength of the sound waves. **[3 marks]**

04 You can use a slinky coil to model waves. The wave on the slinky coil has compressions and rarefactions.

04.1 On **Figure 2** write the letter **C** above a compression, and the letter **R** above a rarefaction. **[2 marks]**

Figure 2

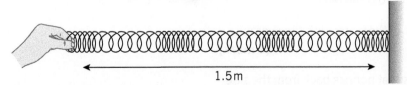

1.5 m

04.2 Show that the wavelength of the wave is 0.5 m. **[2 marks]**

04.3 The wave is travelling at 1.0 m/s. Calculate the frequency of the wave. State the unit. Explain what this means in terms of the motion of the person's hand. **[5 marks]**

05 A student watches a video about different types of wave. The video describes ripples on a water surface and sound waves.

05.1 Write down which of these types of wave is longitudinal. **[1 mark]**

05.2 Describe an experiment to show that, as the wave travels, the air and water particles are not carried with it. Describe the observations that you would make and what those observations show. **[6 marks]**

05.3 Here are some examples of waves. Circle the mechanical waves. **[1 mark]**

> sound   water   electromagnetic   seismic

06 A student sets up a ripple tank to measure the speed of water waves. The student takes a bar with a motor attached to it to make it vibrate. The bar is attached to a power supply and is partly submerged in a tray of water. A lamp above the tray of water projects an image of the ripples onto the desk below the ripple tank.

06.1 Describe a hazard associated with this experiment. Describe a strategy to reduce the risk of injury due to the hazard. **[2 marks]**

> **! Exam Tip**
>
> Even if you've never done this experiment before you can apply your practical skills to this new context. Look at the equipment involved and think of common hazards to do with them.

06.2 The student turns on the motor and sees the image of ripples moving across the desk. The student records that the number of waves passing a point in 10 s is 5 and that the number of waves in 20 cm on the desk is 15. Suggest what can be calculated from this data. Include the units. **[2 marks]**

06.3 Describe how to perform the calculations you have suggested using the data collected by the student. Explain your reasoning. **[4 marks]**

> **! Exam Tip**
>
> You should always match the resolution of your answer to the data given in the question.

06.4 Use the data recorded by the student to calculate the speed of the ripples in the tank. Give your answer in standard form. Explain why the answer should be given to **one** significant figure. **[6 marks]**

07 A student sets up a ripple tank. They use a cylindrical bar to make ripples that move from left to right across the tank.

07.1 Compare the motion of the surface of the water with the overall motion of the wave. **[1 mark]**

07.2 The student notices that the waves that bounce back from the side of the tank are not as high as the waves before they hit it. Name the property of the wave that has changed. **[1 mark]**

07.3 The student puts two barriers in the tank so they make a gap that is 4 cm wide. Describe how the student can make waves that will be diffracted by the gap. **[1 mark]**

07.4 Draw a diagram to show the waves being diffracted. **[2 marks]**

07.5 Sound is diffracted by doorways, but light is not. Suggest why. **[1 mark]**

08 A driver is driving on an icy road.

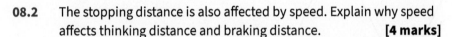

08.1 The stopping distance of a car is affected by the condition of the road surface. Explain why. **[2 marks]**

08.2 The stopping distance is also affected by speed. Explain why speed affects thinking distance and braking distance. **[4 marks]**

08.3 **Figure 3** shows the stopping distances at different speeds on an icy surface and a dry road. Suggest which curve, **A** or **B**, is the graph for an icy surface. Explain your answer. **[2 marks]**

Figure 3

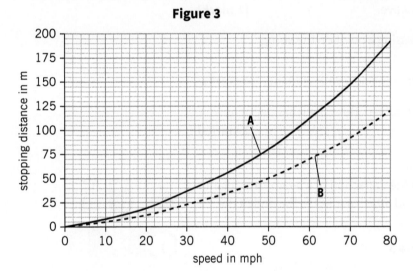

> **(!) Exam Tip**
>
> If you can't tell by looking at the lines, try turning each line into a sentence. For example, when Car A was travelling at 50 mph, the stopping distance was 80 m.

08.4 The car is travelling at 50 mph (22.3 m/s). The reaction time of the driver is 0.4 s. Calculate the thinking distance for the car on each surface. Use the information in **Figure 3** to calculate the braking distance on each surface. **[6 marks]**

09 A wave can be modelled by a person running. The runner's stride length is 2.0 m. The runner takes 180 strides per minute.

09.1 Use the information to work out the speed of the runner in metres per second. **[3 marks]**

09.2 Write down which quantity is analogous to the wavelength. **[1 mark]**

09.3 Write down which quantity is analogous to frequency. Explain your answer. **[2 marks]**

09.4 Compare the method of working out the speed of the runner used in **10.1** with using the wave equation to work out the speed of a wave. **[3 marks]**

09.5 A student considers the limitations of the model. Explain **two** limitations of this model in terms of predicting and explaining what happens when a wave hits a boundary. **[3 marks]**

10 **Figure 4** shows a snapshot of waves on a string.

Figure 4

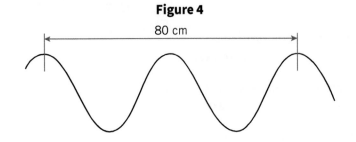
80 cm

10.1 Calculate the wavelength of the wave. **[2 marks]**

10.2 Estimate the amplitude of the wave. **[1 mark]**

10.3 A student counts two waves passing a point on the string per second.
Calculate the frequency and period. Show your working. **[4 marks]**

10.4 The frequency of the waves is doubled. Describe what happens to the period and the amplitude. **[2 marks]**

11 A student wants to investigate the deflection of a beam. They clamp a ruler to the edge of a table, and attach a mass to the end of the ruler as shown in **Figure 5**.

Figure 5

length of ruler

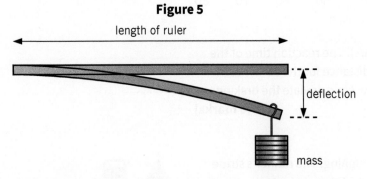

deflection

mass

They decide to investigate how the length of the ruler affects the deflection.

11.1 Write down the independent variable, the dependent variable, and two control variables. **[4 marks]**

11.2 Describe a method that the student could use to collect data to find a relationship between the length of the ruler and the deflection. Assume that the equipment is set up as in **Figure 5**. **[3 marks]**

11.3 The student collects the data in **Table 1**.

Table 1

Length of ruler in m	Deflection in cm
0.20	3.5
0.30	3.8
0.40	4.2
0.50	5.3

The deflection is not proportional to the length. Use the data in **Table 1** to show this. **[2 marks]**

11.4 Suggest a different investigation that the student could carry out using the same equipment. **[1 mark]**

12 A baker uses their car to travel to work, and back home at the end of the day.

12.1 Write down the total displacement from the baker's home. **[1 mark]**

12.2 The distance from the baker's home to their workplace is 4.5 miles. There are 1609 m in one mile. Calculate 4.5 miles in metres. **[1 mark]**

12.3 The total time they spend in the car each day is 20 min. Calculate the average speed of their travel. **[4 marks]**

12.4 Describe why your answer to **12.3** is an average speed. **[1 mark]**

13 A car has broken down. A group of people decide to push the car to try to start it. In order to start, the car needs to be travelling at 5 mph.

13.1 There are 1609 m in a mile. Show that 5 mph is approximately 2.2 m/s. **[3 marks]**

13.2 The group of people push the car with a constant acceleration. It takes 5.0 s to accelerate the car from 0 m/s to 2.2 m/s. Calculate the acceleration of the car. **[2 marks]**

13.3 Calculate the force exerted by the group of people. The mass of the car is 1250 kg. **[3 marks]**

13.4 After the car has started, it travels for a short distance at a constant speed of 5 mph before accelerating to 30 mph. Compare the magnitude of the driving and resistive forces: while travelling at 5 mph, while accelerating to 30 mph. You do not need to include any calculations. **[3 marks]**

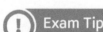

> **(!) Exam Tip**
>
> 2.2 m/s is metres per second, whereas mph is miles per hour. In an hour, you have 60 minutes each with 60 seconds.

P8 Electromagnetic waves

The electromagnetic spectrum

Electromagnetic (EM) waves are transverse waves that transfer energy from their source to an absorber. For example, infrared waves emitted from a hot object transfer thermal energy.

EM waves form a continuous **spectrum**, and are grouped by their wavelengths and frequencies.

All EM waves travel at the same velocity through space or in a vacuum. They travel at a speed of 3×10^8 m/s.

Waves and matter

Electromagnetic waves interact with matter in ways that vary with their wavelength. They can be:

- absorbed
- reflected
- transmitted
- refracted.

Refraction occurs when there is a difference in the velocity of an EM wave in different substances.

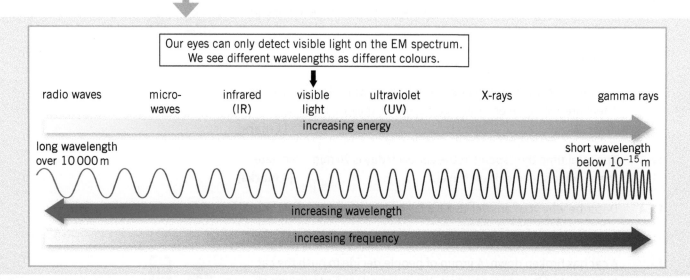

Our eyes can only detect visible light on the EM spectrum. We see different wavelengths as different colours.

radio waves | micro-waves | infrared (IR) | visible light | ultraviolet (UV) | X-rays | gamma rays

increasing energy

long wavelength over 10 000 m

short wavelength below 10^{-15} m

increasing wavelength

increasing frequency

Infrared radiation

All objects **emit** (give out) and **absorb** (take in) infrared radiation.

The higher the temperature of an object, the more infrared radiation it emits in a given time.

A good absorber of infrared radiation is also a good emitter.

For an object at a constant temperature:

- infrared radiation emitted = infrared radiation absorbed
- infrared radiation is emitted across a continuous range of wavelengths.

An object's temperature will increase if it absorbs infrared radiation at a higher rate than it emits it.

- Dark, matt surfaces are good emitters and absorbers of infrared radiation.
- Light, shiny surfaces are poor emitters and absorbers of infrared radiation, but good reflectors.

Black bodies

A **black body** is a theoretical object that absorbs 100% of the radiation that falls on it.

A perfect black body would not reflect or transmit any radiation, and would also be a perfect emitter of radiation.

Effects of EM waves

Low-energy EM waves have a heating effect. Higher energy EM waves can remove electrons from atoms or molecules. They have an **ionising** effect.

Exposure of the human body to EM waves can be harmful. People who use equipment or substances that produce ionising radiation must take precautions to monitor and minimise the levels of radiation they are exposed to.

Type of EM wave	Use	Why is it suitable for this use?	Hazards
radio waves	communication: television and radio signals (including Bluetooth)	• can travel long distances through air • longer wavelengths can bend around obstructions to allow detection of signals when not in line of sight	can penetrate the body and cause internal heating
microwaves	communication: mobile phones, satellite communications; cooking food	• can pass through Earth's atmosphere to reach satellites • can penetrate into food and are absorbed by water molecules in food, heating it	
infrared	night vision devices, heating, communication: TV remote controls	• all hot objects emit infrared waves – sensors can detect these to turn them into an image • can transfer energy quickly to heat rooms and food	can damage or kill skin cells due to heating (skin burns)
visible light	photography, communication: fibre optics	• short wavelength means visible light carries more information	can damage the retina
ultraviolet (UV)	security marking	• carries more energy than visible light • some chemicals emit light in UV radiation and are used in security marker pens to mark valuable objects	can damage skin cells, causing skin to age prematurely and increasing the risk of skin cancer, and can cause blindness
X-rays	medical imaging	• pass easily through flesh, but not through denser materials like bone	form of high-energy ionising radiation – can damage or kill cells, cause mutation of genes, and lead to cancers
gamma rays	sterilising surgical instruments, killing harmful bacteria in food	• high doses kill living cells, so can be used to kill cancer cells	

X-rays

X-rays affect photographic film in the same ways as visible light. For a long time, this is how X-rays were detected. Now sensors and computers are used to produce images.

Medical imaging

When X-rays interact with the human body, they are strongly absorbed by bone, and transmitted by healthy tissue. Simple X-ray images are used to diagnose broken bones and dental problems.

In **computed tomography (CT)**, many X-rays are taken and combined to produce a detailed image that can be used to diagnose disease.

X-rays and risk

Radiologists who administer X-rays take precautions to reduce risk of injury from X-rays. They wear a film badge to show how much ionising radiation they have received. They use lead to shield themselves and parts of the patients from radiation.

 **Key Terms**

Make sure you can write a definition for these key terms.

| absorb | black body | computed tomography | electromagnetic spectrum |

electromagnetic wave   emit   gamma rays   infrared   ionising

microwaves   radio waves   ultraviolet   visible light   X-rays

Retrieval

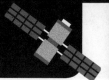

Learn the answers to the questions below then cover the answers column with a piece of paper and write as many as you can. Check and repeat.

	P8 questions	Answers
1	Are electromagnetic (EM) waves longitudinal or transverse waves?	transverse
2	Explain why EM waves are not mechanical waves.	they can travel through a vacuum (don't need a substance to travel through)
3	What do EM waves transfer from their source to an absorber?	energy
4	List the different types of waves in the EM spectrum in order of decreasing wavelength (increasing frequency).	radio, microwave, infrared, visible, ultraviolet, X-rays, gamma
5	Which part of the EM spectrum can humans see?	visible light
6	Which type of radiation do all objects emit and absorb?	infrared
7	Which surfaces are good absorbers and emitters of infrared?	dark, matt surfaces
8	What is black-body radiation?	the range of EM radiation emitted by an object at a particular temperature
9	What are radio waves used for?	transmitting television, mobile phone, and Bluetooth signals
10	What are microwaves used for?	satellite communications, cooking food
11	What is infrared radiation used for?	heating, remote controls, infrared cameras, cooking food
12	Which types of EM waves have a heating effect?	radio, microwaves, infrared
13	What is ionisation?	the removal of an electron from an atom or molecule
14	Which types of EM waves are ionising?	ultraviolet, X-rays, gamma rays
15	What are the hazards of being exposed to ionising radiation?	increase risk of cancer
16	Why are X-rays used for medical imaging?	they pass through flesh but not bone
17	Why are gamma rays used for treating cancer and sterilising medical equipment?	high doses kill cells and bacteria
18	What is computed tomography (CT) scanning used for?	to diagnose medical conditions
19	What precautions do people who use ionising radiation take?	reduce time of exposure, increase distance to source, shielding, wear film badges

Put paper here

Now use the questions below to check your knowledge from previous chapters.

P8

Previous questions

Answers

1 Give an example of a longitudinal wave.

sound waves

2 What can be done to reduce the drag on an object?

streamlining

3 Why is a fuel not 100% efficient?

some energy is transferred to the surroundings

4 What are the main disadvantages of using biofuels?

expensive to produce, use land/water that might be needed to grow food

5 What is a rarefaction?

an area in longitudinal waves where the particles are pulled further apart

Put paper here

Put paper here

 Maths Skills

Practise your maths skills using the worked example and practice questions below.

Estimating	Worked example	Practice

Estimating

You will find it helpful to be able to estimate values in physics. You can use estimates to determine whether your calculated answer is correct or not.

For some quantities, such as the wavelength of electromagnetic waves, it is useful to remember them. However, you don't need to remember them all. You can estimate the rest.

Try to remember the following wavelengths:

- microwaves: 10^{-2} m
- visible light: 10^{-7} m
- X-rays: 10^{-10} m

You know that all EM waves travel at the same speed, 3×10^8 m/s, in a vacuum. Therefore, you can estimate their frequencies using:

speed (m/s) = frequency (Hz) × wavelength (m)

For example:

- microwaves: 3×10^{10} Hz
- visible light: 3×10^{15} Hz
- X-rays: 3×10^{18} Hz

Worked example

A mercury lamp emits ultraviolet light of frequency 5×10^{16} Hz.

1 Calculate the wavelength of these waves. The speed of EM waves in air is 3×10^8 m/s.

Step 1: write down the equation.

speed (m/s) = frequency (Hz) × wavelength (m)

Step 2: rearrange the equation.

$$\text{wavelength (m)} = \frac{\text{speed (m/s)}}{\text{frequency (Hz)}}$$

Step 3: put the numbers into the equation.

$$\text{wavelength} = \frac{3 \times 10^8 \, \text{m/s}}{5 \times 10^{16} \, \text{Hz}} = 6 \times 10^{-9} \, \text{m}$$

Step 4: check that this is the correct wavelength.

UV light is between visible light and X-rays in the EM spectrum. The wavelength should be between 10^{-7} m and 10^{-10} m. The calculated answer is correct.

2 Suggest an object that would diffract these waves.

Answer: An object about 6×10^{-9} m in size. A molecule.

Practice

1 A television studio transmits radio waves at a frequency of 2×10^6 Hz.

   a Calculate the wavelength of these waves. The speed of EM waves in air is 3×10^8 m/s.

   b Suggest an object that would diffract these waves.

2 A remote control emits infrared waves of frequency 6×10^{13} Hz.

   a Calculate the wavelength of these waves. The speed of EM waves in air is 3×10^8 m/s.

   b Suggest an object that would diffract these waves.

Exam-style questions

01 There are lamps that can be used to produce a suntan without needing to sunbathe. The lamps emit ultraviolet radiation.

01.1 Name an electromagnetic wave with longer wavelength than ultraviolet radiation. **[1 mark]**

_____

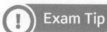

01.2 Name an electromagnetic wave with higher frequency than ultraviolet radiation. **[1 mark]**

_____

> **! Exam Tip**
> Read the question – it is only asking for **one** type of electromagnetic wave. You won't get more marks for writing more types.

01.3 Describe one hazard of using an ultraviolet lamp. **[1 mark]**

_____

_____

01.4 People who work outside are exposed to ultraviolet radiation from the Sun.
Suggest one method of reducing the risk of injury. **[1 mark]**

_____

_____

02 A teacher demonstrates how different materials absorb electromagnetic radiation.

They use a high-power lamp and a solar cell to investigate how sheets of transparent film absorb visible light.

They fix the lamp 10 cm from the solar cell, and connect the solar cell to a voltmeter. The solar cell produces a potential difference that is proportional to the intensity of the light that falls on it.

Table 1 shows the data that they obtained.

> **! Exam Tip**
> Go through the text and pick out the key points before attempting the questions. You may want to highlight the important information.

Table 1

Number of sheets	Potential difference in V			
	Repeat 1	Repeat 2	Repeat 3	Mean
0	5.87	5.05	6.12	5.68
1	4.12	3.61	4.55	4.10
2	3.74	6.75	4.40	
3	3.12	2.81	3.13	3.02
4	2.89	2.02	3.86	2.92
5	2.67	2.64	3.21	2.84

02.1 Explain why the potential difference decreases as the number of sheets of transparent film increases. **[2 marks]**

_____

_____

_____

_____

02.2 Calculate the missing mean in **Table 1**. **[1 mark]**

mean = _____

! Exam Tip

Whenever you're asked to calculate a mean, always check for any outliers.

02.3 Suggest how a source of systematic error might arise in the experiment, and how it could be reduced. **[2 marks]**

_____

_____

_____

02.4 The teacher repeats the experiment with a gamma radiation source.

Suggest why the teacher ensures that all students are standing at least 1 m from the gamma source. **[2 marks]**

_____

_____

_____

! Exam Tip

The marks for **02.3** are for giving an error _and_ saying how to reduce it. Do not give two errors; you will only gain one mark. Don't give two errors and describe how one can be reduced either. You won't gain an extra mark and, if the extra error is wrong, you may lose a mark! Only ever give what is asked for in the question.

02.5 Compare visible light and gamma rays in terms of wavelength and ability to penetrate the human body. **[2 marks]**

_____

_____

_____

_____

03 Radiographers use X-ray machines in hospitals for medical imaging, for example computed tomography (CT) scans.

A narrow X-ray beam circles around one part of your body. It produces lots of 'slices' of the body which the computer puts together to make a detailed image of an organ, bone, or blood vessel.

Table 2 shows the radiation doses from different types of CT scan.

Table 2

Examination	Average effective dose in mSv
head	2
spine	6
chest	15

03.1 A radiographer must leave the room when a CT scan is being taken. Explain why they should leave the room. **[2 marks]**

03.2 X-rays are 'ionising'. Define 'ionisation'. **[1 mark]**

03.3 A traditional X-ray of a foot produces an effective radiation dose of 0.001 mSv.

Suggest why the dose is much smaller than a CT scan of the head. **[1 mark]**

03.4 Calculate the number of foot X-rays that would give a patient the same dose as a CT scan of the head. **[2 marks]**

Exam Tip

Radiographers do several scans in one day, nearly every day of the week.

Exam Tip

We've said it before and we'll say it again. Always show your working! That way, if you make a mistake or get the wrong answer, you can still gain marks.

04 A student has made a list of appliances in their house that use different electromagnetic waves.

The student identifies the television and the electrical heater as two appliances that use electromagnetic waves. However, they cannot find appliances for some of the other waves in the electromagnetic spectrum.

Explain how televisions and heaters use electromagnetic waves.

Suggest uses for **two** of the waves for which the student cannot find appliances. **[6 marks]**

Exam Tip

There are lots of parts to this question. First, identify the EM radiation that can be used in the home. Then work out which EM waves are left over and think of uses for them. The answer needs to include *two* different sources of EM waves.

05 The atmosphere only allows certain wavelengths of the electromagnetic spectrum to reach the Earth's surface.

05.1 Write down the electromagnetic wave that our eyes detect. **[1 mark]**

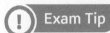

05.2 Radio waves also reach the Earth's surface. People sometimes confuse radio waves and sound waves.

Complete the sentences with words from the box below. Each word can only be used once. **[5 marks]**

| transverse | 340 m/s | matter | air | 300 000 km/s | longitudinal | energy |

Waves of the electromagnetic spectrum are _____ waves that travel at _____.

Sound waves are _____ waves and travel at _____.

All waves transfer _____ without transferring _____.

05.3 Some microwaves reach the surface of the Earth from the Sun.

Write down which wave, radio or microwave, has the lower frequency. **[1 mark]**

05.4 We sometimes use the power of microwaves to cook food.

Write down a use of microwaves other than cooking. **[1 mark]**

06 A radiologist uses an X-ray machine to make an image of a person's leg, as shown in **Figure 1**. The film underneath the leg is developed, and the doctor looks at the image on the film.

Figure 1

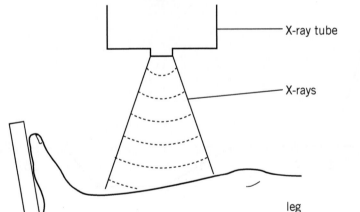

06.1 Name another type of electromagnetic radiation that would produce an image on the film. **[1 mark]**

06.2 Name the parts of the person's leg that X-rays will travel through to reach the film. **[1 mark]**

06.3 Explain why the radiologist covers the rest of the patient's leg with an apron made of lead. **[1 mark]**

06.4 Apart from producing images, describe another use of X-rays in hospitals. **[1 mark]**

07 Electromagnetic waves have many different uses. We use visible light to communicate.

07.1 Name **two** other electromagnetic waves that are used for communication. In each case describe the use. **[2 marks]**

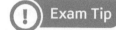

! Exam Tip

The question gives you visible light as an example, so you won't get any marks for that in your answer to question **07.1**.

07.2 Some waves, such as gamma rays, can penetrate the human body. Describe a use of another electromagnetic wave that can penetrate the body. **[2 marks]**

07.3 Some waves, such as infrared, have a heating effect. Describe a use of a different electromagnetic wave that has a heating effect. **[2 marks]**

08 A driver in a car sees an obstacle ahead on the road. The motion of the car is shown in **Figure 2**.

Figure 2

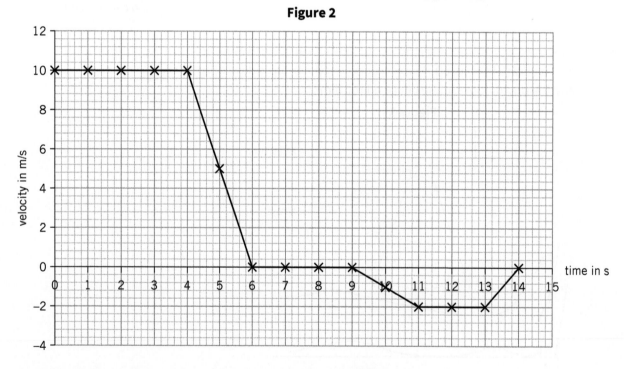

08.1 Identify the time at which the driver saw the obstacle. Give a reason for your answer. **[2 marks]**

08.2 Calculate the distance travelled by the car while it was travelling at its initial constant speed. **[2 marks]**

08.3 Calculate the acceleration of the car between 4 and 6 seconds. Comment on whether the answer is positive or negative. **[3 marks]**

! Exam Tip

Draw lines on the graph to help with your working.

08.4 Compare the acceleration of the car between 9 and 11 seconds with the acceleration that you calculated in **08.3**. **[2 marks]**

09 Electromagnetic waves form a continuous spectrum.

09.1 Write the waves of the electromagnetic spectrum in order from largest to smallest wavelength. **[3 marks]**

09.2 Give the approximate wavelength of radio waves. **[1 mark]**

09.3 Name the wave that has a wavelength of about 10^{-15} m. **[1 mark]**

09.4 Compare the speed of radio waves in a vacuum with the speed of light in a vacuum. **[1 mark]**

10 A student makes the following observation:

'Black clothing gets hotter more quickly than white clothing because it attracts heat'.

(!) Exam Tip

The number of marks gives you important clues as to what you need to do in a question. **10.1** is worth 1 mark so you only need to make a small change.

10.1 Re-write the sentence so that it is correct. **[1 mark]**

10.2 The student makes a second observation:

'Silver surfaces only reflect radiation. They do not absorb or emit radiation.'

Suggest a situation where we use the fact that silver surfaces reflect radiation. **[1 mark]**

10.3 A student sets up a silver can and a black can. They fill the cans with hot water, put a lid on each can, and record the temperature of the water using a data logger.

Describe **two** variables that they need to control in order to make a comparison between the cans. **[2 marks]**

10.4 Sketch the graph of temperature against time that the student would obtain from their experiment. **[4 marks]**

10.5 Suggest whether the experiment supports the student's second observation in **10.2**. **[2 marks]**

11 A gardener wants to purchase a greenhouse. There is a choice of different types of glass to put in the greenhouse.

Figure 3 shows the percentage of sunlight that is transmitted through each type of glass.

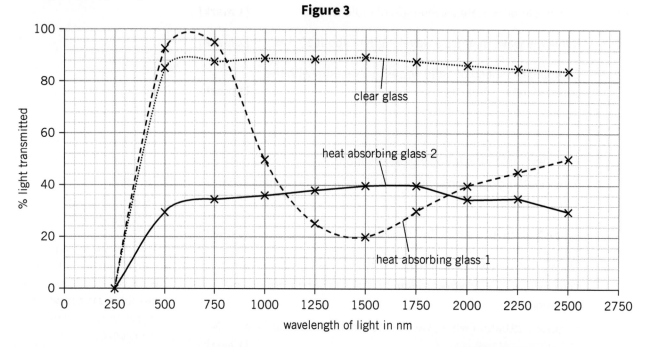

Figure 3

11.1 Ultraviolet radiation has a wavelength from 250 nm to 400 nm. Infrared radiation has a wavelength above 750 nm.

Use this information to write down the range of wavelengths of visible light. **[1 mark]**

Exam Tip

Don't let the very small numbers put you off. Just treat them the same as you would any other number.

11.2 Write down which type of glass is the best at absorbing radiation with a wavelength of 2500 nm.

Justify your answer. **[2 marks]**

11.3 Plants need to absorb radiation in the range 430 nm and 662 nm.

Suggest which type of glass would be best for growing plants.

Justify your answer. **[2 marks]**

11.4 Suggest whether you could get a suntan inside a greenhouse made using heat absorbing glass 2.

Justify your answer. **[3 marks]**

Exam Tip

You need to use data to justify your answer to **11.4**.

12 A student reads that the wavelength of X-rays is about the same as the diameter of an atom. The student recalls that the radius of an atom is 1×10^{-10} m. The speed of electromagnetic radiation is 300 000 km/s.

12.1 Calculate the frequency of X-rays.
Use an equation from the *Physics Equations Sheet*. **[4 marks]**

12.2 Write down the order of magnitude (power of 10) of the frequency of X-rays. **[1 mark]**

12.3 The student learns that the wavelength of microwaves is about 10 cm. Show that the order of magnitude of the frequency of microwaves is 10^9 Hz. **[3 marks]**

 Exam Tip

Be careful with the unit for frequency. You must write the unit correctly, with a capital H and a lowercase z. Anything else and you won't gain the mark.

13 A car and a boat are travelling at 35 mph (16 m/s). The car uses its brakes and comes to a stop in a distance of 30 m. The boat comes to a stop in a distance of 100 m after the engine is turned off. Both the car and the boat have a mass of 1500 kg.

13.1 Identify the force acting on the car and the force acting on the boat that brings them to a stop. **[2 marks]**

13.2 Calculate the kinetic energy of the boat. **[2 marks]**

13.3 The force acting on the boat brings it to a stop over a certain distance. This means the force does work on the boat.
Use the equation that links work, force, and distance to calculate the force required to stop the boat.
Suggest whether the braking force acting on the car is bigger, smaller, or the same size as the force acting on the boat.
Give reasons for your answer. **[6 marks]**

Exam Tip

List all the important information from the question.
car:
- initial speed = 16 m/s
- mass = 1500 kg
- stopping distance = 30 m
boat:
- initial speed = 16 m/s
- mass = 1500 kg
- stopping distance = 100 m

14 A student accelerates a toy car. They use a newtonmeter to apply a constant force. They use light gates to measure the speed at two different times.

Exam Tip

Not all the information you need will be in one location. You'll need to use the data from the main body of the question to answer this.

14.1 The initial velocity is 0.5 m/s. The final velocity is 2.7 m/s. The time between the measurements of velocity is 0.4 s.
Calculate the acceleration of the trolley. **[2 marks]**

14.2 Write down the equation that links mass, force, and acceleration. **[1 mark]**

14.3 The student applies a force of 2.0 N. The mass of the trolley is 400 g (0.4 kg).
Calculate the acceleration of the trolley. **[3 marks]**

14.4 Suggest one practical reason why the two values of acceleration are not the same. **[1 mark]**

Exam Tip

Even if it doesn't specifically ask you to, get into the habit of writing down the equation you are using as your first step whenever you do a calculation.

P9 Sound and ultrasound

Sound waves

Sound waves are:

- mechanical waves – they need a solid, liquid, or gas medium to travel through (cannot travel through a vacuum)
- longitudinal – the oscillations of particles in the medium are *parallel* to the direction of energy transfer.

When sound waves go from air into a solid, they cause vibrations of the same frequency in the solid.

Hearing

Sound waves cause solid parts of the ear (e.g., ear drum) to vibrate.

The brain converts these vibrations into what we hear, but only over a limited frequency range (20 Hz to 20 kHz).

higher frequency = higher pitch

greater amplitude = louder sound

Diffraction of sound

You can hear around corners, but you cannot see around corners. This is because sound waves are diffracted (spread out) when they pass through an opening, such as a doorway. The size of the opening is the same order of magnitude as the wavelength of sound waves, but not of light waves.

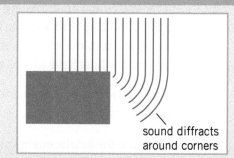

sound diffracts around corners

Reflection of sound

An **echo** is a reflected sound wave.

- If a wall (or barrier) is bare and smooth, sound waves are reflected and an echo is heard.
- If a wall is covered in soft fabric (e.g., in a cinema), the fabric absorbs sound instead of reflecting it. No echoes are heard.
- If a wall surface is rough, reflected sound is broken up and scattered. The echoes are diffuse.

Sound travels at the speed of 340 m/s in air.

The distance between the source of the sound and the reflector can be calculated using:

$$\text{distance (m)} = \frac{1}{2} \times \text{speed of sound (m/s)} \times \text{transit time (s)}$$

$$s = \frac{1}{2} vt$$

Echo sounding

Echo sounding uses high-frequency sound waves (ultrasound) to detect objects in deep water and to measure the depth of water.

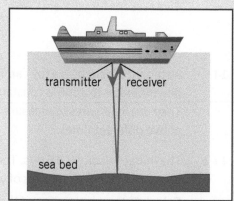

transmitter   receiver

sea bed

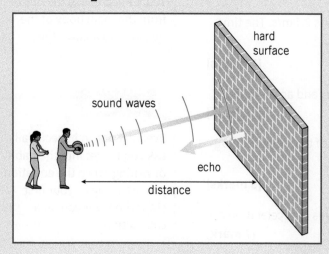

sound waves

hard surface

echo

distance

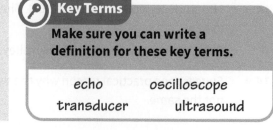

Key Terms

Make sure you can write a definition for these key terms.

echo	oscilloscope
transducer	ultrasound

Ultrasound

Ultrasound waves are acoustic (sound) waves. They have a frequency above the range of human hearing, which means that the frequency is greater than 20 000 Hz.

Animals such as bats produce ultrasound and detect prey using the time of the echo.

Ultrasound transducers

Ultrasound waves are produced by a **transducer**.

- An ultrasonic transducer uses an electrical device that vibrates very fast to produce pulses of ultrasound.

- Another transducer is used to detect the wave and produce an electrical signal.

- Electronic systems are used to record the time between the emitted and received pulses.

In some devices, the transmitting and receiving transducers are the same device.

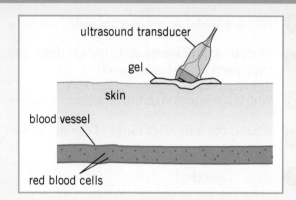

Using an oscilloscope trace to calculate distance

Ultrasound waves can be used to detect a boundary between different media. Ultrasound waves are partially reflected and partially transmitted at a boundary. The pulse and the echo can be seen on an **oscilloscope** screen.

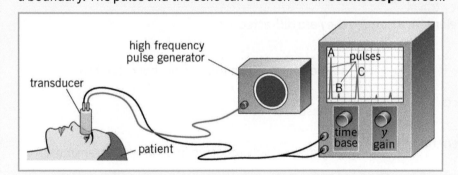

The oscilloscope can be used to measure the transit time of each pulse.

The total distance travelled by the pulse can be calculated using:

$$\text{total distance (m)} = \text{speed (m/s)} \times \text{time (s)}$$

$$s = vt$$

The depth of the boundary below the surface is half the distance travelled by each pulse to and from the boundary:

$$\text{depth of boundary (m)} = \frac{1}{2} \times \text{speed (m/s)} \times \text{transit time (s)}$$

$$s = \frac{1}{2}vt$$

Ultrasound and its uses

Powerful ultrasound waves can be used to break kidney stones into tiny pieces.

Ultrasound waves are also used to produce images of unborn babies.

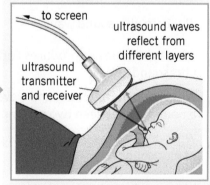

The advantages of using ultrasound waves instead of X-rays for medical imaging are that ultrasound waves:

- are non-ionising and harmless when used for scanning

- are reflected at boundaries between different types of tissue

- can be used to scan organs and other soft tissues in the body.

Learn the answers to the questions below then cover the answers column with a piece of paper and write as many as you can. Check and repeat.

P9 questions

Answers

	P9 questions	Answers
1	Are sound waves transverse or longitudinal?	longitudinal
2	What happens to the frequency of a sound that travels from air into a solid?	it stays the same
3	Why are sound waves mechanical?	need a substance to travel through
4	What do sound waves do to the ear drum and other solid parts of the human ear?	make them vibrate
5	Why is there a limit to the range of human hearing?	conversion of sound waves in air to vibrations in ear (solid) only works over a limited range of frequencies
6	What is the frequency range of normal human hearing?	20 Hz to 20 000 Hz (20 kHz)
7	What is an echo?	a reflection of sound
8	How can you reduce echoes in a large room?	soft carpets, curtains, wall coverings
9	What does the pitch of a sound depend on?	the frequency of vibration of the source
10	What does the loudness of a sound depend on?	the amplitude of vibration of the source
11	What happens to sound waves when they travel through a gap the same size as the wavelength of the sound waves?	they are diffracted
12	What are ultrasound waves?	sound waves with a frequency above 20 000 Hz
13	What type of device produces and detects ultrasound?	a transducer
14	What happens to ultrasound waves when they meet a boundary between two substances?	they are partially reflected and some are transmitted
15	What device can be used to view pulses and echoes of ultrasound?	an oscilloscope
16	What is echo sounding used for?	detecting objects in deep water, measuring the depth of water
17	What equation is used to calculate the depth of the sea?	$s = \dfrac{1}{2}vt$
18	What are two medical uses of ultrasound?	prenatal scanning, removal of kidney stones
19	What are the advantages of using ultrasound waves instead of X-rays for medical imaging?	they are non-ionising, therefore harmless; they are reflected at boundaries between different types of tissue

Put paper here

Now use the questions below to check your knowledge from previous chapters.

P9

Previous questions — Answers

	Previous questions	Answers
1	What are radio waves used for?	transmitting television, mobile phone, and Bluetooth signals
2	What is a transverse wave?	oscillations/vibrations are perpendicular (at right angles) to the direction of energy transfer
3	What are three factors that can affect the braking distance of a vehicle?	speed, road conditions, condition of tyres and brakes
4	What is the resultant force on an object moving at a steady speed in a straight line?	zero
5	What is the difference between distance and displacement?	distance is a scalar quantity and only has magnitude (size); displacement is a vector quantity and has both magnitude and direction
6	Describe the energy transfer when a falling apple hits the ground.	energy is transferred from the kinetic energy of the apple and dissipated to the thermal energy of the surroundings by sound waves

Put paper here

 ## Maths Skills

Practise your maths skills using the worked example and practice questions below.

Calculating with significant figures	Worked example	Practice
In many of the calculations that you do, the answer will be a whole number. Sometimes, it will be a number with two significant figures. Remember that: • non-zero numbers are always significant • leading zeros are not significant • trailing zeros are only significant if there is a decimal point. Using too many significant figures implies a level of precision or accuracy that is not justified. When doing calculations, your answer should match the number of significant figures in the data given in the question.	A student is standing a distance of 250 m from a wall. They clap and detect an echo after 1.5 seconds. Calculate the speed of sound in air at that location. **Step 1:** write down the equation. $$\text{distance (m)} = \frac{1}{2} \times \text{speed of sound (m/s)} \times \text{transit time (s)}$$ **Step 2:** rearrange the equation. $$\text{speed (m/s)} = 2 \times \frac{\text{distance (m)}}{\text{time (s)}}$$ **Step 3:** put the numbers into the equation. $$\text{speed} = 2 \times \frac{250\,\text{m}}{1.5\,\text{s}} = 333.333\,333\,3 \text{ m/s}$$ **Step 4:** round the answer to an appropriate number of significant figures. There are two significant figures in the number 1.5 s. So, the answer should be rounded down. $$\text{speed} = 330 \text{ m/s}$$	1 A boat sends an ultrasound pulse to reflect from a shoal of fish 65 m below the boat. The receiver detects an echo after 8.6×10^{-2} s. Calculate the speed of sound in water at that location. 2 An ultrasonic device is used to find a crack in a piece of metal. The speed of sound in metal is 5400 m/s. The time between sending the pulse and hearing the echo is 3.1×10^{-6} s. Calculate the distance to the crack.

01 **Figure 1** shows a graph of the volume of a sound wave on the screen of an oscilloscope.

Figure 1

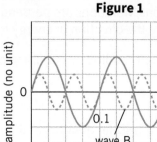

01.1 Use the graph to calculate the time period in seconds of wave A.

[2 marks]

period = _____ s

01.2 Calculate the frequency of wave A. **[2 marks]**

frequency = _____ Hz

> **Exam Tip**
>
> First work out how much each box on the graph represents in seconds. Then write down the equation you're going to use.

01.3 Compare wave A and wave B in terms of how they sound. Explain your answer. **[4 marks]**

_____

_____

_____

_____

02 A guitar has six strings. Each is tuned so that it produces a different note.

Table 1 shows the frequencies of the six strings.

Table 1

Guitar string	Frequency (Hz)
1st	82
2nd	110
3rd	147
4th	196
5th	247
6th	330

02.1 Explain what is meant by '82 Hz'. **[1 mark]**

_____

02.2 Give the string that will produce the note with the highest pitch.

[1 mark]

_____

02.3 Explain why you cannot say which string will produce the loudest note. **[2 marks]**

_____

_____

02.4 The speed of sound in air is 340 m/s. Calculate the wavelength of the sound produced by the 3rd string. **[2 marks]**

! Exam Tip

Show all of your working for every calculation. This will help you get marks even if you make a mistake.

wavelength = _____ m

02.5 Without doing a calculation, compare the wavelength of the 3rd string with the wavelength of the 1st string. **[1 mark]**

_____

_____

! Exam Tip

The question says 'without doing a calculation' so don't waste time doing a calculation because you won't get any extra marks.

02.6 Explain whether the sound from the 3rd string would be diffracted by a doorway. **[1 mark]**

_____

03 A student buys a dog whistle. When the student blows on the whistle, they cannot hear the sound but the dog can hear it.

03.1 Suggest a frequency for the sound that the whistle is producing.

[1 mark]

03.2 The student can hear the dog when it barks. Describe the difference between the sound wave produced by the dog when it barks, and the sound wave produced by the whistle. **[1 mark]**

! Exam Tip

For a compare question, you need to give ways in which the bark and the whistle have both _similar_ effects and _different_ effects on the ear drum.

03.3 Describe the effect of the sound waves on the ear drum. Compare the effect of the sounds of the bark and the whistle on the ear drum. Use your answer to explain why you cannot hear the whistle.

[4 marks]

03.4 Suggest a device that converts the disturbance in a sound wave to the vibration of a solid. **[1 mark]**

03.5 The student and the dog are in a park. There are buildings nearby. The student notices that they can hear the echo of the bark as it is reflected off the buildings. Suggest whether the reflection is clear or diffuse. Give reasons for your answer. **[2 marks]**

04 In 1826, two scientists measured the speed of sound in water. In their experiment, an underwater bell was struck at the same time as a flash of gunpowder went off on the first boat. The sound of the bell and the flash from the gunpowder were observed 15 000 m (about 10 miles) away on a second boat.

The time between the gunpowder flash and the sound reaching the second boat was used to calculate the speed of sound in water. This is shown in **Figure 2**.

Exam Tip

This is a long and wordy question so cross out the bits that aren't relevant to the answer. For example, you can ignore 'in 1826, two scientists' because the year this happened isn't relevant to the questions.

Figure 2

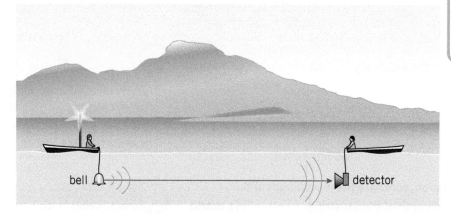
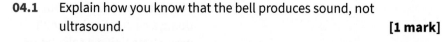

bell / detector

04.1 Explain how you know that the bell produces sound, not ultrasound. **[1 mark]**

04.2 The person in the second boat recorded the sound at the detector after 10 seconds. Calculate the speed of sound in water. **[2 marks]**

04.3 Give **one** assumption the scientists made in this experiment. **[1 mark]**

Exam Tip

This question has links with chemistry. Using your knowledge in an unfamiliar context is something you need to expect in the exams.

04.4 The scientists found that the speed of sound varied with the temperature of the water. Suggest whether the speed of sound increases or decreases with temperature. Explain your suggestion. **[2 marks]**

05 A rocket is launched from Earth towards the Moon. The rocket burns its fuel for 5 minutes and then turns off its engines. The rocket keeps moving through space at a speed of 10 km/s.

05.1 Calculate the rocket's average acceleration during the time that the fuel burns. **[3 marks]**

05.2 Explain in terms of forces why the rocket accelerates. **[1 mark]**

05.3 The Moon is approximately 3.8×10^5 km from Earth. Assuming that the rocket continues at a speed of 10 km/s, calculate how long it will take to reach the Moon. Give your answer in an everyday unit. **[4 marks]**

05.4 Suggest a reason why
- it may take **less** time than you have calculated
- it may take **more** time than you have calculated. **[2 marks]**

06 A scientist attempted to measure the speed of sound experimentally by measuring the time difference between spotting the flash of a gun and hearing the sound produced by the gun. The experiment was carried out over a long distance on a day without any wind. The value obtained was 478.4 m/s.

06.1 Describe **one** assumption made when doing this experiment.
[1 mark]

06.2 Describe the measurements made and how they were used to calculate the speed of sound. **[2 marks]**

06.3 The accepted speed of sound is 340 m/s. Calculate the percentage difference between the accepted value and the value calculated by the scientist. Show your working. **[3 marks]**

06.4 Another scientist stood 29 km away from a cannon. This scientist measured the time interval between the cannon being fired and hearing the cannon. They calculated the speed of sound as 332 m/s. Calculate the time interval between the cannon being fired and the scientist hearing the sound from the cannon. Use the speed of sound calculated by the scientist. **[4 marks]**

06.5 Suggest why the difference between the measured and accepted values of the speed of sound calculated in **06.4** is much smaller than for the first scientist's experiment. **[2 marks]**

07 The driver of a car reacts to a car braking suddenly in front of them. The car is initially travelling at 45 mph (20 m/s) and comes to a complete stop.

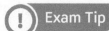

07.1 Describe the process by which energy is transferred from kinetic energy to thermal energy. **[1 mark]**

07.2 When energy is transferred to thermal energy, objects get hot. Write down which objects get hotter when the driver brakes. **[1 mark]**

07.3 The speed of the car changes over a time of 4.3 seconds. Calculate the deceleration of the car. Give **one** assumption that you make when you do this calculation. Suggest whether this assumption is likely, or not likely, to be correct. Explain your answer. **[5 marks]**

07.4 The mass of the car is 1250 kg. Calculate the braking force.
[2 marks]

08 A wave in a ripple tank is reflected from a barrier.

08.1 Explain why the amplitude of the wave that hits the barrier is bigger than the amplitude of the wave reflected from the barrier.

[2 marks]

08.2 Give the name that describes a 'reflection of sound'. [1 mark]

08.3 Sound is a wave. Sound waves can be reflected from barriers, such as walls and windows. Suggest **one** observation that you have made that shows that sound can also be transmitted through barriers. [1 mark]

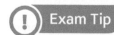

Exam Tip

Even though this isn't a maths question, an equation will help you work out the answer.

08.4 A sound wave is transmitted through a concrete wall. The velocity of the sound wave increases. Write down what happens to the frequency and wavelength of the sound wave as it moves from the air into the wall. [2 marks]

09 A block of stone has a mass of about 10 tonnes. One tonne = 10^3 kg. The block has to be moved a vertical distance of 2 m.

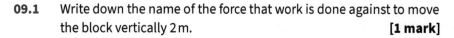

09.1 Write down the name of the force that work is done against to move the block vertically 2 m. [1 mark]

09.2 Calculate the weight of the block.
Gravitational field strength = 9.8 N/kg. [3 marks]

09.3 Calculate the work done lifting the block a vertical distance of 2 m. [3 marks]

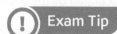

Exam Tip

The units for work done are the same as the units for energy.

09.4 The block is pulled up a 4 m long ramp. The top of the ramp is 2 m above the ground. Describe how a student can use a scale diagram to calculate the magnitude of the component of the weight parallel to the slope. [3 marks]

09.5 A student works out that the component of the weight parallel to the slope is 50 000 N. As the block is being pulled, the force acting on the block due to friction is 3000 N. Calculate the work done pulling the stone up the ramp using the resultant of these two forces. [3 marks]

09.6 The work done using the ramp is larger than the work done lifting the stone directly. Suggest why a ramp is used. [1 mark]

10 A boat uses ultrasound to find the depth of a lake.

10.1 Define ultrasound. [1 mark]

10.2 Write down the equation that links speed, distance, and time. [1 mark]

Exam Tip

Remember the sound wave has to go to the bottom of the lake and back before it is detected.

10.3 The speed of sound in water is 1500 m/s. The boat sends out a pulse of ultrasound. The pulse is detected after 16 ms. Calculate the depth of the lake. [5 marks]

10.4 A student uses an ultrasonic emitter and receiver to investigate how to use sound to measure distance. They measure the time for the beam to be reflected from an object, and calculate the distance. The student then measures the actual distance with a ruler and writes the data in **Table 2**.

Table 2

Time for reflection in ms	Calculated distance in m	Actual distance in m
9	1.53	1.51
6	1.02	1.00
3	0.51	0.49

The student thinks that there could be an error in the ultrasonic distance measurement. Use the data to suggest the type of error. Explain your answer. **[2 marks]**

(!) Exam Tip

Calculate the differences between the actual and calculated distances.

11 A technician in a hospital uses an ultrasonic transducer to produce an image of a foetus. An ultrasonic transducer emits a series of pulses of ultrasound. The transducer also contains a receiver that can convert a reflected pulse into a potential difference. The path of one of the pulses is shown in **Figure 3A**.

Figure 3

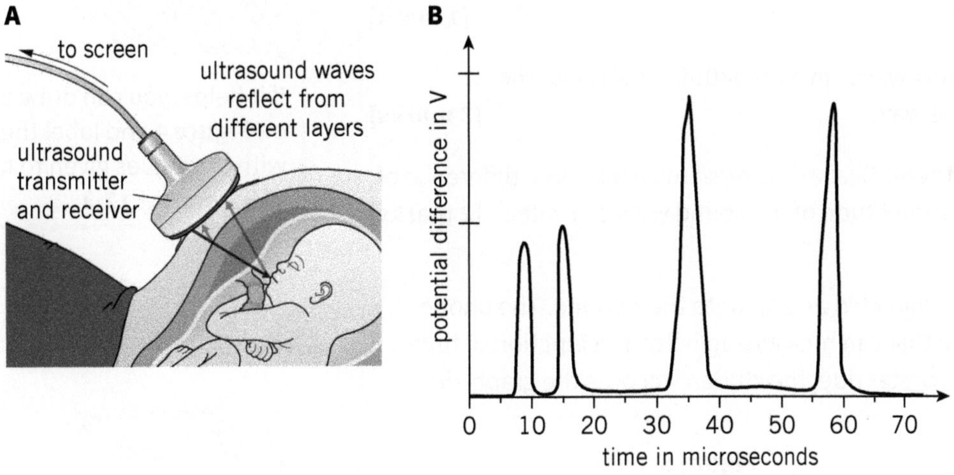

A
- to screen
- ultrasound waves reflect from different layers
- ultrasound transmitter and receiver

B
potential difference in V

time in microseconds (0, 10, 20, 30, 40, 50, 60, 70)

11.1 Suggest why there are four peaks in **Figure 3B**. Explain your answer. **[2 marks]**

11.2 The fetus' mouth produces the third pulse. Calculate the distance between the bottom of the transducer and the fetus. Assume that the speed of sound in the tissue is 1540 m/s. **[5 marks]**

11.3 The resolution of the transducer is 1 mm. Define resolution. **[1 mark]**

11.4 The resolution of the transducer is approximately the same as the wavelength of the ultrasound. Write down the equation that links the wavelength, speed, and frequency of a wave. **[1 mark]**

(!) Exam Tip

Try to relate the peaks in **Figure 3B** to the image in **3A**.

11.5 Calculate the frequency of the ultrasound. Write your answer in standard form. **[5 marks]**

Exam Tip

Read the question carefully. It asks for standard form, so one mark is for giving the answer in the correct format.

12 An oscilloscope can be used to display sound waves. The oscilloscope is connected to a microphone. The microphone converts sound waves into an alternating potential difference which is displayed on the screen (**Figure 4**).

Figure 4

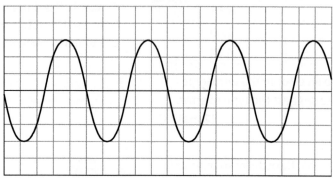

Exam Tip

ms is milliseconds, not to be confused with m/s, which is speed in metres per second.

12.1 Each square on the horizontal axis represents a time of 0.1 ms. Calculate the period of the sound waves. Give your answer in standard form. **[3 marks]**

12.2 Write down the equation that links wave speed, frequency, and wavelength. **[1 mark]**

12.3 The speed of sound waves in air is 340 m/s. Calculate the wavelength of the wave. **[3 marks]**

12.4 Each square on the vertical axis represents a potential difference of 2 V. Calculate the amplitude of the sound waves in volts. **[2 marks]**

Exam Tip

If it helps, you can draw axes on **Figure 4** and label them with the values given to help you work out **12.3**.

13 A student has downloaded an app onto their phone. The phone contains a device that can measure velocity as a function of time. While on a rollercoaster ride, the student records the graph shown in **Figure 5**.

Exam Tip

You can divide the graph into sections, with a different behaviour happening in each section. You might find it helpful to highlight the different sections in different colours.

Figure 5

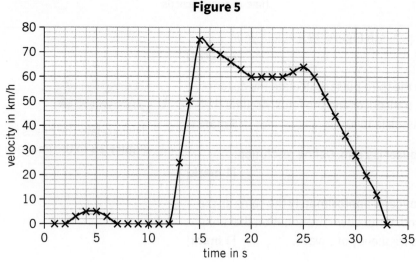

13.1 Write down a time interval during which the acceleration was large and positive. **[1 mark]**

13.2 Write down a time interval during which the acceleration was large and negative. **[1 mark]**

13.3 Write down what the student was doing between 7 seconds and 12 seconds. **[1 mark]**

13.4 Write down the time interval, after 13 seconds, where the net force on the student was zero. Explain your answer. **[2 marks]**

13.5 Use the information in **Figure 5** to estimate the distance travelled on the ride between 12 seconds and 33 seconds. Give your answer to an appropriate number of significant figures. **[5 marks]**

13.6 Suggest why you cannot use the equation 'distance = speed × time' to do this calculation. **[1 mark]**

Exam Tip

Divide the graph up into different sections, and then work out the area of each shape individually.

14 A company makes solid metal blocks. They need to ensure that there are no cracks or defects in the blocks. A device that emits ultrasound is placed on the end of a block.

14.1 Name the device that emits ultrasound. **[1 mark]**

14.2 If there is a crack in the block, the device will detect two echoes. Explain why. **[2 marks]**

14.3 The first echo is detected after a time of 0.4 ms. The speed of sound in the metal is 4500 m/s. Calculate the distance of the crack from the device. **[3 marks]**

14.4 The company then makes a block of different metal that has a crack in the same place as the block in **14.3**. The speed of sound in that metal is smaller. State and explain what would happen to the times for the echo detected by the device. **[1 mark]**

⚙ Knowledge

P10 Reflection and refraction of light

Reflection

When reflection happens at a surface, the **angle of incidence** is always equal to the **angle of reflection**:

$$i = r$$

This is the law of reflection.

The **normal** is a construction line that we draw perpendicular (at 90°) to the surface at the point of incidence.

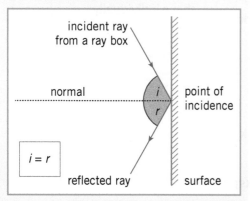

Ray diagrams for reflection

Ray diagrams can be used to show what happens when a wave is reflected at a surface.

To draw a ray diagram for reflection:

1 use a ruler to draw all lines for the rays

2 draw an arrow on the rays to show the direction the wave is travelling

3 draw a dotted line at right angles to the surface at the point of incidence (this line is normal to the surface)

4 apply the law of reflection.

For an image at a **plane mirror**:

1 repeat the above for a second line from the object to the mirror

2 trace the lines back using dashed lines until they meet to find the same point on the image.

The image formed in a mirror is:

- upright
- virtual
- the same size, colour, shape
- laterally inverted.

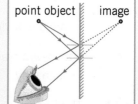

Refraction and ray diagrams

The velocity (speed and direction) of waves is affected by the medium they travel through. This is **refraction**.

A wave is refracted (changes direction) at the boundary between two different substances.

- If a wave slows down when it enters a more dense medium, the refracted ray will bend towards the normal.
- If a wave speeds up when it enters a less dense medium, the refracted ray will bend away from the normal.
- If a wave travels at a right angle to the boundary (along the normal), it will change speed but not direction.

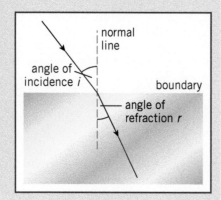

Wavefront diagrams for refraction

Wavefront diagrams can be used to explain refraction in terms of the change of speed that occurs when a wave travels from one substance to another.

The wavefront is an imaginary line at right angles to the direction the wave is moving.

- If a wave slows down as it crosses a boundary, the wavefronts become closer together.
- When a wave crosses a boundary at an angle, one end of the wavefront changes speed before the other, so the wave changes direction.

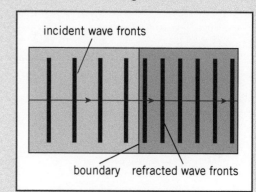

Refractive index

The **refractive index** of a material is a measure of how much the speed of light slows down in the material.

The refractive index, n, of a material can be calculated using:

$$\text{refractive index, } n = \frac{\text{speed of light in a vacuum (air)}}{\text{speed of light in a medium}}$$

A material with a higher refractive index will slow down light more, and light will bend towards the normal more.

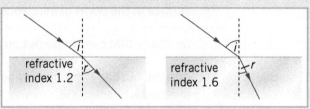

refractive index 1.2

refractive index 1.6

Snell's Law

The refractive index of a material is linked to the angles of incidence and refraction of light. This is Snell's Law.

The refractive index, n, of a material can be calculated using:

$$n = \frac{\sin(\text{angle in air})}{\sin(\text{angle in medium})}$$
$$= \frac{\sin i}{\sin r}$$

Total internal reflection

When light starts inside a medium of higher refractive index than the medium on the other side of the boundary then:

• If the angle of incidence in the medium (e.g., glass) is equal to the **critical angle**, the refracted ray emerges along the boundary ($r = 90°$).

• At angles above the critical angle, light is **totally internally reflected**.

$$n = \frac{\sin(\text{angle in air})}{\sin(\text{angle in medium})} = \frac{\sin 90°}{\sin c} = \frac{1}{\sin c}$$

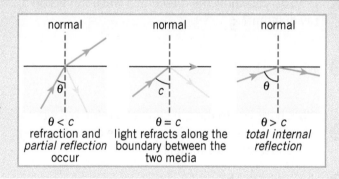

normal | normal | normal

$\theta < c$
refraction and *partial reflection* occur

$\theta = c$
light refracts along the boundary between the two media

$\theta > c$
total internal reflection

Uses of total internal reflection

Total internal reflection is used in **optical fibres**. An optical fibre is like a light pipe.

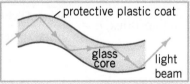

protective plastic coat

glass core

light beam

Optical fibres transmit light or infrared radiation. They are used in communications.

Endoscopes use optical fibres and visible light to see inside the human body.

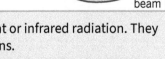

Revision Tip

Ray diagrams may look confusing, but drawing them step-by-step can make them logical and simple.

Learn the rules to draw them rather than memorising the diagrams themselves.

Dispersion

When a beam of white light goes through a prism, it is split into a continuous spectrum. This is **dispersion**.

• Light with a long wavelength (e.g., red) is refracted less.

• Light with a short wavelength (e.g., violet) is refracted more.

• A **spectrum** can be produced on a screen.

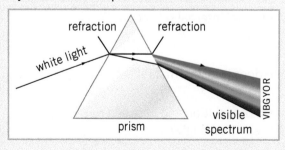

refraction   refraction

white light

prism

visible spectrum

VIBGYOR

Key Terms   **Make sure you can write a definition for these key terms.**

angle of incidence/reflection   critical angle   dispersion   normal   optical fibre   plane mirror
ray diagram   refraction   refractive index   spectrum   total internal reflection   wavefront diagram

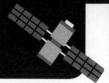

Learn the answers to the questions below then cover the answers column with a piece of paper and write as many as you can. Check and repeat.

	P10 questions	Answers
1	What rule do waves follow when they reflect off a surface?	angle of incidence = angle of reflection
2	What is the normal (on a ray diagram)?	a construction line perpendicular to the reflecting surface at the point of incidence
3	What is a virtual image?	an image that cannot be put on a screen
4	List the properties of an image formed in a plane mirror.	upright, virtual, same size/colour/shape, laterally inverted
5	What does *laterally inverted* mean?	an image that is reversed left to right
6	How do you show the direction a wave travels on a ray diagram?	draw a single arrow on the ray, pointing in the direction of travel
7	What is refraction?	waves change speed and direction as they cross the boundary from one substance to another due to the change in velocity
8	What happens to the direction of a refracted wave when it slows down as it crosses the boundary from one substance to another?	bends towards the normal
9	What does a prism do to white light?	it disperses white light to produce a spectrum
10	Which colour of light is refracted most by a prism?	violet
11	How do you calculate refractive index in terms of speed?	refractive index, $n = \dfrac{\text{speed of light in a vacuum (air)}}{\text{speed of light in a medium}}$
12	How do you calculate refractive index in terms of angles?	$n = \dfrac{\sin i}{\sin r}$
13	What is total internal reflection?	the total reflection of a light ray inside a transparent material when it reaches a boundary with air or another transparent material
14	When does total internal reflection happen?	when the angle of incidence is greater than the critical angle at the boundary between two media
15	What is the relationship between refractive index and the critical angle?	$n = \dfrac{1}{\sin c}$
16	Which types of radiation are transmitted through optical fibres?	visible light or infrared
17	What is refraction in optical fibres used for?	communications and seeing inside the human body using an endoscope

Put paper here

Now use the questions below to check your knowledge from previous chapters.

P10

Previous questions

Answers

Put paper here

1	Is force a vector or scalar quantity?	vector
2	How can the distance travelled by an object be found from its velocity–time graph?	calculate the area under the graph
3	What is the unit of momentum?	kg m/s
4	What is the amplitude of a wave?	maximum displacement of a point on the wave from its undisturbed position
5	List the different types of waves in the electromagnetic spectrum in order of decreasing wavelength (increasing frequency).	radio, microwave, infrared, visible, ultraviolet, X-rays, gamma

🧪 Required Practical Skills

Practise answering questions on the required practicals using the example below. You need to be able to apply your skills and knowledge to other practicals too.

Reflection and refraction	**Worked example**	**Practice**
In this practical, you should have traced rays of light from a ray box as they interact with different surfaces or materials. This includes investigating how light refracts as it passes through different materials, and how light is reflected by different surfaces. To carry out accurate and precise investigations you need to: • use low-light conditions • place the slit in the ray box as far from the bulb as possible • use a sharp pencil and ruler to draw the rays • draw a line at 90° to any surface or boundary and measure all angles from this line to the ray • mark either side of the solid block to work out the path of a ray inside the block.	A student wants to determine the angle of reflection for a particular angle of incidence. They set up a ray box and a mirror, and mark on paper the paths of the rays. 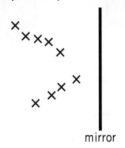 mirror **1** Explain how you know the student has drawn the mirror in the wrong place. **Answer:** The rays will not meet on the line where the mirror is placed. **2** Suggest one reason why the marks for each ray are not in a straight line. **Answer:** The beam from the ray box was very broad because the slit was too close to the bulb, or the classroom lights were on.	A student sets up a ray box and directs the ray at a glass block. They produce the drawing shown. 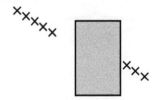 outline of glass block **1** Complete the diagram by drawing in the rays using the marks that the student put on the paper. **2** Label the angle of incidence, the angle of refraction, and the normal. **3** Explain why the rays entering and leaving the block are parallel.

Exam-style questions

01 Here are some statements about images. **[2 marks]**
Tick the correct statements.

The image you see in a plane mirror is virtual. ☐

A virtual image cannot be put on a screen. ☐

Your image in a plane mirror is the same size and inverted. ☐

The distance between you and your image in a plane mirror is twice the distance between you and the mirror. ☐

> **! Exam Tip**
>
> This question hasn't told you how many to tick, but look at the number of marks available for a clue.

02 A student investigates the light-transmitting properties of some materials.

First, they put the light meter on the other side of the material, as shown in **Figure 1**. Then they read the light level on the light meter.

Figure 1

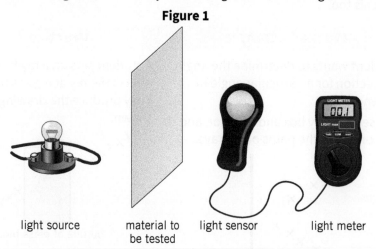

light source   material to   light sensor   light meter
be tested

The student uses this equipment to collect data to answer this question:

How does the type of material affect the light intensity detected by the light meter?

02.1 Name the independent variable in this investigation. **[1 mark]**

_____

02.2 Name the dependent variable in this investigation. **[1 mark]**

_____

> **! Exam Tip**
>
> Use highlighter pens to pick out the variables in the question.

P10

02.3 Suggest two control variables in this investigation. **[2 marks]**

_____

_____

02.4 The student then puts the light meter on the *same* side as the light source, pointing it at the material, and reads the light level.

They change the materials and measure the reflected light intensity. The materials they test are a mirror, a light-coloured material, and a dark-coloured material.

Table 1 shows the reflected light intensity, measured in lux, for each material.

Table 1

Material	Reflected light intensity in lux
A	25
B	85
C	65

Use the data in **Table 1** to identify materials A, B, and C. Explain your reasoning. **[3 marks]**

_____

_____

_____

_____

> **! Exam Tip**
> Before you start your answer make notes next to the table to help you work out the identity of A, B, and C.

03 You can achieve magic tricks with the reflection of light. In this trick, you can make it appear that a candle is burning in a beaker of water.

In **Figure 2**, object O is a burning candle.

Figure 2

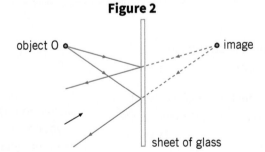

03.1 Explain what happens to the rays of light from object O when they hit the sheet of glass. **[2 marks]**

03.2 Describe what you see if you look in the direction of the black arrow. **[1 mark]**

P10 Practice 109

03.3 Suggest **one** difference between what you see and the appearance of object O. Explain the difference. **[2 marks]**

03.4 Describe where you should put a beaker of water to make it appear that the candle is burning underwater. Describe the direction you should look in to see this illusion. **[2 marks]**

> **Exam Tip**
>
> Here you need to describe how you would add to an image, so be very clear with your wording so the examiner understands what you mean.

04 Mirages are very common in deserts. You see what appears to be a sheet of water a short distance ahead of you.

On a hot day, you can see the same effect on a road (**Figure 3**). The road in front of you may appear wet or shiny. However, no matter how far you travel, you never reach the water because it is an optical illusion.

Figure 3

What you are seeing is an image of the sky, which looks like water to us (**Figure 4**).

Figure 4

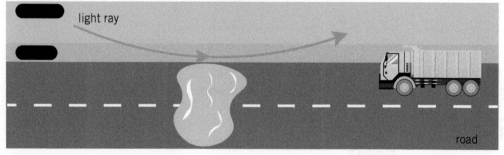

pool mirage

04.1 The brain works by assuming that light travels in straight lines. Describe where the light appears to come from. **[1 mark]**

04.2 As the light travels toward the road, it is moving from cool air to hot air. Describe what happens to a ray of light in terms of a normal to the boundary at the point of incidence. **[1 mark]**

04.3 Explain why the light changes direction in this way. **[2 marks]**

04.4 Explain why the ray of light is reflected from the boundary between the hot air and the road. **[2 marks]**

> **Exam Tip**
>
> This topic has a lot of key words. You need to use them in your answer to show the examiner you know what you're talking about.

05 The refractive index tells us how much light is slowed down by a medium such as air or glass.

Table 2 shows data for a vacuum and glass.

Table 2

Material	Speed of light in a vacuum in km/s	Speed of light in the material in km/s	Refractive index
vacuum	300 000		1
glass	300 000	200 000	

! Exam Tip

Read the second part of the question to give you a clue about the first part.

05.1 Use the data in **Table 2** to write down the speed of light in a vacuum. **[1 mark]**

05.2 Explain why you do not need to do a calculation. **[2 marks]**

05.3 Explain why refractive index does not have a unit. **[1 mark]**

05.4 Calculate the refractive index of glass. **[3 marks]**

05.5 Suggest whether it is possible to have a material with a refractive index of less than 1.0. Explain your answer. **[2 marks]**

06 **Figure 5** shows the change in direction of waves as they move between two different media.

Figure 5

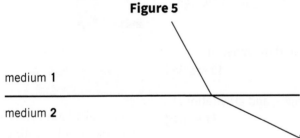

medium **1**

medium **2**

06.1 Add **three** lines to show the wavefronts of waves moving in medium **1**. **[2 marks]**

06.2 Add **three** lines to show the wavefronts of waves moving in medium **2**. **[3 marks]**

! Exam Tip

Whether the waves bend towards or away from the normal depends on whether the waves speed up or slow down as they pass into medium 2. This is the first thing you have to work out.

06.3 Describe what happens to the speed and frequency of the waves when they move from medium **1** to medium **2**. **[2 marks]**

06.4 Suggest a situation where waves would behave as shown in the diagram. **[1 mark]**

07 A ray of light enters two media at the same angle of incidence (**Figure 6**).

Figure 6

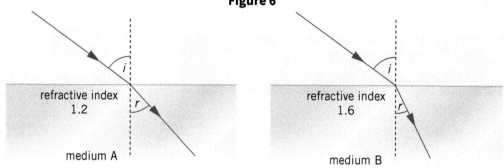

07.1 The angle of incidence is 45°. Show that the angle of refraction of the ray in medium A is 36°. **[2 marks]**

The refractive index of medium B is bigger than the refractive index of medium A.

07.2 Calculate the angle of incidence of a ray of light entering medium B if the angle of refraction is 36°. **[3 marks]**

07.3 Explain how you know that the answer to **07.2** must be bigger than 45°. **[3 marks]**

08 A student finds a website that shows how much they would weigh on different planets.

08.1 Describe one difference between the weight and the mass of an object. **[2 marks]**

08.2 Write down the equation that links mass, weight, and gravitational field strength. **[1 mark]**

08.3 The website says that the student's weight on Mercury would be 179 N. The gravitational field strength on Mercury is 3.8 N/kg. Calculate the mass of the student. **[3 marks]**

08.4 The student sits on a sofa. The sofa contains springs that compress when the student sits down. Describe the relationship between the weight of the student and the compression of the springs. **[2 marks]**

> **! Exam Tip**
>
> In a calculation you can get a mark for substituting in the correct values and a mark for rearranging the equation. Make sure you clearly demonstrate both steps in your working.

09 A skateboarder is travelling at 2.0 m/s. The mass of the skateboarder is 54 kg.

09.1 Calculate the momentum of the skateboarder. Use an appropriate number of significant figures. **[4 marks]**

09.2 As the skateboarder moves along, they grab their backpack from the ground and continue moving forward. When no other forces act, their velocity decreases. Explain why. **[2 marks]**

09.3 The skateboarder comes to a stop using friction between their shoe and the ground. The frictional force is 80 N. Calculate the acceleration of the skateboarder. **[3 marks]**

10 A student has been studying what happens when light goes into a glass block.

They measure the angle of incidence and the angle of refraction. Their results are shown in **Table 3**.

Table 3

Angle of incidence in degrees	Angle of refraction in degrees
10	7
20	13
30	37
40	25
50	31

10.1 Write down the angle of refraction when the angle of incidence is zero. **[1 mark]**

10.2 Give the result that does not fit the pattern. **[1 mark]**

10.3 The student replaces the block with one that has a lower refractive index.

Write a prediction that they could make about what will happen to the angles of refraction shown in **Table 3**. Explain your answer.

[2 marks]

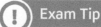

> **! Exam Tip**
>
> This is a one mark question, so all you need to do is give the result. No other explanation is needed, so don't waste time writing more.

11 Light travels in straight lines, but can travel around corners in an optical fibre.

11.1 Complete **Figure 7** to show the path of the light ray. Explain what you have drawn. **[2 marks]**

Figure 7

> **! Exam Tip**
>
> Use a ruler to complete this question. Draw the light ray with a pencil so that you can erase if you need to.

11.2 Describe the link between the refractive index and critical angle. **[1 mark]**

11.3 **Table 4** shows the speed of light in different materials.

Table 4

Material	Speed of light in the material in million km/s
air	300
diamond	125
glass	200
plastic	187

Exam Tip

You'll need to include all of the materials to get the marks.

Put the materials in order in terms of biggest to smallest critical angle. **[1 mark]**

11.4 Explain why it would be better to have an optical fibre made of material with a very small critical angle. **[1 mark]**

12 **Figure 8** shows a ray of white light being dispersed by a prism.

Figure 8

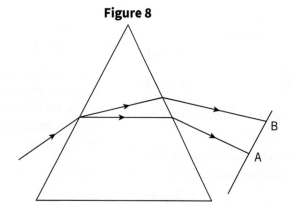

12.1 Name the effect seen on the screen as a result of the light being dispersed. **[1 mark]**

12.2 Give the colour of the light at **A** and at **B**. **[1 mark]**

12.3 Describe the position of the points on the diagram that show light being refracted. **[1 mark]**

12.4 You can add another prism to recombine the light and produce white light. Describe where you would put the second prism, and which way up you would put it. **[2 marks]**

Exam Tip

Think about the colour of light that went in and the order of colours that will be coming out.

13 Many optical instruments use prisms.

Figure 9 shows how light travels through binoculars.

Figure 9

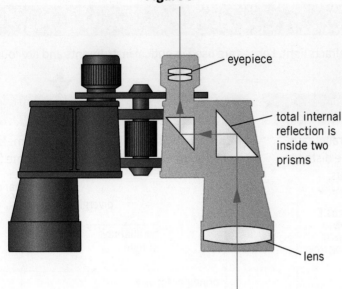

eyepiece

total internal reflection is inside two prisms

lens

13.1 Explain why the light is not dispersed as it goes through the prisms.

[2 marks]

13.2 Suggest a value for the critical angle of the material of the prisms. Explain your answer. **[2 marks]**

13.3 Suggest **one** benefit of using prisms rather than lenses in binoculars. **[1 mark]**

14 Motorbikes have a suspension system. Springs are connected between the wheel and the frame. A motorcyclist of mass 80 kg gets on a motorcycle.

14.1 Calculate the weight of the motorcyclist.

Gravitational field strength = 9.8 N/kg. **[2 marks]**

14.2 There are four springs on the motorbike. The motorcyclist's weight is supported by all four springs. Calculate the force applied to each spring. Show your working. **[2 marks]**

14.3 When the motorcyclist sits on the bike, each spring compresses a distance of 3.4 cm. Use the equation that links force, extension, and spring constant to calculate the spring constant of the spring.

[4 marks]

14.4 When the motorcyclist gets off the bike the springs return to their original length. Suggest whether the work done on the spring is bigger than, smaller than, or equal to the stored elastic potential energy. Explain your answer. **[2 marks]**

> **! Exam Tip**
>
> Units can give you a clue to the rest of the equation. The units of gravitational field strength are N/kg. This is saying that to calculate gravitational field strength, you need to divide Newtons by kilograms. This is a big hint to the equation.

> **! Exam Tip**
>
> Remember there are four springs!

P11 Lenses and the eye

Lenses

A **lens** is a piece of glass or other material that refracts light. Lenses are used in optical instruments and are found in the eye.

Convex lenses

Convex lenses curve outwards. They make parallel rays of light **converge** at a point. **Focal length** is the distance from the centre of the lens to the principal focus.

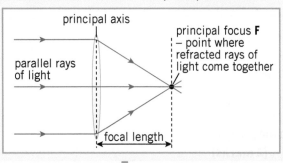

Concave lenses

Concave lenses curve inwards. They make parallel rays of light **diverge** (so they appear to come from a point).

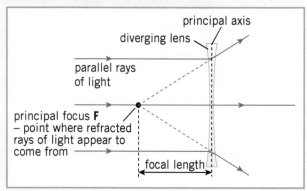

Forming images

Images formed by convex lenses can be either real or virtual. **Real images** can be projected onto a screen. **Virtual images** appear to come from behind the lens.

If the object is beyond the principal focus, the image is real. It can be diminished, magnified, or the same size as the object.

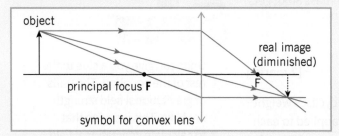

If the object is between the principal focus and the lens, the image is virtual and magnified. This is a magnifying glass.

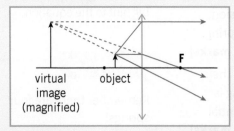

Forming images

Images formed by concave lenses are always virtual.

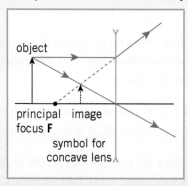

Magnification

The **magnification** of an image can be calculated using:

$$\text{magnification} = \frac{\text{image height}}{\text{object height}}$$

Magnification has no units because it is a ratio. Magnified images have a magnification greater than one. Diminished images have a magnification less than one.

🔑 Key Terms

Make sure you can write a definition for these key terms.

concave	converge	convex	diverge	focal length	laser	lens
long sight	magnification	range of vision	real image	short sight	virtual image	

The eye

Our eyes only detect visible light. Light entering the eye is refracted by the cornea and the lens.

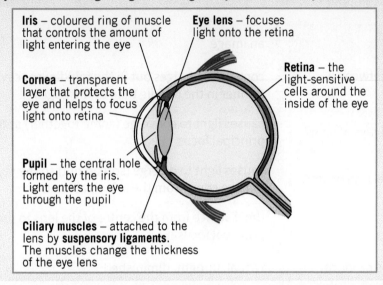

Iris – coloured ring of muscle that controls the amount of light entering the eye

Eye lens – focuses light onto the retina

Cornea – transparent layer that protects the eye and helps to focus light onto retina

Retina – the light-sensitive cells around the inside of the eye

Pupil – the central hole formed by the iris. Light enters the eye through the pupil

Ciliary muscles – attached to the lens by **suspensory ligaments**. The muscles change the thickness of the eye lens

Near and far

The normal eye has:

- a near point at 25 cm
- a far point at infinity.

The eye can focus on objects between 25 cm and infinity. The distance between these points is called the **range of vision**.

Ciliary muscles adjust the thickness of the lens to focus light arriving from different distances.

Correcting vision

In normal vision, light is focused on to the retina.

Short sight occurs when an eye cannot focus on distant objects.

This is because the eyeball is too long, or the eye lens is too powerful, causing it to refract light from objects too much.

It is corrected using a concave (diverging) lens.

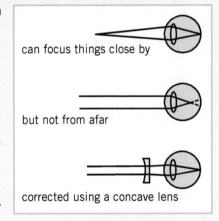

can focus things close by

but not from afar

corrected using a concave lens

Long sight occurs when an eye cannot focus on nearby objects.

This is because the eyeball is too short, or the eye lens is too weak. The lens cannot refract light enough to form an image on the retina.

It is corrected using a convex (converging) lens.

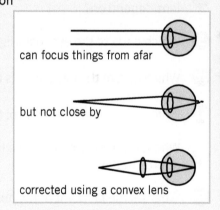

can focus things from afar

but not close by

corrected using a convex lens

Laser eye surgery can be used to correct sight. A **laser** produces a narrow, concentrated beam of light that is used to cut, cauterise, or burn tissue.

Cameras and the eye

In a camera, an image is brought to focus on film or a CCD sensor by adjusting the distance between the lens and the film or sensor.

Part of eye	Part of camera
lens	lens
pupil	aperture
retina	photographic film or CCD sensor

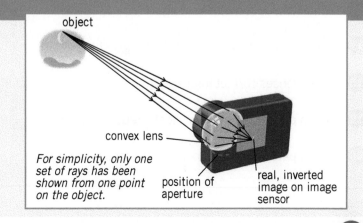

object

convex lens

For simplicity, only one set of rays has been shown from one point on the object.

position of aperture

real, inverted image on image sensor

Retrieval

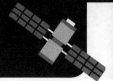

Learn the answers to the questions below then cover the answers column with a piece of paper and write as many as you can. Check and repeat.

Put paper here

	P11 questions	Answers
1	What does a lens form?	an image
2	What is the difference in appearance between a concave and convex lens?	convex lens bulges out in the middle; concave lens is thinner in the middle than at the edges
3	What does a convex lens do to parallel rays of light?	causes light to converge (come together) at the principal focus
4	What does a concave lens do to parallel rays of light?	causes light to diverge (spread out) so the rays appear to have come from the principal focus
5	What is the focal length of a lens?	the distance from the centre of the lens to the principal focus
6	What kind of images do concave lenses produce?	virtual, upright, diminished
7	What kind of images do convex lenses produce?	real or virtual; upright or inverted; diminished, magnified, or the same size
8	What does the type of image produced by a convex lens depend on?	the distance between the object and the lens
9	Which parts of the eye focus light?	the cornea and the lens
10	Which part of the eye controls the size of the pupil?	the iris
11	Which parts of the eye control the shape of the lens?	ciliary muscles and suspensory ligaments
12	Where is the near point of the human eye, approximately?	25 cm from the eye
13	Where is the far point of the human eye?	infinity
14	What is the range of vision of a human?	the distance between the near point and the far point
15	What causes some people to be short-sighted?	the eyeball is too long or the lens is too powerful
16	Which lenses correct short sight?	concave (diverging) lenses
17	What causes some people to be long-sighted?	the eyeball is too short or the lens is too weak
18	Which lenses correct long sight?	convex lenses
19	Which part of a camera is like the retina of the eye?	the film or CCD sensor
20	Which part of the camera is like the lens of the eye?	the lens

Now use the questions below to check your knowledge from previous chapters.

P11

Previous questions

Answers

1	What is the name for the force acting on an object due to gravity?	weight
2	What is the resultant force on an object moving at a steady speed in a straight line?	zero
3	What is the centre of mass?	the point through which the weight of an object can be considered to act
4	Give an example of a transverse wave.	electromagnetic waves
5	Which types of surface are poor absorbers and emitters of infrared radiation?	light, shiny surfaces

Put paper here (between questions and answers)

 ## Maths Skills

Practise your maths skills using the worked example and practice questions below.

Sense checking calculations	Worked example	Practice

Sense checking calculations

When you do a calculation to produce a number, you should do a 'sense check'. This is to see if your answer agrees with other information in the question, or with what you know about the topic.

There are many examples of ways that you can do this. For example:

- a speed cannot be greater than the speed of light
- a magnification of more than one means the image is bigger than the object
- a larger refractive index means the critical angle is smaller
- a larger frequency means a smaller wavelength
- a larger specific heat capacity means a smaller temperature rise (for the same energy in and mass).

Worked example

An image is produced by a convex lens. Calculate the magnification.

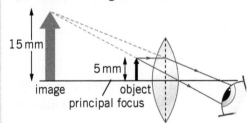

Step 1: take information from the image.

image height = 15 mm

object height = 5 mm

Step 2: write the equation.

$$\text{magnification} = \frac{\text{image height}}{\text{object height}}$$

Step 3: put the numbers into the equation.

$$\text{magnification} = \frac{15\,\text{mm}}{5\,\text{mm}} = 3$$

Step 4: do a sense check.

In the diagram, the image is bigger than the object. Therefore, the magnification should be greater than 1, which it is.

Practice

1 A convex lens is placed in line with a filament lamp to produce an image on a screen. The filament in the lamp is 6 mm high.

A student moves the lens until the magnification is 0.4. Calculate the size of the image on the screen.

2 A rocket manufacturer claims that a rocket motor has an acceleration of 500 000 m/s², and it will function for 800 s. Check the accuracy of this claim.

3 The critical angle of a material is 24°. This is much smaller than that of glass, which has a refractive index of 1.42. Calculate the refractive index of the material.

01 A student is looking through convex and concave lenses.

01.1 Complete the sentences. Use the words in the box. **[4 marks]**

concave	convex

The student sees only a virtual image when they look through a

_____ lens. The image through a _____ lens
can be real or virtual.

A _____ lens spreads light rays out. A _____
lens brings light rays to a focus.

> **! Exam Tip**
>
> Each 'fill in the gaps' question is different. For this one you have to use words given more than once. In other ones, you can only use each word one time. Always read the question carefully.

01.2 The student notices that an image is magnified.

The image height is 1.2 cm. The object height is 0.7 cm.

Calculate the magnification.

Use an equation from the *Physics Equations Sheet*. **[2 marks]**

magnification = _____

01.3 Suggest why magnification has no unit. **[1 mark]**

_____

_____

01.4 Draw a diagram to show how light from a distant object is refracted by a concave lens. **[3 marks]**

> **! Exam Tip**
>
> Use a ruler and a pencil for **01.4**. It requires accuracy and you won't get that if you draw it free hand.

02 When you look at an object a long way away, like a distant mountain, you see an image in focus.

02.1 Write down the parts of the eye that focus light. **[2 marks]**

_____

_____

02.2 Complete **Figure 1** to show what happens to light from a distant point that enters the eye. Assume the person has normal vision.

[2 marks]

Figure 1

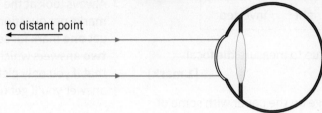

to distant point

02.3 When you look at the writing on this page, you see an image that is in focus.

Describe the change to the lens that means the image is in focus.

[1 mark]

_____

_____

02.4 You hold the page 10 cm from your eye. Would you expect it to be in focus? Explain your answer. **[2 marks]**

_____

_____

03 A child is sitting in a supermarket trolley. Their brother is pushing the trolley.

The brother exerts a force of 20 N.

The total distance travelled by the trolley is 30 m.

03.1 Calculate the work done by the brother. **[2 marks]**

03.2 There are **two** units for work done. Name them both. **[1 mark]**

03.3 When you lift an object, you do work against gravity.

The brother is doing work when he pushes the trolley at a steady speed.

Name the force against which he is doing work. **[1 mark]**

03.4 Describe the energy changes when the brother is moving the trolley at a steady speed. **[2 marks]**

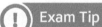

> ! **Exam Tip**
>
> The equation might give you a clue to one of the units.

> ! **Exam Tip**
>
> What force would cause the trolley to slow down?

04   A teacher finds a box of lenses. The focal lengths of the lenses are not shown.

The teacher holds up a piece of paper and the lens, and forms an image of a distant house on the paper.

04.1   Choose **two** of these words to describe the image they will see on the paper.   [1 mark]

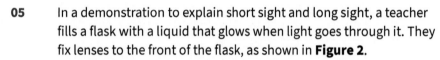

| diminished | magnified | upright | inverted |

04.2   Explain how they can use this technique to measure the focal length of the lens.   [1 mark]

04.3   Explain why they cannot form an image on the paper with some of the lenses in the box.   [1 mark]

04.4   A student asks why they cannot do the experiment inside, using a light source close to the lens and a screen. Explain the problem with this method.   [1 mark]

05   In a demonstration to explain short sight and long sight, a teacher fills a flask with a liquid that glows when light goes through it. They fix lenses to the front of the flask, as shown in **Figure 2**.

Lens **A** will focus the rays from a light source onto the back of the flask.

If you look at the back of the flask, you will see a dot.

Figure 2

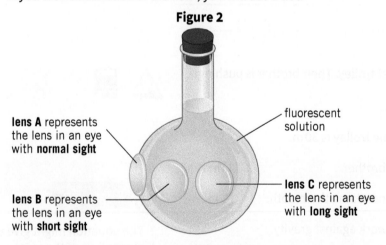

lens **A** represents the lens in an eye with **normal sight**

fluorescent solution

lens **C** represents the lens in an eye with **long sight**

lens **B** represents the lens in an eye with **short sight**

05.1   Compare the strength of lens **A** and lens **B**. Explain your answer.   [2 marks]

05.2   Suggest what you would see on the back of the flask with lens **C**. Explain your answer.   [2 marks]

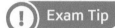
Exam Tip

Always look at the number of marks per question. Here you get **one** mark for selecting **two** answers which means that if you only pick one answer you'll get nothing.

Exam Tip

This is just talking about lenses in a new context so apply what you know and you'll be fine.

05.3 In one of the experiments, the teacher uses a concave lens to correct the defect, as shown in **Figure 3**.

Figure 3

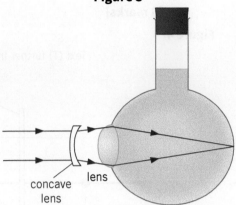

concave lens   lens

Give the name of the defect, and explain how the concave lens corrects it. **[2 marks]**

06 A theme park rollercoaster vehicle travels along a track. The forces acting on the vehicle are shown in **Table 1**.

Table 1

Section of straight track	Driving force in N	Resistive force in N
A	3000	2500
B	3000	3500
C	3500	3500

06.1 Write down the section of track where the vehicle is decelerating. **[1 mark]**

06.2 Write down the section of track where the vehicle is travelling at a steady speed. **[1 mark]**

06.3 At the end of the ride the only force acting on the vehicle is the resistive force due to the brakes. The mass of the vehicle and passengers is 3500 kg. Calculate the force required to stop the vehicle with a deceleration of 4 m/s². **[3 marks]**

06.4 On one section of the track a resultant force does not produce the change in speed predicted. Suggest why. **[1 mark]**

07 A student looks through a thick perspex rod at some text on a piece of paper. They notice that when the rod is close to the text, the image of the text is magnified. However, when the rod is further from the text, the image is diminished. The rod is behaving like a lens.

07.1 Write down which type of lens shows the same behaviour. **[1 mark]**

07.2 Complete the diagrams in **Figure 4** to show how the image changes as the student moves the rod away from the text. The focal points are shown as 'f'. **[6 marks]**

Figure 4

Text (T) closer to rod:

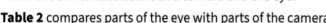

Text (T) further from rod:

perspex rod

07.3 The student makes another observation about the change to the image as they move the rod away. Use the diagrams to describe the second observation about the image. **[2 marks]**

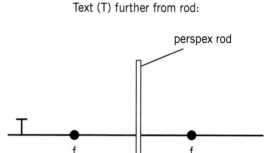

! Exam Tip

The steps for drawing ray diagrams are the same no matter where the object is. Just follow the rules and you should see the differing results.

08 There are similarities between a camera and the eye.

Table 2 compares parts of the eye with parts of the camera.

Table 2

Part of eye	Part of camera
lens	
pupil	
retina	

08.1 Complete **Table 2**. **[3 marks]**

With both the eye and the camera you can focus on a near and distant object.

08.2 Compare what happens in the camera when you adjust the focus with what happens in the eye. **[2 mark]**

08.3 The eye also contains ciliary muscles. Explain why there is no part of the camera that matches the ciliary muscles. **[2 marks]**

08.4 The camera often has a lens cap. Suggest which part of the eye this is most like, and why it is not exactly like it. **[2 marks]**

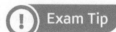

! Exam Tip

Remember to answer both parts of this question.

09 The spy hole in a door is a concave lens. When you look through the hole you see an image of the person on the other side.

09.1 Complete **Figure 5**. **[4 marks]**

Figure 5

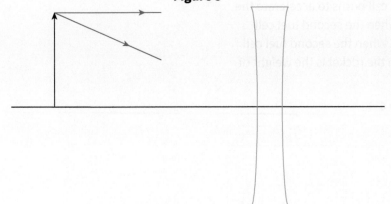

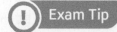
Exam Tip

Always use a ruler for ray diagrams and follow the rules slowly and carefully.

09.2 Describe the type of image that you see. **[2 marks]**

09.3 The person on the other side of the door moves away from the door. Describe what happens to the image. **[2 marks]**

09.4 Describe what you would see if someone accidentally placed a convex lens in the door instead, and the person stood close to the door. **[2 marks]**

10 If you go to the opticians to get eyeglasses, you will be asked lots of questions. One of the questions will be about the material you would like the optician to use to make the lenses.

10.1 'High-index' lenses are usually more expensive. Suggest what the 'index' in 'high-index' refers to. **[1 mark]**

Exam Tip

Even if you've never heard of 'high-index' before, the index part is similar to something you've studied in this unit.

10.2 Suggest a physical difference between a 'high-index' lens and a normal lens. Explain your answer. **[2 marks]**

A student has both eyeglasses and contact lenses. A contact lens is a very thin piece of plastic that is placed directly on the eye.

10.3 Suggest how a contact lens can be concave and still cover the front of the eyeball. **[1 mark]**

10.4 The strength of the contact lens will always be less than the strength of the eyeglass lens for the same person. Suggest why. **[1 mark]**

11 A model rocket contains two fuel cells. When the fuels burn, they force air from the rocket. This produces a force upwards on the rocket. **Figure 6** shows the first 13 seconds of the rocket's journey. Section **AB** shows when the first fuel cell burns to accelerate the rocket upwards. Section **BC** shows when the second fuel cell burns to accelerate the rocket again. When the second fuel cell has finished, the only force acting on the rocket is the weight of the rocket.

Figure 6

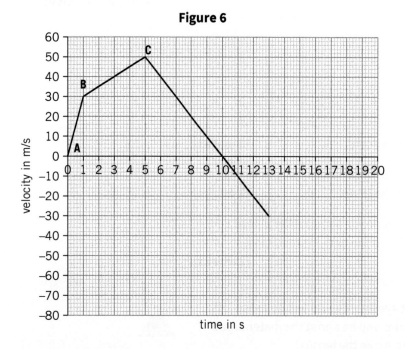

11.1 Suggest which of the fuel cells burns more quickly. Explain your answer in terms of energy. **[2 marks]**

11.2 Use **Figure 6** to calculate the acceleration of the rocket during section **BC**. **[2 marks]**

11.3 Use **Figure 6** to write down the time at which the rocket reaches the maximum distance from the ground. Give reasons for your answer. **[2 marks]**

11.4 The equipment recording the velocity of the rocket stopped recording after 13 seconds. Explain how you know that the rocket had not hit the ground at that time. **[2 marks]**

12 A student investigates the magnification of an object by a lens. They set up a lamp, a lens, and a screen as shown in **Figure 7**. The student sees an image of the filament of the lamp on the screen.

Figure 7

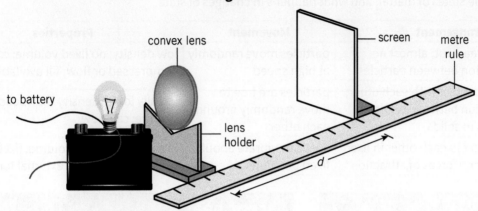

The student uses a ruler to measure the distance d between the lens and the screen and the size of the image on the screen.

12.1 Estimate the uncertainty in measurement when using a ruler to measure distance. **[1 mark]**

> ⚠ Exam Tip
>
> Look at the divisions on a ruler.

12.2 As the student moves the lamp away from the lens, the image becomes more blurred. Suggest why. **[1 mark]**

12.3 Describe what the student needs to do to produce an image in focus, with the lens and lamp in their new positions. Give reasons for your answer. **[2 marks]**

12.4 **Table 3** shows the student's data.

Table 3

d in cm	Image size in cm			
	Measurement 1	Measurement 2	Measurement 3	Mean
12.1	2.9	3.1	3.0	3.0
12.3	3.4	3.6	3.7	3.6
12.5	3.9	3.6	3.8	3.8
13.0	4.8	5.0	4.7	4.8

Describe how to use the range of measurements of image size to calculate the uncertainty in the measurement. **[1 mark]**

12.5 Calculate the uncertainty in the image size at $d = 13.0\,\text{cm}$. Compare this uncertainty with the uncertainty in **12.1**. **[2 marks]**

12.6 The width of the filament of the lamp is 4 mm. Calculate the magnification of the lens when $d = 13.0\,\text{cm}$. Use an equation from the *Physics Equations Sheet*. **[3 marks]**

P12 Kinetic theory and energy transfer

Kinetic theory

Kinetic theory explains the states of matter, and what happens in changes of state.

State	Arrangement	Movement	Properties
gas	particles are spread out; almost no forces of attraction between particles	particles move randomly at high speed	low density; no fixed volume; can be compressed or flow; fill available space
liquid	particles are in contact with each other; forces of attraction between particles are weaker than in solids	particles are free to move randomly around each other	usually lower density than solids; fixed volume; can flow
solid	particles held next to each other in fixed positions by strong forces of attraction	particles vibrate about fixed positions	high density; fixed volume; fixed shape (unless distorted by external forces)

Internal energy

Heating a substance increases its **internal energy**.

Internal energy is the sum of the total kinetic energy due to the particles' motion and the total potential energy due to the particles' positions.

Specific heat capacity

When a substance is heated or cooled the temperature change depends on: the substance's mass, the type of material, and how much energy is transferred to it.

Every type of material has a **specific heat capacity** – the amount of energy needed to raise the temperature of 1 kg of the substance by 1 °C.

The energy change can be calculated using:

change in thermal energy (J) = mass (kg) × specific heat capacity (J/kg°C) × temperature change (°C)

$$E = m\,c\,\Delta\theta$$

Change of state and impurities

Only a **pure** substance produces a horizontal line on a temperature–time graph of change of state.

Melting points and boiling points are affected by **impurities**.

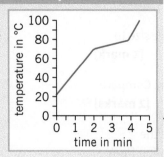

Latent heat

The graph shows the temperature change over time, when a substance is heated or cooled. While the substance is changing state, the energy transferred does not change the temperature, but it does change the internal energy. So these show as flat sections on the graph.

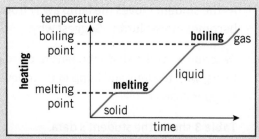

The energy transferred when a substance changes state is called the **latent heat**.

Specific latent heat is the energy required to change the state of 1 kg of a substance with no change in temperature.

This can be calculated using:

thermal energy for a change in state (J) = mass (kg) × specific latent heat (J/kg)

$$E = m \times L$$

Specific latent heat of fusion is the energy required to melt 1 kg of a substance with no change in temperature.

This can be calculated using: $E = m \times L_F$

Specific latent heat of vaporisation is the energy required to evaporate 1 kg of a substance with no change in temperature.

This can be calculated using: $E = m \times L_V$

🔑 Key Terms

Make sure you can write a definition for these key terms.

condensation   conduction   conductor   convection   evaporation   expansion   impurities   insulator   internal energy   kinetic theory   latent heat   pure   specific heat capacity   specific latent heat

Energy transfer – conduction

In solids, energy is mainly transferred by **conduction**.

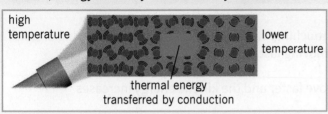

high temperature

lower temperature

thermal energy transferred by conduction

In a metal, energy is transferred by the movement of free electrons. Metals are **conductors**.

Insulators do not have electrons that can move easily.

Energy transfer – convection

When a fluid (liquid or gas) is heated, the particles move further apart and the density of the fluid decreases.

Warm fluid floats above cooler fluid.

This is **convection**.

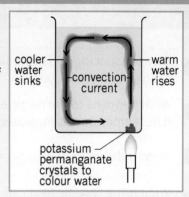

cooler water sinks

convection current

warm water rises

potassium permanganate crystals to colour water

Energy transfer – evaporation and condensation

When a liquid **evaporates**, the faster moving molecules escape. This reduces the average energy per molecule in the liquid. The temperature decreases. Energy is transferred *from* the liquid *to* the surroundings. The surroundings heat up.

Evaporation is used in systems to cool houses, and cools the human body when we sweat.

When a gas **condenses** to a liquid, the molecules slow down and move closer together. Energy is transferred *from* the gas *to* the surroundings. The surroundings heat up.

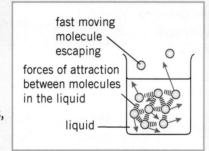

fast moving molecule escaping

forces of attraction between molecules in the liquid

liquid

Rate of evaporation

A liquid will evaporate more quickly if:

* the temperature difference between the liquid and the surroundings is greater
* the surface area of the liquid is larger
* there is wind or air movement near the surface
* the liquid has a low boiling point.

Rate of energy transfer

Hot objects transfer energy to the surroundings. The rate of transfer depends on:

* the surface area and volume of the object
* the material from which the object is made
* the nature of the surface with which the object is in contact.

Elephants have large ears to increase the surface area available for cooling. Engines and computers have devices with 'cooling fins' to increase the surface area.

Moving a liquid over a surface, or blowing air over a surface, will allow it to cool more quickly.

Heating and expansion

Most solids expand when they are heated. The amount of **expansion** for each increase of 1 °C in temperature can be different. This can be useful.

Bimetallic strips can be used in systems that control temperature. The strip consists of two metals stuck together.

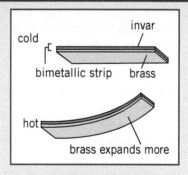

cold

invar

bimetallic strip

brass

hot

brass expands more

Thermal expansion can cause bridges, roofs, and railway lines to buckle.

Expansion joints enable sections to move together safely.

Retrieval

Learn the answers to the questions below then cover the answers column with a piece of paper and write as many as you can. Check and repeat.

	P12 questions	Answers
1	Give the spacing and movement of particles in solids, liquids, and gases.	solids: touching, vibrating; liquids: touching, moving around; gases: moving fast, far apart
2	What happens to the particles in a substance if its temperature is increased?	they move faster and the kinetic energy increases
3	What is the internal energy of a substance?	the total kinetic energy and potential energy of all the particles in the substance
4	What is the specific heat capacity of a substance?	the amount of energy needed to raise the temperature of 1 kg of the substance by 1 °C
5	Why is the mass of a substance conserved when it changes state?	the number of particles does not change
6	On a graph showing the change in temperature of a substance as it cools, why is the section when the substance is changing state flat?	the energy transferred during a change in state causes a change in the internal energy of the substance
7	What is the name given to the energy transferred when a substance changes state?	latent heat
8	What is the specific latent heat of a substance?	the energy required to change the state of 1 kg of the substance with no change in temperature
9	What is the specific latent heat of fusion of a substance?	the energy required to change 1 kg of the substance from solid to liquid at its melting point, without changing its temperature
10	What is the specific latent heat of vaporisation of a substance?	the energy required to change 1 kg of the substance from liquid to vapour at its boiling point, without changing its temperature
11	On a graph of temperature against time for a substance being heated up or cooled down, what do the flat (horizontal) sections show?	the time when the substance is changing state and the temperature is not changing
12	How is energy transferred by conduction in metals?	free electrons move through the metal
13	How is energy transferred by convection?	hot gas or liquid is less dense and floats above colder gas or liquid
14	What happens to the temperature of a liquid as it evaporates?	it decreases
15	Describe four factors that affect the rate of evaporation of a liquid.	surface area, temperature difference, boiling point, air movement across surface
16	Describe three factors that affect the rate of transfer of energy.	surface area to volume ratio, type of material, type of surface
17	Describe one use of thermal expansion.	bimetallic strips
18	Describe one situation where thermal expansion is a problem.	buckling of roads/bridges/railway tracks

Put paper here

Now use the questions below to check your knowledge from previous chapters.

P12

Previous questions | Answers

	Previous questions	Answers
1	According to Newton's Second Law, what is the acceleration of an object inversely proportional to?	mass
2	Name the four ways in which energy can be transferred.	heating, waves, electric current, mechanically (by forces)
3	What do electromagnetic waves transfer from their source to an absorber?	energy
4	What is a virtual image?	an image that cannot be put on a screen
5	Which parts of the eye control the shape of the lens?	ciliary muscles and suspensory ligaments

Put paper here *Put paper here*

Required Practical Skills

Practise answering questions on the required practicals using the example below. You need to be able to apply your skills and knowledge to other practicals too.

Melting point	Worked example	Practice

Melting point

To determine the melting point of stearic acid, you need to measure the temperature of stearic acid as it is heated.

To do this, you use a thermometer and a timer.

In the experiment, you need to:

- use a thermometer that is already in a boiling tube of stearic acid
- clamp the tube so the stearic acid is surrounded by water in a beaker
- use a Bunsen burner to heat the water, and stir the water to maintain an even temperature
- plot the data as you go until the temperature reaches 70 °C
- wear eye protection.

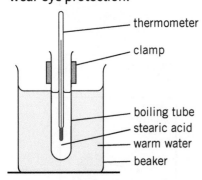

thermometer
clamp
boiling tube
stearic acid
warm water
beaker

If there are impurities in the stearic acid, the line on the graph when the stearic acid is melting will not be horizontal.

Worked example

A student heats a boiling tube of stearic acid in a water bath.

They measure the temperature of the stearic acid as it is heated, and plot this graph.

1 Write down the time interval between measurements.

Answer: The measurements are one minute apart.

2 Estimate the melting point of stearic acid. Explain how you arrived at your answer.

Answer: 70 °C

This is the horizontal section of the graph.

3 Sketch the graph for freezing a sample of stearic acid, with

  a a few impurities

  b lots of impurities.

Answer:

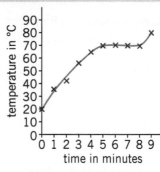

lots of impurities
few impurities

Practice

A student wants to work out if a sample of water contains impurities.

1 Describe the experimental procedure that would enable them to do this.

2 Sketch a temperature–time graph for a sample of pure water.

3 Describe how the student will use the temperature–time graph for the sample to decide if it is pure.

Practice

Exam-style questions

01 A block of aluminium has a mass of 1.2 kg.

It is at room temperature, which is 20 °C.

A student uses a heater to increase the temperature to 50 °C.

01.1 Calculate the difference between the initial and final temperatures. **[1 mark]**

temperature change = _____

01.2 The specific heat capacity of aluminium is 900 J/kg °C.

Calculate the energy transferred to the aluminium to raise its temperature.

Use the correct equation from the *Physics Equations Sheet*. **[2 marks]**

_____ J

> **! Exam Tip**
>
> The first thing you must do is write down the equation.
>
> This is a key skill and you need to get into the habit of always doing this first.

01.3 A student does this experiment and finds that the energy they need to transfer is bigger than the energy calculated in **01.2**.

Suggest why. **[1 mark]**

_____

_____

02 A student is learning about internal energy.

They draw two diagrams, **A** and **B**, as shown in **Figure 1**.

02.1 Complete the sentences using the words in the box. **[4 marks]**

| kinetic | vibrating | moving fast |
| potential | gravitational | moving slowly |

In diagram **A**, the particles are _____. Most of the

internal energy is due to the _____ energy of the

particles. In diagram **B**, the particles are _____. Most

of the internal energy is due to the _____ energy of the

particles.

02.2 The sample shown in **Figure 1A** is heated for a long time.

Describe how the internal energy of the sample changes. **[2 marks]**

_____

_____

_____

Figure 1

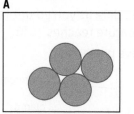

The particles in a solid.

The particles in a gas.

02.3 The sample shown in **Figure 1B** is heated.

The student decides to use the particle model to describe and explain what happens.

Which statement is correct? **[1 mark]**

Tick **one** box.

As the gas is heated, the average kinetic energy of the molecules decreases. ☐

The average kinetic energy of the molecules is independent of the temperature of the gas. ☐

If the temperature of a gas increases, the pressure that the gas exerts decreases (if the volume stays the same). ☐

The particles in a gas are in random motion. ☐

03 A swimming pool is heated by the Sun.

A paddling pool next to the swimming pool is also heated by the Sun.

A student notices that the temperature of the paddling pool is higher than the temperature of the swimming pool.

The student makes the estimates shown in **Table 1**.

Table 1

	Swimming pool	Paddling pool
energy transferred by the Sun	88 000 MJ	28.8 MJ
temperature of pool	25 °C	28 °C
starting temperature	18 °C	18 °C
specific heat capacity of water	4200 J/kg °C	4200 J/kg °C

03.1 Use **Table 1** to find the ratio of the mass of water in the paddling pool to the mass of water in the swimming pool.

Use the correct equation from the *Physics Equations Sheet*.

Use an appropriate number of significant figures. **[6 marks]**

03.2 At the end of the day the pool owner puts an identical cover over each pool.

If energy transfer is only through the cover, suggest why

- the swimming pool might take longer to cool down
- the paddling pool might take longer to cool down. **[2 marks]**

04 A student is comparing the specific heat capacities of two liquids **A** and **B**. Both liquids have the same mass. They use a heater to change the temperature of the liquids, and an energy meter to measure the energy transferred to each liquid by the electric current.

It takes 1.8 kJ of energy to raise the temperature of 10 g of liquid **A** by 50 °C. Calculate the specific heat capacity of liquid **A**. Use the correct equation from the *Physics Equations Sheet*.

Liquid **B** has a specific heat capacity that is twice that of liquid **A**. Suggest **two** differences that the student would observe if they heat the 10 g of liquid **B** using the same heater. Justify your answer.

[6 marks]

! Exam Tip

Pull all the key information out of the text first, for example:

Liquid A

mass =

energy used =

temperature change =

05.1 What quantities do you need to find to work out kinetic energy? Choose **one** answer. **[1 mark]**

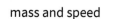

mass and speed	mass and time	speed and time

05.2 Car **A** and car **B** are both moving in different ways. Car **A** accelerates under a constant force for three seconds at the start of a race. During the same three seconds, car **B** is travelling at a steady speed on a motorway.

Compare:

- the ways energy is stored for each car at the start and end of the three seconds

- the way energy is transferred. **[6 marks]**

! Exam Tip

Break your answer up into two paragraphs – one paragraph for each bullet point in the question.

05.3 All cars require that you add oil to the engine. Suggest **one** benefit of adding oil to the engine. Use the idea of energy to explain your answer. **[2 marks]**

06 An electric iron switches off when it gets to the required temperature. The iron contains a bimetallic strip.

In **Figure 2**, a current is flowing and the heater is on.

Figure 2

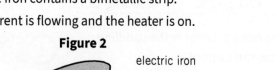

electric iron with base plate removed

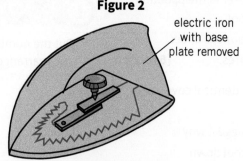

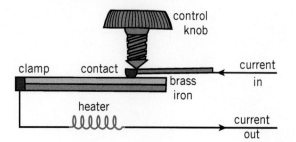

control knob

clamp   contact

brass
iron

current
in

heater

current
out

06.1 Describe what happens to materials when they are heated.

[1 mark]

06.2 Explain how the bimetallic strip ensures that the iron turns off at the correct temperature. **[2 marks]**

06.3 The control knob is turned so that it pushes the contact down and bends the bimetallic strip.

Suggest what happens to the temperature at which the circuit is switched off. Explain your answer. **[2 marks]**

07 A student is investigating the purity of an unknown solid. They are given a boiling tube with the solid and a temperature probe embedded in it. The temperature probe is connected to a data logger that records the temperature every minute. The student places the tube in a beaker of water on top of a hot plate. They turn the hot plate on and start the data logger.

07.1 Name the type of energy transfer between the hot plate and water. **[1 mark]**

07.2 Explain why the water at the bottom of the beaker will rise. **[2 marks]**

07.3 Describe the observation that will indicate to the student that the solid is pure. **[1 mark]**

07.4 At the end of the experiment, the student notices that the water level in the beaker is lower even though the water has not boiled.

Explain why, in terms of particles. **[2 marks]**

07.5 Which of the following statements are correct?

Choose **two** answers. **[2 marks]**

If the water was at a lower temperature, the evaporation rate would be higher.

If the room temperature was higher, the evaporation rate would be higher.

If the liquid had a lower boiling point, the evaporation rate would be higher.

If the surface area of the liquid was higher, the evaporation rate would be higher.

Exam Tip

Lots of the words in this topic sound very similar. It's important that things are spelt correctly and that your handwriting is clear so the examiner can see exactly which word you mean.

08 A student set up an experiment to measure the specific heat capacity of a 1 kg solid block of an unknown material, as shown in **Figure 3**.

The immersion heater was connected to a power supply.

Figure 3

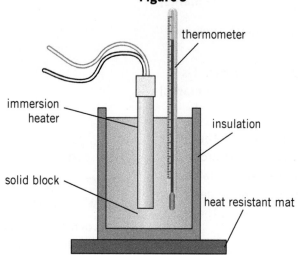

 **Exam Tip**

You might be familiar with this practical but you may not have seen it drawn like this before.

Here we show you what is going on inside the practical.

The student measured the starting temperature of the solid block. Then they turned on the power supply and started a stopwatch.

The results are shown in **Table 2**.

Table 2

Time in minutes	Temperature in °C
0	20
2	35
4	45
6	50
8	52

08.1 Plot a graph of temperature against time on **Figure 4**. **[3 marks]**

Figure 4

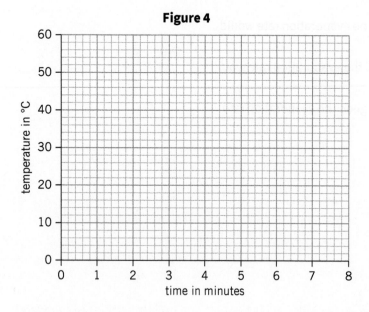

 **Exam Tip**

Always use crosses to plot points, and draw a line of best fit.

08.2 Describe the change in the rate of temperature increase over time. Explain your answer. **[2 marks]**

08.3 After 8 minutes, the energy transferred to the block was 15 800 J. Use the data in **Table 2** to calculate the specific heat capacity of the block. Use the correct equation from the *Physics Equations Sheet*. Give your answer to **three** significant figures. **[3 marks]**

Exam Tip

The first step is to write down the equation.

08.4 **Table 3** lists the specific heat capacity of some materials.

Table 3

Material	Specific heat capacity in J/kg °C
aluminium	900
iron	452
magnesium	1020
nickel	440
zinc	390

Use **Table 3** to identify which material the block is most likely to be made of. **[1 mark]**

Exam Tip

Use your answer from **08.3**.

09 A teacher is showing a class a method for finding the specific latent heat of vaporisation of water. The teacher puts a kettle containing water on a set of digital scales and measures its mass.

The kettle is turned on to allow the water to boil. At the same time, the teacher turns on a stopwatch. After two minutes the kettle is turned off and the teacher notes the new reading on the scales (see **Table 4**).

Table 4

Mass at the start of the two minutes	1.276 kg
Mass at the end of the two minutes	1.180 kg

The power of the kettle is 2 kW.

09.1 Calculate the energy transferred from the kettle to the water. **[4 marks]**

Exam Tip

Make sure you use the correct equation from the *Physics Equations Sheet*.

09.2 Use the correct equation from the *Physics Equations Sheet* to calculate the specific latent heat of vaporisation of water. Give your answer in kJ/kg. **[5 marks]**

Exam Tip

Look at the difference in values in **Table 4**.

09.3 The textbook value for the specific latent heat of vaporisation of water is 2265 kJ/kg. Suggest a reason for the difference between the value that you have calculated and the textbook value. Explain your answer. **[3 marks]**

10 A student noticed that when they finished having a shower, the mirror was 'fogged up'.

10.1 Explain in terms of energy why the mirror is covered by a thin layer of water. **[3 marks]**

Exam Tip

First use the equation for specific latent heat of vaporisation to find the mass of water.

10.2 The student estimates that the mirror is a square with sides measuring 60 cm. The density of water is 1×10^3 kg/m³. The specific latent heat of vaporisation of water is 2265 kJ/kg. While the fog was forming, a total of 730 kJ of energy was transferred. Calculate the thickness of the layer of water on the mirror. **[6 marks]**

11 A teacher shows data from an experiment involving heating oil and water (**Figure 5**).

The teacher wants to compare the liquids in terms of their specific heat capacity.

Figure 5

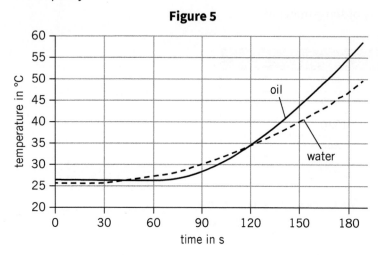

11.1 The teacher does not allow the students to conduct an experiment involving heating oil with a Bunsen burner. Suggest why. **[1 mark]**

11.2 Explain why the heater used to heat the liquids needs to have the same power. **[1 mark]**

11.3 Compare the relationships between temperature and time for the liquids. **[3 marks]**

11.4 Use the differences between the graphs to compare the specific heat capacity of oil and water.

State any assumptions that you have made. **[4 marks]**

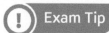 **Exam Tip**

Look at the differences in the lines on the graph.

12 A student sees a demonstration involving gallium.

Gallium has a melting point of 29.8 °C.

A small piece of gallium, with mass 0.005 kg, melts in the palm of the demonstrator's hand.

12.1 Calculate the energy needed to raise gallium to its melting point.

Room temperature = 20 °C.

The specific heat capacity of solid gallium is 371 J/kg°C. **[3 marks]**

12.2 The demonstrator uses a second piece of gallium.

It has three times the mass of the first piece of gallium.

Calculate how much energy would need to be transferred to the second piece to raise it to its melting point. **[2 marks]**

12.3 Aluminium has a greater specific heat capacity than gallium.

Describe what you would notice about the temperature rise of 5 g of aluminium if you transferred the same amount of energy as calculated in **12.1**.

Explain your answer. **[2 marks]**

 **Exam Tip**

You don't need to know the temperature of the demonstrator's hand, you only need to work out the temperature change.

13 One way to heat milk is to pass steam through it.

13.1 Suggest how a jet of steam heats a cup of milk. **[2 marks]**

13.2 The mass of milk in a cup is 242 g. The specific heat capacity of milk is 3.93 kJ/kg°C. Show that the energy required to heat the milk from 20°C to 70°C is about 48 kJ. Use an equation from the *Physics Equations Sheet*. **[4 marks]**

13.3 The specific latent heat of vaporisation of water is 2260 kJ/kg. Calculate the mass of steam that would need to condense into water to produce the energy calculated in **13.2**. **[4 marks]**

13.4 Write down one assumption that you made when doing the calculation. **[1 mark]**

14 A substance is heated. **Figure 6** shows how the temperature of the substance changes with time. The straight-line sections of the graph are labelled **A**, **B**, **C**, **D**, and **E**.

Figure 6

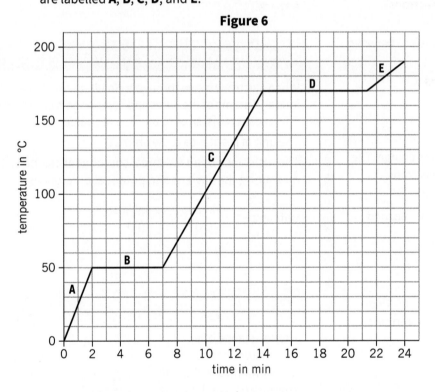

14.1 Write the letters of all the sections of the graph that show a change of state.

Explain why you have chosen these sections. **[4 marks]**

14.2 Did the substance start out as a solid or a liquid?

Explain your answer. **[2 marks]**

14.3 Write down the section of the graph where the vibration of the particles is increasing. **[1 mark]**

14.4 Write down the **two** sections of the graph where the kinetic energy of the particles is increasing. **[2 marks]**

P13 Electric circuits

Charge

An atom has no **charge** because it has equal numbers of positive protons and negative electrons.

When electrons are removed from an atom, it becomes *positively* charged. When electrons are added to an atom, it becomes *negatively* charged.

Static electricity

Insulating materials can become charged when they are rubbed with another insulating material. This is because electrons are transferred from one material to the other. Materials that gain electrons become negatively charged and those that lose electrons become positively charged.

Positive charges do not usually transfer between materials.

Electric charge is measured in **coulombs** (C).

Electric current

Electric **current** is the rate of flow of electric charge. The charge in an electric circuit is carried by electrons.

The unit of current is the **ampere** (amp, A).

1 ampere = 1 coulomb of charge flow per second

The current can be calculated using:

$$\text{current (A)} = \frac{\text{charge flow (C)}}{\text{time taken (s)}} \qquad I = \frac{Q}{t}$$

In circuit diagrams, current flows from the positive terminal of a cell or battery to the negative terminal. This is known as conventional current.

Voltage or potential difference

The **voltage** of a source is the energy supplied by a source in driving charges round a complete circuit.

Potential difference (pd) is a measure of how much energy is transferred between two points in a circuit. For electrical charge to flow through a circuit there must be a source of potential difference. The unit of potential difference is the volt (V).

The pd across a component measures the energy transferred by charges. It can be calculated using:

$$\text{potential difference across} \atop \text{the component (V)} = \frac{\text{energy transferred (J)}}{\text{charge (C)}}$$

$$V = \frac{E}{Q}$$

Moving charge

In insulating materials, charge has no conducting route to travel along. Conducting materials, such as metals, contain charges (electrons) that are free to move. They are delocalised electrons. If a route is provided, there is a **discharge**.

Lightning

Friction due to air movement in clouds can set up areas that are charged. When there is a large build up of charge, the air can conduct. This discharge is what we see as lightning. On a small scale, when the air conducts, we see a spark.

Resistance

When electrons move through a circuit, they collide with the ions and atoms of the wires and components in the circuit. This causes **resistance** to the flow of charge.

The unit of resistance is the ohm (Ω).

The resistance of an electrical component can be found by measuring the current and potential difference:

$$\text{potential} \atop \text{difference} \atop (V) = \text{current} \atop (A) \times \text{resistance} \atop (\Omega)$$

$$V = IR$$

Thermistors and LDRs

The resistance of a thermistor changes as the temperature changes. Thermistors can be used in thermostats to control temperature.

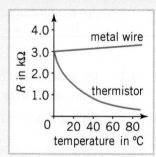

The resistance of a light-dependent resistor (LDR) decreases as the temperature changes. LDRs can be used to switch lights on when it gets dark.

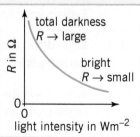

Current–potential difference graphs

A graph of current through a component against the pd across it (*I–V* graph) is known as the component characteristic.

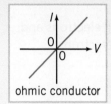

ohmic conductor

Current is directly proportional to the pd in an ohmic conductor at a constant temperature. The resistance is constant.

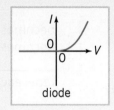

diode

The current through a diode only flows in one direction – called the forward direction. There needs to be a minimum voltage before any current will flow. An LED emits light when a current flows in the forward direction. LEDs use a much smaller current than other light bulbs.

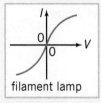

filament lamp

As more current flows through the filament, its temperature increases. The atoms in the wire vibrate more, and collide more often with electrons flowing through it, so resistance increases as temperature increases.

Circuit components

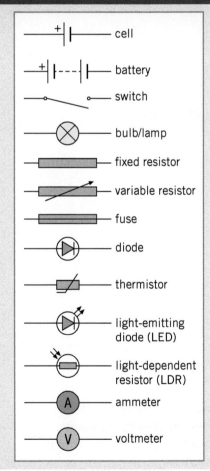

- +|| — cell
- +||---|| — battery
- switch
- bulb/lamp
- fixed resistor
- variable resistor
- fuse
- diode
- thermistor
- light-emitting diode (LED)
- light-dependent resistor (LDR)
- (A) ammeter
- (V) voltmeter

Series circuits

In a **series** circuit, the components are connected one after the other in a single loop. If one component in a series circuit stops working, the whole circuit will stop working. Components with a higher resistance will transfer a larger share of the total pd because $V = IR$.

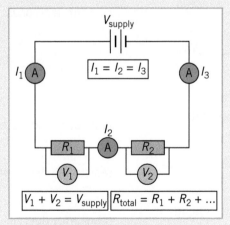

V_{supply}

I_1 (A) $I_1 = I_2 = I_3$ (A) I_3

I_2

R_1 (A) R_2

V_1 V_2

$V_1 + V_2 = V_{supply}$ $R_{total} = R_1 + R_2 + ...$

- The total voltage in a circuit is the *sum* of all the sources.
- The total resistance is the sum of the resistance of each component.
- The current is the *same* in each component.
- The total pd of the power supply is shared between the components.

Parallel circuits

A **parallel** circuit is made up of two or more loops through which current can flow. If one branch of a parallel circuit stops working, the other branches will not be affected.

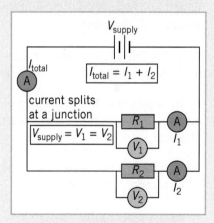

V_{supply}

I_{total}
(A) $I_{total} = I_1 + I_2$

current splits at a junction

$V_{supply} = V_1 = V_2$ R_1 (A)

V_1 I_1

R_2 (A)

V_2 I_2

- The current from the supply splits in the branches.
- The pd across each component is the *same*.
- The combined resistance of the components is *less* than that of the smallest component. This is because adding a loop to the circuit provides another route for the current to flow, so more current can flow in total even though the pd has not changed.

🔑 **Key Terms**   **Make sure you can write a definition for these key terms.**

ampere	charge	coulomb	current	discharge	parallel
potential difference		resistance	series	static	voltage

Learn the answers to the questions below then cover the answers column with a piece of paper and write as many as you can. Check and repeat.

P13 questions	Answers
1 How does a material become charged?	becomes negatively charged by gaining electrons and becomes positively charged by losing electrons
2 What will two objects carrying the same type of charge do if they are brought close to each other?	repel each other
3 When will a charged object discharge?	when there is a conducting route to travel along
4 What is electric current?	rate of flow of charge
5 What is the unit of charge?	coulombs (C)
6 What is the unit of current?	amperes (A)
7 What is the same at all points when charge flows in a closed loop?	current
8 What must there be in a closed circuit so that electrical charge can flow?	source of potential difference (pd)
9 Which two factors does current depend on and what are their units?	resistance in ohms (Ω), pd in volts (V)
10 What happens to the current if the resistance is increased but the pd stays the same?	current decreases
11 What happens to the resistance of a wire as the current increases if the temperature does not change?	it stays the same
12 What happens to the resistance of a filament lamp as its temperature increases?	resistance increases
13 What happens to the resistance of a thermistor as its temperature increases?	resistance decreases
14 What happens to the resistance of a light-dependent resistor when light intensity increases?	resistance decreases
15 What are the main features of a series circuit?	same current through each component, total pd of power supply is shared between components, total resistance of all components is the sum of the resistance of each component
16 What are the main features of a parallel circuit?	pd across each branch is the same, total current through circuit is the sum of the currents in each branch, total resistance of all resistors is less than the resistance of the smallest individual resistor

Put paper here

Now use the questions below to check your knowledge from previous chapters.

P13

Previous questions

Answers

	Previous questions	Answers
1	What is one joule of work?	the work done when a force of 1 N causes an object to move 1 m in the direction of the force
2	What is the period of a wave?	the time for one wave to pass a fixed point
3	What is the focal length of a lens?	distance from the centre of the lens to the principal focus
4	What is the name given to the energy transferred when a substance changes state?	latent heat

Put paper here ... *Put paper here* ... *Put paper here*

🧪 Required Practical Skills

Practise answering questions on the required practicals using the example below. You need to be able to apply your skills and knowledge to other practicals too.

I–V graphs	Worked example	Practice
You need to be able to determine the relationship between current and potential difference (pd) for a lamp, resistor, and diode.	A student uses a circuit to measure values of current and pd for component **X**. They decide to use a variable resistor to change the current.	A student has set up an experiment to collect data to plot an *I–V* graph for a piece of resistance wire.

You need to be able to
determine the relationship
between current and potential
difference (pd) for a lamp,
resistor, and diode.

You should be able to draw and
interpret *I–V* graphs – the shape
of the graph is characteristic of
the component. The gradient
of the graph is not related to
the resistance, but resistance
can be calculated from values
for pd and current.

A variable power supply
or resistor should be used
to change the current in
both directions.

The diode needs to be
connected with a protective
resistor so it does not get
too hot.

A student uses a circuit to measure values of current
and pd for component **X**. They decide to use a
variable resistor to change the current.

1 Below is some data for the component. Plot a
   graph of the data and draw a line of best fit.

pd in V	0.1	0.4	0.6	0.8	1
Current in A	0.38	0.59	0.64	0.69	0.72
pd in V	−0.1	−0.4	−0.6	−0.8	−1
Current in A	−0.38	−0.59	−0.64	−0.69	−0.72

Answer:

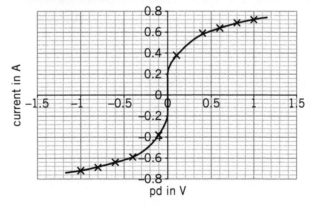

2 Suggest the name of component **X**. Use the
   graph and data to explain your answer.

   Answer: X is a lamp as the graph is symmetrical:

   $$\text{resistance} = \frac{\text{pd}}{\text{current}}$$

   $$R = \frac{0.1\,\text{V}}{0.38\,\text{A}} = 0.26\,\Omega \qquad R = \frac{1\,\text{V}}{0.72\,\text{A}} = 1.39\,\Omega$$

   So as pd increases, resistance increases.

A student has set up an
experiment to collect
data to plot an *I–V*
graph for a piece of
resistance wire.

1 Give two changes
   the student will need
   to make to repeat
   the experiment with
   a diode.

2 Sketch the *I–V* graph
   for a diode. Explain
   the shape of the
   graph in terms of
   resistance.

Practice

Exam-style questions

01 A student finds a box of different resistors. One of the resistors is not marked.

The student wants to find the resistance. They place the unknown resistor in the circuit shown in **Figure 1**.

Figure 1

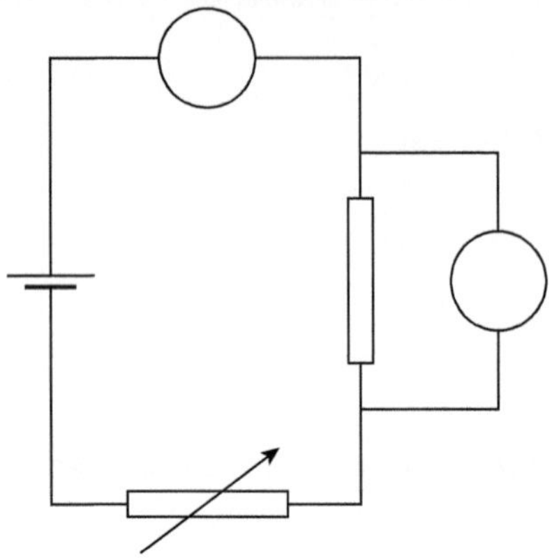

01.1 The student has not labelled the diagram.

The ammeter and voltmeter need to be in the correct places.

Write the letters **A** and **V** in the circles in **Figure 1** to show where to put the meters.

Label the resistor.

Label the variable resistor. **[4 marks]**

01.2 The student measures a current of 0.3 A.

Define current. **[1 mark]**

____

01.3 Write down the equation that links current, potential difference, and resistance. **[1 mark]**

____

01.4 The student measures a potential difference of 6 V.

Calculate the resistance of the resistor. **[3 marks]**

resistance = ______________________

> **Exam Tip**
>
> Look back at the Knowledge page – this is practice, not the real exam, so you are allowed to look back.

> **Exam Tip**
>
> For all maths questions:
>
> Step 1 – write down the equation you are using
>
> Step 2 – put the numbers into the equation
>
> Step 3 – rearrange the equation if necessary
>
> Step 4 – do the maths
>
> Step 5 – write down the answer *with units.*

02   **Figure 2** shows four circuits drawn by a student.

Figure 2

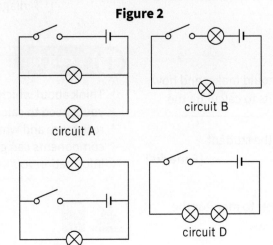

circuit A

circuit B

circuit C

circuit D

02.1   Here are some statements about the circuits in **Figure 2**.
Which statement is correct?   **[1 mark]**

Tick **one** box.

Circuit A is a series circuit.   ☐

Circuits A and C are parallel circuits.   ☐

Only circuit A is a parallel circuit.   ☐

Circuits C and D are series circuits.   ☐

02.2   Complete these sentences about the three circuits.
Use the letters **A**, **B**, **C**, or **D**.   **[3 marks]**

The bulbs in circuits _____ and _____ are the brightest.

If one of the bulbs in circuit _____ or _____ breaks, the other bulb will go out.

An ammeter placed anywhere in circuit _____ or _____ will measure the same current.

02.3   The student looks at circuit **B** and says: '*I think that when you press the switch, the bulb nearer the battery will be brighter than the bulb that is further away.*'

Do you agree? Explain your answer.   **[3 marks]**

_____

_____

_____

_____

03 A student wants to demonstrate the difference between the resistance of two circuits that contain two resistors in series and in parallel.

Describe how a student could set up two circuits, one in series and one in parallel, to show the difference.

You need to:

- draw a circuit diagram for each circuit
- describe the measurements the student should make, and how the student should use those measurements to calculate the resistance of each circuit
- describe the differences in resistance that the student should find. **[6 marks]**

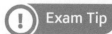

Always use a ruler for circuit diagrams.

Exam Tip

Think about which equations you'll need to calculate resistance and which circuit components can give you the information you'll need.

04 A student is using a thermistor and a data logger to monitor the change in temperature in the school greenhouse.

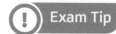

04.1 Describe how the resistance of a thermistor depends on temperature. **[1 mark]**

Exam Tip

This is a 'Describe' question, so you need to say *what* will happen but not *why*.

04.2 The student connects the thermistor in the circuit shown in **Figure 3**.

Figure 3

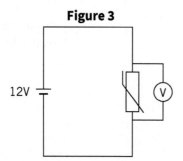

They think that if the temperature changes, the reading on the voltmeter will change.

Explain why this would **not** happen. **[2 marks]**

04.3 Another student sets up the circuit shown in **Figure 4**.

Figure 4

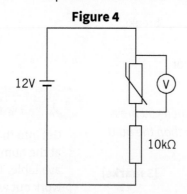

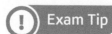

Exam Tip

This question isn't as hard as it looks – just think logically and use your maths skills.

They measure the highest and lowest voltmeter readings.

The highest reading is 8V. The lowest reading is 3V.

Use proportion to calculate the resistance of the thermistor when it is very hot, and when it is very cold.

Explain your method. **[7 marks]**

05 **Figure 5** shows a lamp and a resistor connected in series.

Figure 5

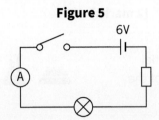

05.1 The potential difference across the lamp is 4V.

Calculate the potential difference across the resistor. **[2 marks]**

05.2 The reading on the ammeter is 0.2A.

Calculate the resistance of the lamp. **[3 marks]**

05.3 Show that the resistance of the resistor is 10Ω. **[2 marks]**

05.4 The student now connects another identical resistor in series with the resistor and lamp in the circuit.

Select the correct word to complete this sentence:

The ammeter reading will **increase / stay the same / decrease**.

Explain your answer. **[2 marks]**

> **(!) Exam Tip**
>
> To answer **05.3** you'll need to use your answer from **05.1** (pd) and the information in **05.2** (0.2A). Show questions are great, because you know what the answer is, and if you write your working out clearly, you know you've got the marks!

06 **Figure 6** shows the current–potential difference graph for two components: **A** and **B**.

Figure 6

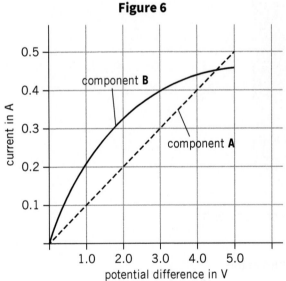

06.1 Write down which component is ohmic. **[1 mark]**

06.2 Calculate the resistance of component **A**. **[3 marks]**

> **(!) Exam Tip**
>
>
> Find the gradient of the graph.

06.3 Describe what happens to the resistance of each component as the potential difference across it increases.

Explain how you used the graph to work out your answer. **[4 marks]**

06.4 A student connects the two components in parallel across a 3V battery.

Calculate the total current in the circuit. **[2 marks]**

> **(!) Exam Tip**
>
>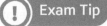
> Use data from the graph.

06.5 Calculate the resistance of the circuit as set up in **06.4**.

Give your answer to **two** significant figures. **[2 marks]**

07 A student takes measurements of the current and potential difference of an LDR in the light and in the dark. They plot the results on a graph, as shown in **Figure 7**.

Figure 7

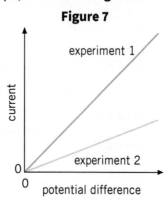

07.1 Suggest and explain which experiment was done in the light, and which in the dark. **[4 marks]**

The student now connects the LDR to a resistance meter, as shown in **Figure 8**.

Figure 8

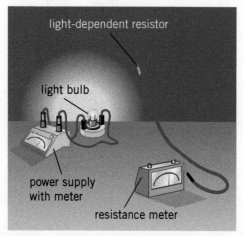

They decide to investigate how the resistance changes with distance from the lamp.

07.2 Name the independent and dependent variables in this investigation. **[2 marks]**

07.3 Name one variable that would need to be controlled. Describe how you would control it. **[1 mark]**

07.4 Sketch the graph that you would expect to plot using their data. **[3 marks]**

08 Student **A** rubs a balloon on their jumper. The balloon becomes negatively charged.

08.1 Name the particle that moves when objects become charged.

[1 mark]

08.2 Explain why the balloon becomes negatively charged. **[2 marks]**

08.3 Student **A** places the charged balloon on the wall.

It appears to 'stick' to the wall.

Student **B** says: '*The wall must be positively charged to make the balloon stick to it*'.

Do you agree? Explain your answer. **[2 marks]**

08.4 Student **B** rubs another balloon on the same jumper, and then holds the two balloons close together.

Describe what will happen to the balloons. Explain your answer.

[3 marks]

09 A student has been given some samples of dough.

The dough conducts electricity because it has been made with salt.

The student connects one sample of dough in a series circuit with an ammeter and a battery marked 6 V, as shown in **Figure 9**.

Figure 9

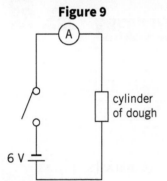

The student then measures the current through the dough. The current is 15 mA.

09.1 Calculate the time it takes 0.6 C of charge to flow through the dough. **[3 marks]**

09.2 The other samples of dough contain different masses of salt.

The student measures the current through these samples.

The data is shown in **Table 1**.

Table 1

Mass of salt per 100 g of dough in g	Current in mA
25	15
30	25
40	32
55	37
75	40
80	41

Sketch a graph of current against mass of salt from the data in **Table 1**. **[2 marks]**

09.3 Use the data in **Table 1** to suggest how the resistance of the dough changes with the mass of salt.

Justify your answer with calculations. **[6 marks]**

10 The resistance of a light-dependent resistor (LDR) changes with light intensity.

Light intensity is measured in lux.

10.1 Sketch a graph of the resistance of an LDR against light intensity. **[3 marks]**

10.2 Suggest a situation where you might need to use a light-dependent resistor. **[1 mark]**

10.3 Using your answer to **10.2**, describe how the LDR can be used in that situation and explain why the changing resistance of the LDR would be useful.

You should include a circuit diagram to illustrate your answer. **[5 marks]**

11 Two students investigated the effect of length on the resistance of a wire.

They measured the resistance of different lengths of metal wire (see **Table 2**).

Table 2

Length in cm	Resistance in Ω
5	1.5
10	3.8
15	4.6
20	5.9
25	7.8

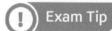

11.1 Plot the data from the table on graph paper. **[4 marks]**

11.2 Identify the independent variable, the dependent variable, and **one** control variable. **[3 marks]**

11.3 Estimate the resistance of a piece of wire that is 22 cm long. **[1 mark]**

11.4 Suggest **one** improvement that the student could make to improve the precision of the data. **[1 mark]**

11.5 Student **A** looked at the graph and said 'the resistance is directly proportional to length'.

Student **B** looked at the graph and said 'there is a linear relationship between resistance and length'.

Which student has made a correct statement?

student **A**	student **B**	both students

Explain your answer. **[3 marks]**

12 A juggler is throwing a ball upwards and catching it.

12.1 Describe all the changes in the way that energy is transferred from the moment the ball leaves the juggler's right hand, to the moment the ball lands in their left hand after travelling through the air. **[4 marks]**

12.2 Write down the equation for calculating gravitational potential energy. **[1 mark]**

12.3 The maximum change in gravitational potential energy is 0.4 J.

Gravitational field strength, $g = 9.8\,N/kg$.

The mass of the ball is 0.1 kg.

Calculate the maximum height that the ball reaches. **[3 marks]**

13 **Table 3** shows data about two types of electric vehicle.

Table 3

Vehicle	Journey length in km	Useful energy transferred in kJ	Energy content of fuel used in kJ
A	100	4000	10 000
B	100	6000	

13.1 Calculate the efficiency of vehicle **A**. Give your answer as a percentage. **[3 marks]**

13.2 Vehicle **B** is twice as efficient as vehicle **A**.

Calculate the energy content of the fuel used by vehicle **B**. **[3 marks]**

13.3 Vehicle **B** completes the journey in a time of 2 hours.

Calculate the power of vehicle **B**.

Give your answer to **two** significant figures. **[4 marks]**

14 A student sketches graphs of current against potential difference for three circuit components, **A**, **B**, and **C**, as shown in **Figure 10**.

Figure 10

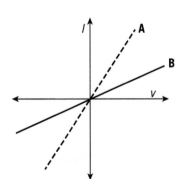

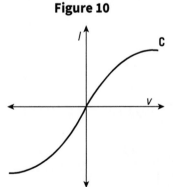

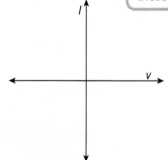

14.1 Match the descriptions with the correct graph from **Figure 10**.

[2 marks]

Description		Graph
the graph for a resistor with a large resistance		A
the graph for a filament lamp		B
the graph for a resistor with a small resistance		C

14.2 On the empty axes in **Figure 10**, sketch the graph of current against potential difference for a diode. [2 marks]

14.3 A student connects some LEDs in a circuit as shown in **Figure 11**.

Figure 11

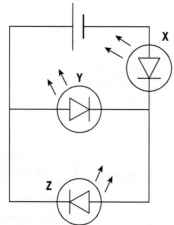

! **Exam Tip**

To answer this question, think about what the symbol for a diode is actually showing.

Write down which LEDs (**X**, **Y**, **Z**), if any, will light up.

Explain your answer. [2 marks]

15 A student rubs a polythene rod with a cloth.

15.1 Explain why the rod becomes negatively charged. [2 marks]

The student brings the rod close to the cap of an electroscope (**Figure 12**). The cap is connected to a rod. At the end of the rod is a piece of metal leaf that rises.

Figure 12

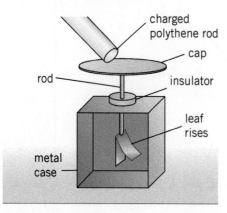

charged polythene rod

cap

rod

insulator

leaf rises

metal case

15.2 Explain in terms of electrons why the leaf rises. [2 marks]

15.3 Describe and explain what would happen if the student removed the rod. **[3 marks]**

15.4 Describe what would happen if there was no insulator between the rod, cap, and leaf in the apparatus in **Figure 12**. **[3 marks]**

15.5 Suggest and explain what would happen if the student brought the cloth near the cap. **[4 marks]**

16 Some events involving static electricity can be dangerous.

16.1 Suggest why flowing petrol might become charged. **[1 mark]**

16.2 Sometimes a spark can jump from the nozzle to the car. State what a spark is. **[1 mark]**

16.3 Explain why a spark would be dangerous. **[1 mark]**

16.4 Some petrol nozzles have a metal wire connected from the nozzle to the ground along the fuel line. Explain how that would reduce the chance of producing a spark. **[1 mark]**

17 A student wires up this circuit. They leave the switch open.

Figure 13

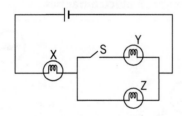

17.1 When the switch, S, is open, is this a series or a parallel circuit? Explain your answer. **[2 marks]**

The battery has a pd of 6.0 V. A current of 2.0 A flows in the circuit when the switch is open.

17.2 If the resistance of lamp X is 2 Ω, show that the resistance of lamp Z is 1.0 Ω. **[5 marks]**

The student now closes the switch, S, and measures the current in lamps Y and Z.

17.3 Complete the **Table 4**. **[1 mark]**

Table 4

Current in lamp Y in A	Current in lamp Z in A	Current in lamp X in A
1.2	1.2	

17.4 Are lamps Y and Z the same? Explain your answer. **[2 marks]**

17.5 Is the total resistance of the circuit bigger or smaller than it was before the switch was closed? Explain your answer. **[2 marks]**

Magnets

Magnets have a north (N) and a south (S) pole.

When two magnets are brought close together, they exert a non-contact force on each other.

Repulsion – If the poles are the same (N and N or S and S), they will repel each other.

Attraction – If the poles are different (N and S or S and N), they will attract each other.

The force between a magnet and a magnetic material (iron, steel, cobalt, or nickel) is always attractive.

Induced and permanent magnets

A **permanent** magnet produces its own magnetic field which is always there.

An **induced** magnet is an object that becomes magnetic when it is placed in a magnetic field.

The force between an induced magnet and a permanent magnet is *always attractive* (it doesn't matter which pole of the permanent magnet the induced magnet is near).

If the induced magnet is removed from the magnetic field it will quickly lose most or all of its magnetism.

Magnetic fields

A **magnetic field** is the region around a magnet where another magnet or magnetic material will experience a force due to the magnet.

A magnetic field can be represented by magnetic field lines.

Field lines show the direction of the force that would act on a north pole at that point.

Field lines always point from the north pole of a magnet to its south pole.

A magnetic field's strength is greatest at the poles and decreases as distance from the magnet increases.

The closer together the field lines are, the stronger the field.

In a uniform field, the field lines are parallel.

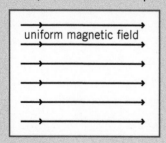

uniform magnetic field

Plotting magnetic fields

A magnetic compass contains a small bar magnet that will line up with magnetic field lines pointing from north to south.

A compass can be used to plot the magnetic field around a magnet or an **electromagnet**.

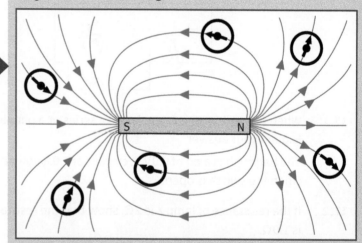

If it is not near a magnet, a compass will line up with the Earth's magnetic field, providing evidence that the Earth's core is magnetic.

As a compass points towards a south pole, the magnetic pole near the Earth's geographic North Pole is actually a south pole.

🔑 Key Terms

Make sure you can write a definition for these key terms.

attraction   electromagnet   induced   magnetic field

permanent   repulsion   solenoid

⚙ Revision Tip

The lines on a diagram that show magnetic field lines will always point from north to south.

Electromagnetism

If an electric current flows through a wire (or other conductor), it will produce a magnetic field around the wire.

The field strength increases:

- with greater current
- closer to the wire.

Reversing the direction of the current reverses the direction of the field.

The field around a straight wire takes the shape of concentric circles at right angles to the wire.

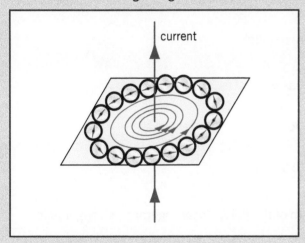

If the wire was gripped by someone's right hand so that the thumb pointed in the direction of the current, the fingers would curl in the direction of the magnetic field.

Solenoids

A **solenoid** is a cylindrical coil of wire.

Bending a current-carrying wire into a solenoid increases the strength of the magnetic field produced.

The shape of the magnetic field around a solenoid is similar to a magnetic field around a bar magnet.

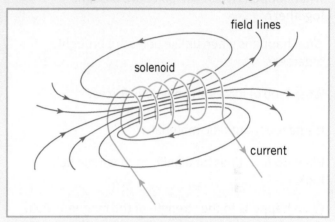

Inside a solenoid the magnetic field is *strong* and *uniform*, which means it has the same strength and direction at all points.

The strength of the magnetic field around a solenoid can be increased by putting an iron core inside it.

If the wire is gripped by someone's right hand so that the fingers curl in the direction of the current in the coil, the thumb will point towards the north pole of the field.

Electromagnets are often solenoids with an iron core.

Advantages of electromagnets

- An electromagnet can be turned on and off.
- The strength of an electromagnet can be increased or decreased by adjusting the current.

Uses of electromagnets

- Scrap-yard crane for lifting heavy objects containing magnetic materials
- Electric bell
- Circuit breaker.

Retrieval

Learn the answers to the questions below then cover the answers column with a piece of paper and write as many as you can. Check and repeat.

	P14 questions		Answers
1	What is a magnetic field?	Put paper here	the region of space around a magnet where a magnetic material will experience a force
2	What happens when like poles are brought together?		they repel
3	What happens when unlike poles are brought together?	Put paper here	they attract
4	What type of forces are magnetic forces?		non-contact forces
5	Name four magnetic materials.	Put paper here	iron, nickel, steel, cobalt
6	What do field lines for a uniform magnetic field look like?		they are parallel
7	What happens to the strength of the magnetic field as you get further away from the magnet?	Put paper here	it decreases
8	Where is the magnetic field of a magnet strongest?		at the poles
9	In which direction do magnetic field lines always point?	Put paper here	north to south
10	What does the distance between magnetic field lines indicate?		strength of the field; closer together = stronger field
11	What is a permanent magnet?	Put paper here	material that produces its own magnetic field
12	What is an induced magnet?		material that becomes magnetic when it is put in a magnetic field, and loses its magnetism quickly when it is removed from the field
13	What does a magnetic compass contain?	Put paper here	small bar magnet
14	Where is the Earth's magnetic field most concentrated?		at the North and South Poles
15	What is produced around a wire when an electric current flows through it?	Put paper here	a magnetic field
16	The strength of the magnetic field around a straight wire depends upon which factors?		size of current, distance from wire
17	What effect does reversing the current have on an electromagnet?	Put paper here	it swaps the poles/reverses the magnetic field lines
18	What shape is the magnetic field at the centre of a solenoid?		uniform
19	What effect does shaping the wire into a solenoid have on the magnetic field strength?	Put paper here	increases strength of magnetic field

Now use the questions below to check your knowledge from previous chapters.

P14

Previous questions | Answers

	Previous questions		Answers
1	What is ionisation?		the removal of an electron from an atom or molecule
2	What causes long-sightedness?	Put paper here	the eyeball is too short or the lens cannot make a sharp image on the retina
3	Define specific heat capacity.		the amount of energy needed to raise the temperature of 1 kg of a material by 1 °C
4	What is the unit of charge?		coulomb (C)

 # Required Practical Skills

Practise answering questions on the required practicals using the example below. You need to be able to apply your skills and knowledge to other practicals too.

Strength of an electromagnet	Worked example	Practice
To investigate the factors affecting the strength of an electromagnet, you need to use a method of quantifying the 'strength'.	A student changes the current flowing in an electromagnet and measures the paperclips that it can pick up. The solenoid is wrapped around a wooden rod. These are the results.	A student wants to work out how the number of coils affects the strength of an electromagnet.

To investigate the factors affecting the strength of an electromagnet, you need to use a method of quantifying the 'strength'.

In the experiment, you need to:

- make an electromagnet by coiling wire around a nail or piece of iron (the core)
- connect the ends of the wire to a battery or power supply (but do NOT connect it for long as the wire will get hot)
- connect an ammeter to measure the current in the wire
- use paperclips or small pieces of iron; pick them up
- turn off the current and measure the mass of the paperclips or metal, or count the paperclips.

You can change:

- the number of coils on the electromagnet
- the current in the wire
- the type of material of the core.

A student changes the current flowing in an electromagnet and measures the paperclips that it can pick up. The solenoid is wrapped around a wooden rod. These are the results.

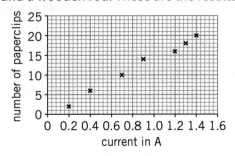

1 Draw a line of best fit on the graph.

Answer:

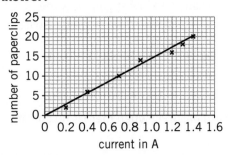

2 The student doubles the number of coils on the solenoid and repeats the experiment. Describe where the line of best fit would be now.

Answer: The line would be steeper/have double the gradient.

A student wants to work out how the number of coils affects the strength of an electromagnet.

1 Describe the experimental procedure that would enable them to do this.

2 Sketch a graph to show what you would expect to get in this experiment.

3 Another student uses much larger paperclips in the experiment. Suggest one problem and one benefit of doing so.

Practice

Exam-style questions

01 A student investigates the magnetic field around two magnets. They draw the diagrams shown in **Figure 1**.

Figure 1

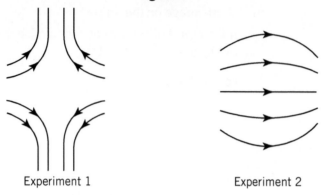

Experiment 1   Experiment 2

01.1 Add magnets to the diagrams in **Figure 1** to show how the student produced the patterns. Label the poles with 'N' and 'S'. **[4 marks]**

01.2 Explain your labelling of the poles in **01.1**. **[1 mark]**

_____

_____

01.3 Describe a piece of equipment the student could have used to produce the patterns. **[1 mark]**

_____

01.4 Look at the field lines in Experiment 2. Describe and explain where the magnetic field is strongest. **[2 marks]**

_____

_____

02 A student uses a magnetic field sensor to investigate how the magnetic field strength varies with distance from an electric wire.

02.1 When there is no current flowing in the wire the field sensor measures a magnetic field of 49 μT.

$1\,\mu T = 10^{-6}\,T$

Write down what the sensor is measuring when there is no current passing through the wire.

Write down the name of this type of error. **[2 marks]**

_____

_____

 Exam Tip

μT are microteslas. There are 1 000 000 μT in one tesla.

 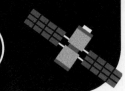

P14

02.2 The student records their data in **Table 1**.

Table 1

Distance in cm	Magnetic field strength in mT			
	1	2	3	Mean
1	0.190	0.210	0.210	0.203
2	0.095	0.105	0.105	0.102
3	0.063	0.070	0.070	0.068
4	0.048	0.053	0.053	0.051

Suggest what the student should do about the sensor reading in **02.1** before recording the data. **[1 mark]**

_____

_____

> **(!) Exam Tip**
>
> The error will have shown up in every result that the student recorded.

02.3 Suggest why the student does not start measuring at zero centimetres. **[1 mark]**

_____

_____

02.4 The student concludes that the magnetic field strength is inversely proportional to the distance from the wire.

Use the data in **Table 1** to explain why. **[3 marks]**

_____

_____

_____

_____

03 A tool set contains a screwdriver. The screwdriver attracts the screw so that the person using it is less likely to lose it.

03.1 The end of the screwdriver is magnetic. The screw is an induced magnet.

Explain the difference between a permanent magnet and an induced magnet. **[2 marks]**

03.2 There is a magnetic field around the end of the screwdriver.

Predict whether there is a magnetic field around the screw when it is attached to the screwdriver.

Justify your answer. **[2 marks]**

03.3 On **Figure 2** write N (north) and S (south) in the blank boxes to show the induced poles on the screw. **[1 mark]**

Figure 2

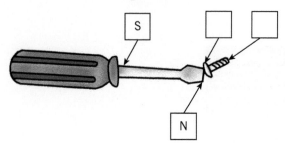

03.4 The screw is put back into a box containing other screws.

Predict whether it will attract the other screws in the box.

Justify your answer. **[2 marks]**

04 A student investigates the strength of an electromagnet. They make a solenoid with different materials for the core and measure the mass of iron filings that the solenoid can pick up.

04.1 Write down the independent and dependent variables. **[2 marks]**

04.2 Write down **two** control variables. **[2 marks]**

04.3 The results are in **Table 2**.

Table 2

Material	Mass of iron filings in g			
	1	2	3	Mean
nickel alloy	0.10	1.0	0.10	0.10
steel	1.20	1.38	1.36	1.31
aluminium	0.03	0.02	0.02	0.02
iron	1.26	1.43	1.38	1.36

One of the values is an outlier. Identify the outlier.

Write down what the student did about this outlier when they calculated the mean. **[2 marks]**

04.4 Nickel is a magnetic material.

Suggest whether the amount of nickel in the nickel alloy is large or small.

Give reasons for your answer. **[2 marks]**

04.5 The student learns that some high-voltage machines, such as X-ray machines, use solenoids. These machines are operated by a switch that is not in the same circuit as the high-voltage source (**Figure 3**).

Figure 3

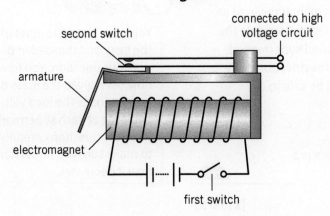

second switch

connected to high voltage circuit

armature

electromagnet

first switch

Suggest a suitable material for the core and armature. **[1 mark]**

04.6 Describe what happens when the first switch is pressed. **[3 marks]**

05 A student winds some wire around a wooden rod to make a coil and connects the coil to a battery.

05.1 Identify a hazard when doing this experiment. Suggest a method of reducing the risk of harm. **[2 marks]**

05.2 On solenoid **A** in **Figure 4**, draw lines to show the shape of the magnetic field around the coil. You do **not** need to draw arrows on the field lines. **[1 mark]**

Figure 4

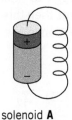 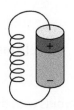

solenoid **A**   solenoid **B**

05.3 Write down which solenoid, **A** or **B**, has the stronger magnetic field around it. Give reasons for your answer. **[2 marks]**

05.4 The student takes a compass and places it in the centre of the solenoid. They move it up and down in the middle of the coil.

Will the compass needle move when it is in the solenoid? Justify your answer. **[2 marks]**

06 A company that transports food to supermarkets requires that lorry drivers are aware of how fast they are accelerating. The acceleration of a lorry should not exceed 1.5 m/s².

06.1 The engine of a lorry produces a force of 10 kN. Typical resistive forces are about 2 kN. A lorry and its load have a total mass of 8400 kg. A driver uses the maximum force possible. Determine whether the acceleration of the lorry exceeds the acceleration expected by the company. Justify your answer with a calculation.

[5 marks]

> **! Exam Tip**
> Make sure you clearly indicate which switch and circuit you are talking about. If it is not clear you won't get the marks.

> **! Exam Tip**
> Be careful with the non-standard units here.

06.2 The lorry starts off fully loaded. The mass of the load is 3200 kg. The lorry stops at two supermarkets. It drops off half the load at each supermarket before going back to the depot. Calculate the acceleration of the lorry on its way to the second supermarket, and on its way back to the depot. Each time the driver uses the maximum force. Suggest whether this would be safe to do.

[6 marks]

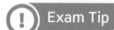

Exam Tip

You were given the mass of the lorry *and* the load in the previous question. You have now been given the mass of just the load. The load will decrease at each supermarket. Read the question carefully to make sure you understand how it decreases.

07 There is a region around a magnet where there is a magnetic field.

07.1 Describe what is meant by magnetic field. **[1 mark]**

07.2 A student puts two magnets, **A** and **B**, together so that their north poles are facing each other.

Draw a diagram to show the magnetic field between the two magnets.

Draw arrows to show the direction of the magnetic field. **[2 marks]**

07.3 The magnetic field is stronger near the poles. Describe how this is shown on a diagram. **[1 mark]**

07.4 There is a 'neutral point' between the magnets where you can place a piece of magnetic material and it will not move.

Suggest where the neutral point is in relation to the two magnets, **A** and **B**, when

- the magnets are equally strong
- magnet **B** is stronger than magnet **A**.

Explain your answers. **[5 marks]**

Exam Tip

A carefully annotated diagram can get marks in **07.4**. If you struggle to explain things with words then this is a perfect question to use a diagram.

08 There are craters produced from the impact of asteroids with the Earth's surface. Astronomers use telescopes to try to work out the position of asteroids that could collide with the Earth.

They send a pulse of radio waves to an asteroid. The radio waves are reflected by the asteroid.

They use the time it takes to detect the reflected radio waves to work out the distance to the asteroid.

08.1 A telescope detects a reflected wave from an asteroid 0.2 s after a pulse of radio waves is emitted.

Calculate the distance to the asteroid. The speed of electromagnetic radiation is 3.0×10^8 m/s. **[4 marks]**

08.2 The uncertainty in the measurement of time is 1×10^{-4} s. Define uncertainty in this context. **[1 mark]**

08.3 The asteroid is moving. Suggest how the astronomers could use pulses of radio waves to calculate the speed of the asteroid. **[3 marks]**

Exam Tip

If you're not used to using standard form in science then take time to look it up in your maths books and practise it. It will come up in an exam somewhere.

09 A scientist notices that a compass needle is deflected when they turn on a circuit containing a battery and a wire.

09.1 Identify the direction in which the compass was pointing before the scientist turned on the circuit.

Explain why the compass points in this direction. **[2 marks]**

09.2 Compare the strength of the Earth's magnetic field with the strength of the magnetic field around the wire.

Give reasons for your answer. **[2 marks]**

09.3 Choose the correct description of a compass needle.

Choose **one** answer. **[1 mark]**

A compass needle always points to the South Pole.

A compass needle is a magnet.

A compass needle can be made from any metal.

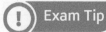

> **! Exam Tip**
>
> *Compare* means you need to write about the similarities or difference of two things.

10 The Earth has a magnetic field.

10.1 Explain the difference between geographic North and magnetic north. **[2 marks]**

10.2 In 1600, William Gilbert published a paper in which he proposed that the Earth behaved like a giant magnet. Gilbert used a small physical model of the Earth with a magnet inside it.

Suggest the equipment he could have used to develop his ideas about the Earth. **[2 marks]**

10.3 Since Gilbert's idea was published, different scientists have proposed different models to explain the mechanism behind the bar magnet.

Suggest **one** reason why the models have changed. **[2 marks]**

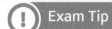

> **! Exam Tip**
>
> This is a very wordy question. Don't worry about the person, it won't help you answer the question. However, the year will give you a clue about the type of equipment available.

11 A student makes a model electric motor by winding wire around a wooden block that can spin between the poles of two magnets. They decide to change the number of turns that they wind around the block while keeping the current in the wire the same.

11.1 Suggest what happens to the speed of the motor if the number of turns increases. **[1 mark]**

11.2 Use magnetic fields to explain your answer to **11.1**. **[2 marks]**

11.3 Suggest why the model motor will not work when the coil is in a magnetic field produced by two north poles. **[1 mark]**

11.4   The student changes the type of block that they are using, and measures the speed of rotation. **Table 3** shows their results.

Table 3

Material	Speed in rev/min
wood	60
aluminium	200
steel	310

Figure 5

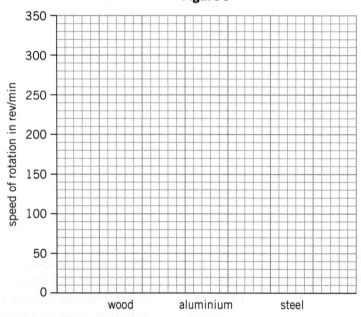

Plot the results on the graph in **Figure 5**.   **[4 marks]**

11.5   Suggest a reason for the pattern shown in the graph.   **[2 marks]**

12   A teacher demonstrates what is meant by 'work' in science. They lift a 1 kg mass a distance of 1 m.

12.1   Use the equation that links weight, mass, and gravitational field strength to calculate the force needed to lift the mass. Gravitational field strength is 9.8 N/kg.   **[3 marks]**

12.2   Use the equation that links work, force, and distance to calculate the work done.   **[3 marks]**

12.3   The teacher holds the mass without moving it. Write down the force the teacher uses to hold the mass.   **[1 mark]**

13   Humans can jump vertically to a height of about 50 cm.

13.1   Estimate the mass of a human.

Use your estimate to calculate the gravitational potential energy of a human being at a distance of 50 cm off the ground.

Gravitational field strength on Earth = 9.8 N/kg.   **[3 marks]**

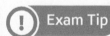

Exam Tip

Make sure you use the correct equation from the *Physics Equations Sheet*.

13.2 The energy to make this jump is stored in the tendons and muscles of the legs. Assume that the muscles and tendons behave like a spring. Assume that the extension of the muscles and tendons is 1 cm.

Calculate the spring constant of the muscles and tendons. Write down **one** assumption that you need to make in doing this calculation. Use the correct equation from the *Physics Equations Sheet*. **[4 marks]**

> **!** **Exam Tip**
>
> When you estimate the mass of a human, it needs to be a sensible value. For example, 10 g would be much too small. But don't spend a long time worrying over that bit, as it won't get you any marks.

13.3 A frog jumps vertically to the same height as the human.

The mass of a frog is about 2000 times smaller than that of a human.

Suggest whether the spring constant of the muscles and tendons in a frog's leg is bigger, smaller, or the same as that of the human. Assume that the muscles and tendons stretch by the same amount. Explain your answer. **[4 marks]**

14 A student watches a video that shows that some insects can detect ultraviolet light.

14.1 Explain why you cannot write down a single number for the wavelength of UV light. **[1 mark]**

14.2 The video explains that humans can see red light but some insects cannot.

Describe the difference between red light and ultraviolet light in terms of frequency and wavelength. **[2 marks]**

> **!** **Exam Tip**
>
> You need to give two differences between red light and UV light. You can structure your answer like this:
>
> The frequency of red light is … whereas for ultraviolet it is … .
>
> The wavelength of red light is … whereas for ultraviolet it is … .

14.3 Ultraviolet light is hazardous to the human body. Describe **one** reason why. **[1 mark]**

14.4 Describe **one** use of ultraviolet light. **[1 mark]**

15 A teacher uses a magnetic field sensor to investigate the magnetic field strength inside a coil with 1000 turns on it. They tell the class that the Earth's magnetic field can be ignored.

15.1 Suggest why the teacher said this. **[1 mark]**

15.2 Inside the coil, the magnetic field strength is 1.2 T when the current is 3 A. Use ratios to calculate the field strength when the current is 1 A. State your assumption. **[2 marks]**

15.3 Calculate the number of *additional* turns of wire that would need to be added to increase the field strength to its original value. **[3 marks]**

15.4 Compare the shape of the magnetic field inside the coil and outside the coil. **[2 marks]**

⚙ Knowledge

P15 Electricity

The generator effect

A potential difference is **induced** (created) across the ends of a conductor if:

- the conductor is moving relative to a magnetic field
- the magnetic field around the conductor changes.

In a complete circuit, there will be an induced current. The **generator effect** can be seen by:

① moving a wire in a magnetic field so that it cuts across the field lines

movement of wire

ammeter

② moving a magnet in and out of a coil of wire.

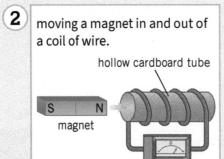

hollow cardboard tube

S N

magnet

Factors affecting induced current

The direction of the induced potential difference and induced current reverse if:

- the movement of the wire or magnet is reversed
- the **polarity** of the magnet is reversed.

If this reversal happens repeatedly, an alternating current/alternating potential difference is produced.

The induced potential difference/current will *increase* if the speed of movement, strength of the magnetic field, area of the coil, or number of turns in the coil are increased.

An induced current will generate a magnetic field around the conductor that always opposes the original change producing it. This acts to slow down or stop any movement or change in magnetic field.

Generating and transmitting electricity

In a power station, turbines turn wire coils between magnets to generate electricity. A network of cables and transformers links power stations to homes, offices, and other consumers of mains electricity.

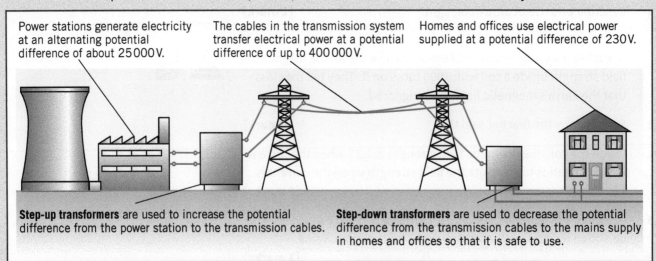

Power stations generate electricity at an alternating potential difference of about 25 000 V.

The cables in the transmission system transfer electrical power at a potential difference of up to 400 000 V.

Homes and offices use electrical power supplied at a potential difference of 230 V.

Step-up transformers are used to increase the potential difference from the power station to the transmission cables.

Step-down transformers are used to decrease the potential difference from the transmission cables to the mains supply in homes and offices so that it is safe to use.

Alternators and dynamos

An **alternator** produces a pd that changes direction. This produces **alternating current** in a circuit.

A **dynamo** produces a pd (and current) that is **direct current**.

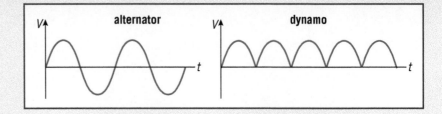

Transformers

A **transformer** is a device that can change the size of an alternating potential difference.

A basic transformer consists of two coils wound round an iron core.

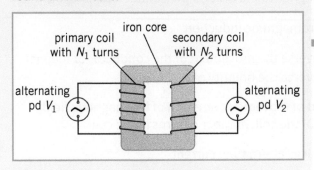

primary coil with N_1 turns — iron core — secondary coil with N_2 turns

alternating pd V_1 — alternating pd V_2

Iron is used for the core because it is easily magnetised and demagnetised.

How a transformer works

- An alternating current passes through the primary coil producing an alternating magnetic field in the iron core.

- The alternating magnetic field in the iron core induces an alternating pd in the secondary coil.

••

The ratio of potential differences across the primary and secondary coils is the same as the ratio of number of turns on each coil:

$$\frac{\text{potential difference across primary coil (V)}}{\text{potential difference across secondary coil (V)}} = \frac{\text{number of turns on primary coil}}{\text{number of turns on secondary coil}}$$

$$\frac{V_p}{V_s} = \frac{N_p}{N_s}$$

In a step-up transformer:
- there are more turns on the secondary coil than on the primary coil so $V_s > V_p$
- current in the secondary coil I_s must be less than the current in the primary coil I_p for the power to be the same.

In a step-down transformer:
- there are fewer turns on the secondary coil than on the primary coil (N_p) so $V_s < V_p$
- current in the secondary coil I_s must be greater than current in the primary coil I_p for power to be the same.

•••

If a transformer is 100% efficient: *power output of secondary coil = power input to primary coil* $V_s \times I_s = V_p \times I_p$

Remember that $P = V \times I$

Why do transformers improve efficiency?

A high potential difference across the transmission cables means that a lower current is needed to transfer the same amount of power, since:

power (W) = current (A) × potential difference (V)

$$P = IV$$

A lower current in the cables means less electrical power is wasted due to heating of the cables.

Switch mode transformer

Switch mode transformers are transformers that:

- operate at a high frequency, often between 50 kHz and 200 kHz

- are much lighter and smaller than traditional transformers that work from a 50 Hz mains supply, making them useful for applications such as mobile phone chargers

- use very little power when they are switched on, but no load is applied.

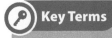 **Key Terms**

Make sure you can write a definition for these key terms.

alternating current   alternator   direct current   dynamo   generator effect
induced   polarity   switch mode transformer   transformer

Retrieval

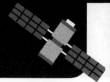

Learn the answers to the questions below then cover the answers column with a piece of paper and write as many as you can. Check and repeat.

	P15 questions	Answers
1	Give two ways that a potential difference (pd) is induced in a conductor.	• conductor moving relative to a magnetic field • magnetic field around the conductor changing
2	What is another name for the generator effect?	electromagnetic induction
3	How can the direction of an induced pd or current be reversed?	• reverse the movement of the conductor or magnet • reverse the polarity of the magnet
4	What affects the size of an induced pd or current?	speed of movement, strength of the magnetic field, area of the coil, number of turns in the coil
5	How does an alternator use the generator effect?	produces alternating current
6	Which kind of current is produced by the generator effect in a dynamo?	direct current
7	How is electricity generated?	turbines turn coils of wire between magnets
8	How is electricity transmitted?	a network of cables and transformers link power stations to customers
9	What does a transformer do?	changes the magnitude of the alternating pd
10	What does a basic transformer consist of?	two coils of wire wound around an iron core
11	Why is iron used for the core of a transformer?	iron is easily magnetised and demagnetised
12	How does a transformer work?	alternating pd across the primary coil produces an alternating magnetic field in the iron core which induces an alternating pd in the secondary coil
13	How is the ratio of pd across the primary coil and secondary coil related to the ratio of the number of turns on each coil?	the ratios are the same: $\frac{V_p}{V_s} = \frac{N_p}{N_s}$
14	Which type of transformer has more turns on its secondary coil than on its primary coil?	step-up transformer
15	What is the efficiency of a transformer if the power output from the secondary coil is the same as the power input to the primary coil?	100%
16	How is a step-up transformer used in transmitting electricity?	to increase the pd from the power station to the transmission cables
17	How is a step-down transformer used in transmitting electricity?	to decrease the pd from the transmission cables to the electricity supply in buildings so that it is safe to use
18	How does having a large potential difference in the transmission cables help to make the transmission of electricity more efficient?	large pd means a small current is needed to transfer the same amount of power; small current in the transmission cables means less electrical power is wasted due to heating

Put paper here

Now use the questions below to check your knowledge from previous chapters.

P15

Previous questions | Answers

1	What will an object experience if the resultant force on it is not zero?	acceleration/change in velocity
2	What causes short-sightedness?	the eyeball is too long or the lens cannot make a sharp image on the retina
3	On a graph of temperature against time for a substance being heated up or cooled down, what do the flat (horizontal) sections show?	the time when the substance is changing state and the temperature is not changing
4	What happens to the resistance of a thermistor as its temperature increases?	resistance decreases
5	What does the distance between magnetic field lines indicate?	strength of the field; closer together = stronger field
6	What is the frequency of a wave?	number of waves passing a fixed point per second
7	In which direction do magnetic field lines always point?	north to south

Put paper here

Maths Skills

Practise your maths skills using the worked example and practice questions below.

Area and volume	Worked example	Practice
The unit of **area** is the square metre (m²). Since 1 m = 100 cm = 1000 mm, an area of 1 m² = 10 000 cm² = 1 000 000 mm². The area of a rectangle can be calculated using: area of rectangle = width × length The area of a triangle can be calculated using: $$\text{area of triangle} = \frac{(\text{height} \times \text{length of base})}{2}$$ The unit of **volume** is the cubic metre (m³). Since 1 m = 100 cm = 1000 mm, a volume of 1 m³ = 1 000 000 cm³ = 1 000 000 000 mm³. The volume of a cuboid can be calculated using: volume of cuboid = length × width × height	A tank of water has the dimensions 2 m width, 4 m height, and 6 m length. **1** What is the area of the base of the tank? **Answer:** area of rectangle = width × length = 2 m × 6 m = 12 m² **2** What is the volume of the tank? **Answer:** volume of cuboid = length × width × height = 6 m × 2 m × 4 m = 48 m³	**1** A triangle is 2.5 m long and 1.25 m tall. Calculate the area of the triangle. **2** A rectangular container has a base that is 0.30 m by 0.60 m. Calculate the area of the container's base. Give your answer in mm². **3** The largest fish tank a pet shop sells is 200 cm long, 60 cm wide, and 90 cm tall. Calculate the volume of the fish tank. Give your answer in m³.

✏ Practice

Exam-style questions

01 There are many devices that rely on a potential difference being induced.

01.1 Describe what is meant by an induced potential difference. **[1 mark]**

_____

_____

01.2 Draw **one** line from each statement to the correct equipment to complete the sentences. **[3 marks]**

Statement	Equipment
A device that produces an alternating potential difference is a…	…dynamo.
A device that changes the potential difference is a…	…generator.
A device that produces a direct potential difference is a…	…transformer.

> **! Exam Tip**
>
> Draw clear lines. If the examiner is confused about where your lines go they can't give you any marks.

01.3 The potential difference that is used by domestic appliances is produced by a generator in a power station.

Circle the correct words or phrases in the sentences below. **[4 marks]**

The type of generator that is found in a power station is **an alternator** / **a dynamo**.

Transformers **step-up** / **step-down** the potential difference from a power station to the power transmission system.

They do this when a changing potential difference in the **primary** / **secondary** coil produces a changing **current** / **magnetic field** in the iron core.

> **! Exam Tip**
>
> Approach this one sentence at a time. If you can't choose between the options in the first sentence, don't give up. Try the next one.

02 A student has a magnet and a coil of wire that is connected to a voltmeter.

They observe that when they move the magnet into the coil it produces a potential difference that is positive.

02.1 Describe how the student can increase the potential difference produced. **[1 mark]**

_____

_____

> **! Exam Tip**
>
> This is a one-mark question so only needs a simple answer. Don't feel pressured to fill two lines with your answer.

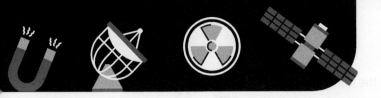

02.2 Suggest how the student could model the production of alternating potential difference using the voltmeter, magnet, and coil.

Explain your answer. **[2 marks]**

_____

_____

_____

02.3 When the student replaces the voltmeter with a resistor, a current flows in the coil when a magnet moves in or out of the coil.

The coil becomes an electromagnet.

Describe the link between the direction of the magnetic field inside the coil and the direction of the magnetic field of the moving magnet. **[1 mark]**

_____

_____

03 A student lies on a plank of wood that is supported at one end by a brick. The other end of the plank is on a scale.

03.1 Use Newton's First Law to explain why the student is stationary. **[2 marks]**

03.2 Using the information below, draw a diagram that shows the clockwise and anticlockwise moments acting on the plank. Assume that the brick is acting like a pivot, and ignore the weight of the plank. Label the distances from the pivot.

- The distance from the brick to the scale is 2.0 m.
- The centre of mass of the student is 1.2 m from the brick.
- The scale reads 400 N. **[4 marks]**

03.3 Use the law of moments to calculate the weight of the student. Give your answer to **two** significant figures. **[3 marks]**

03.4 Write down the equation that links mass, weight, and gravitational field strength. **[1 mark]**

03.5 Calculate the mass of the student. Gravitational field strength = 9.81 N/kg. **[2 marks]**

04 A student is investigating the effect of changing the number of turns in the secondary coil of a transformer on the induced potential difference across the secondary coil.

04.1 Describe what happens in a transformer to produce an induced potential difference. **[2 marks]**

04.2 The data from their experiment is shown in **Table 1**.

Table 1

Number of turns on the secondary coil	Induced pd in V			
	Repeat 1	Repeat 2	Repeat 3	Mean
0	0.0	0.0	0.0	0.0
10	2.5	2.4	2.6	2.5
20	4.8	5.2	5.0	5.0
30	7.3	7.4	7.8	7.5

Give **two** control variables in this experiment. **[2 marks]**

04.3 Describe the relationship between the number of turns on the secondary coil and the induced potential difference. Use the data to justify your conclusion. **[2 marks]**

04.4 The student wants to connect a bulb that requires a potential difference of 3V at the secondary coil.

Suggest the number of turns on the secondary coil that the student needs in order to light the bulb. Explain your reasoning. **[2 marks]**

05 A teacher shows a mobile phone charger with the cover removed. A student says: *'I can see that the charger contains a transformer.'*

05.1 Identify what the student saw inside the charger that prompted them to make that observation. **[1 mark]**

05.2 The teacher gives the following data about the charger:

$N_p = 2000$ $N_s = 100$ $V_s = 12V$

Use the correct equation from the *Physics Equations Sheet* to calculate V_p. **[3 marks]**

05.3 The student says: *'This is a step-up transformer because N_p is bigger than N_s.'*

Do you agree? Give reasons for your answer. **[2 marks]**

05.4 Explain why the core of the transformer is made of iron. **[2 marks]**

06 A student makes a model generator. A coil of wire spins in a magnetic field, as shown in **Figure 1.**

Figure 1

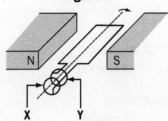

The student puts a voltmeter between points **X** and **Y**. They measure a changing potential difference when the coil spins.

06.1 Explain why a potential difference is produced. **[2 marks]**

06.2 A graph of potential difference against time is shown in **Figure 2.**

Figure 2

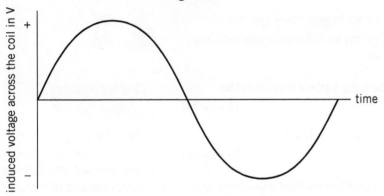

> **Exam Tip**
>
> Even though there are no numbers on this graph you still need to use data from it in your answer.

State whether the potential difference is alternating or direct. Explain your answer. **[2 marks]**

06.3 The student changes the permanent magnets for two electromagnets. Suggest changes that the student could make to the experimental set-up to produce the same graph as in **Figure 2** without spinning the coil. **[2 marks]**

06.4 Suggest **two** reasons why the output of a power station generator is bigger than the output of a model generator. **[2 marks]**

07 A student looks at the ac adapter that they use for their laptop. The label on the adapter is shown in **Figure 3.**

Figure 3

ac adapter
Input: 100–240 V ∼ 1.8 A
Output: 19.5 V — 4.62 A

The adapter is connected to the mains and to the student's laptop.

07.1 Suggest what the following symbols mean in relation to the input and output current: ── and ∿ **[2 marks]**

07.2 Calculate the input power of the adapter. Use the value of current given on the label.

Give your answer to **two** significant figures. Assume that the mains potential difference is 230 V. **[3 marks]**

07.3 Use the values given on the label to calculate the output power. **[2 marks]**

07.4 The student observes that the adapter gets hot when it is connected to the mains.

Compare the values of input and output power that you calculated in **07.2** and **07.3**.

Suggest how the student's observation can be explained. **[3 marks]**

> **!** Exam Tip

Think back to other topics on energy.

08 A student connects a dynamo to a data logger. They spin the dynamo and look at the graph of potential difference against time that is produced by the data logger.

08.1 Sketch the graph of potential difference against time that the student sees. **[3 marks]**

08.2 Explain how you can tell from the graph that the device is a dynamo. **[3 marks]**

08.3 Describe the changes to the graph that the student would see when they spin the coil in the opposite direction. **[1 mark]**

08.4 Describe the changes to the graph that the student would see when they spin the coil twice as fast. **[2 marks]**

> **!** Exam Tip

Sketching a graph means showing the general shape of the line and labelled axes. You don't have to plot points.

09 An electricity transmission system uses a variety of transformers. There are losses in energy due to heating.

09.1 Suggest why there is thermal energy loss when a transformer is in operation. **[2 marks]**

09.2 Write down the equation that links power, potential difference, and current in a circuit. **[1 mark]**

09.3 The output of a transformer supplies 120 MW of power to a transmission system at a potential difference of 400 kV.

Calculate the current in the secondary coil of a transformer connected to the transmission system. **[4 marks]**

> **!** Exam Tip

You can write the equation with words or symbols, whichever you find less confusing.

10 An electricity transmission system is used to transmit electricity from power stations to homes and businesses.

10.1 Select all the essential parts of this system from the list below.
[2 marks]

step-up transformers
transmission cables
microphones
voltmeters
step-down transformers

10.2 Describe the appearance of the parts you selected in **10.1**.
[2 marks]

11 A company making steel pipes uses ultrasound to find cracks in the pipes. Ultrasound has a frequency beyond the range of human hearing.

11.1 Write down the range of human hearing. **[1 mark]**

11.2 Write down the equation that links the speed, frequency, and wavelength of a wave. **[1 mark]**

11.3 Calculate the wavelength of ultrasound with a frequency of 400 kHz. The speed of sound in steel is 5000 m/s. **[3 marks]**

11.4 A technician uses ultrasound with a frequency of 400 kHz to measure the distance to the crack. The ultrasonic transducer detects a reflected pulse after 8.4×10^{-7} seconds.

Calculate the total distance travelled by the pulse. **[3 marks]**

11.5 Use your answer to **11.4** to calculate the distance to the crack in the pipe. **[2 marks]**

> **! Exam Tip**
>
> It is important to write the unit for hertz correctly: a capital H and a lowercase z. HZ will not get marks; nor will hz.

12 A single piece of wire is moved between the poles of a magnet, as shown in **Figure 4**.

Figure 4

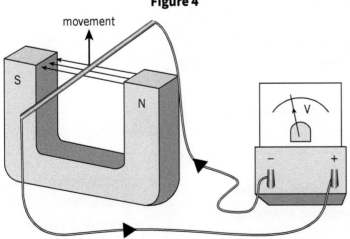

The speed of motion is increased and the induced potential difference is measured. The data is shown in **Table 2**.

Table 2

Speed in m/s	Induced pd in V			
	Repeat 1	Repeat 2	Repeat 3	Mean
0	0.00	0.00	0.00	0.00
1	0.70	0.67	0.68	0.68
2	0.90	1.01	1.20	1.04
3	1.60	1.80	1.45	1.62
4	1.85	2.00	1.90	

12.1 Complete **Table 2** by calculating the mean induced potential difference for a speed of 4 m/s. **[1 mark]**

 Exam Tip

Give your answer to 2 decimal places. Always try to match the number of decimal places of your answer to the data given in the question.

12.2 Plot a graph of the data on **Figure 5**. Draw a line of best fit. **[2 marks]**

Figure 5

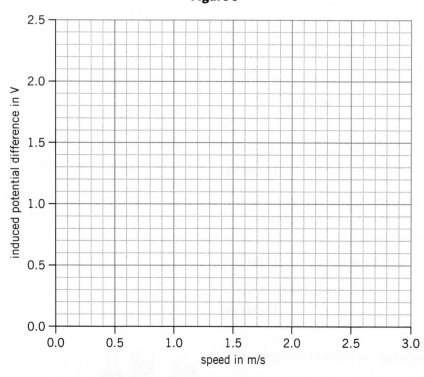

! **Exam Tip**

Plot the mean induced potential difference, not each repeat.

12.3 Use **Figure 5** to find the potential difference that would be obtained at a speed of 1.5 m/s. **[1 mark]**

12.4 There is a spread in the data in **Table 2**. Name the type of error that produces this type of uncertainty in the data. **[1 mark]**

13 An electricity transmission system is made up of substations that contain transformers.

13.1 Describe the role of a transformer. **[1 mark]**

13.2 A power station supplies 80 MW to the transmission system.

Some parts of the transmission system operate at very high potential differences.

! **Exam Tip**

You'll need to do two calculations for this question.

Make it clear which section of information each calculation is referring to in your answer.

Compare the power losses of transmitting power using a potential difference of 400 000 V with using a potential difference of 4000 V.

Assume that the wires have a resistance of about 4 Ω.

Use your calculations to explain why it is important to transmit power in the transmission system at a high potential difference rather than low potential difference. **[6 marks]**

14 A motorboat is in the middle of a lake. It is stationary. When the engines are turned on, the boat accelerates.

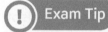

14.1 Write down the equation that links force, mass, and acceleration. **[1 mark]**

14.2 The engine provides a force of 3000 N. The mass of the boat is 860 kg. Assume that there are no resistive forces acting on the boat.

Calculate the acceleration of the boat. **[3 marks]**

14.3 The actual acceleration of the boat is 2.7 m/s².

Calculate the magnitude of the drag forces acting on the boat. **[5 marks]**

14.4 Use an equation from the *Physics Equations Sheet* to calculate the time it takes the boat to reach a speed of 14 m/s.

Give your answer to **two** significant figures. **[3 marks]**

> **(!) Exam Tip**
>
> There are lots of different parts to the calculations in question **14**. You might find it helpful to make a list of all the numbers you know before starting.

15 A student does a survey of some of the devices in their house that use a mains adapter. They use the mains adapter label to look at the output voltage. They notice that the adapters are warm.

15.1 Use the structure of an adapter to explain why they are warm. **[2 marks]**

15.2 The input voltage to a laptop adapter is 230 V. The laptop requires a voltage of 23 V. Calculate the ratio of the number of turns on the secondary coil to the number of turns on the primary coil. **[2 marks]**

15.3 There are 4000 coils on the primary coil. Calculate the number of turns on the secondary coil. **[3 marks]**

15.4 Describe one difference between this adapter and a mobile phone adapter. **[2 marks]**

Knowledge

P16 Household electricity and motors

Mains electricity

A cell or a battery provides a **direct current (dc)**. The current only flows in one direction and is produced by a **direct potential difference**.

Mains electricity provides an **alternating current (ac)**. The current repeatedly reverses direction and is produced by an **alternating potential difference**.

The positive and negative terminals of an alternating power supply swap over with a regular frequency.

The ac of mains electricity has a set frequency and voltage.

Diagrams of mains electricity show:

- the period (the time for one oscillation), from which you can calculate the frequency:

$$\text{frequency (Hz)} = \frac{1}{\text{time (s)}}$$

- the peak potential difference (the highest or lowest value of the pd).

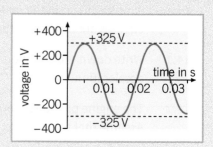

Plugs

The Earth wire is a safety wire to stop the appliance becoming live. The potential difference of the Earth wire is 0V. It only carries a current if there is a fault.

The neutral wire completes the circuit. It has a potential difference of 0V.

Plastic is used for the wire coatings and plug case because it is a good electrical insulator.

Fuse connected to the live wire. If the live wire inside an appliance touches the neutral wire a very large current flows. This is called a **short circuit**. When this happens the fuse melts and disconnects the live wire from the mains, keeping the appliance safe.

The live wire is dangerous because it has a high potential difference. This would cause a large current to flow through you if you touched it.

Most electrical appliances are connected to the mains using a three-core cable. Copper is used for the wires because it is a good electrical conductor and it bends easily.

Circuit breaker

A **circuit breaker** is a switch that is in series with an electromagnet.

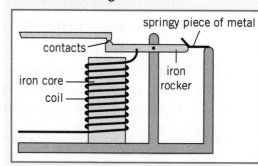

The switch is held closed by a spring, but if the current becomes too large, the electromagnet becomes strong enough to pull the switch into the open position, turning the current off.

Electrical safety

Some appliances have a metal case. If there is a fault, the case can become live (attached to the mains pd) and therefore dangerous to touch. An **earth wire** ensures any current goes safely to earth not through a person. In this case, the high current melts a **fuse**, or trips a circuit breaker, which disconnects the **live wire**. A circuit breaker can be reset.

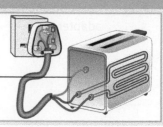

The earth wire is connected to the metal case of the appliance.

 **Key Terms**

Make sure you can write a definition for these key terms.

alternating current (ac)	alternating potential difference	circuit breaker
direct current (dc)	direct potential difference	earth wire	electric motor
fuse	live wire	mains electricity	motor effect	power

The motor effect

When a current-carrying wire (or other conductor) is placed in a magnetic field, it experiences a force.

The force is due to the interaction between the field created by the current in the wire and the magnetic field in which the wire is placed. It is called the **motor effect**.

The magnet producing the field will experience an equal-sized force in the opposite direction.

- The direction of the force is reversed if the current is reversed or if the direction of the magnetic field is reversed.
- The force is bigger if the current or field strength is bigger.
- There is no force if the wire and field are parallel.

Fleming's left-hand rule

The direction of the force/motion of the wire is always at right angles to both the current and the direction of the magnetic field it is within.

It can be worked out using Fleming's left-hand rule:

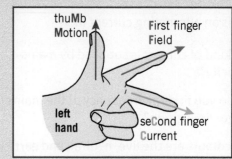

Electric motors

A current-carrying coil of wire in a magnetic field will tend to rotate. This is the basis of an **electric motor**.

The diagram shows a simple motor made of one rectangular piece of wire. When there is a current in the wire, it spins because:

- each side of the coil experiences a force due to being a current-carrying conductor in a magnetic field
- the forces on each side of the coil are in opposite directions.

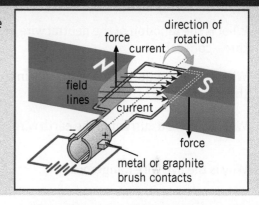

Energy transfer in electrical appliances

When you turn an electrical appliance on, the potential difference of the mains supply causes charge (carried by electrons) to flow through it.

You can find the energy transferred to an electrical appliance when charge flows through it using:

energy transferred (J) = charge flow (C) × potential difference (V)

$$E = QV$$

The rate at which energy is transferred by an appliance is called **power**. You can find the energy transferred per second using the equation:

$$\text{power (W)} = \frac{\text{energy transferred (J)}}{\text{time (s)}}$$

$$P = \frac{E}{t}$$

The power transfer is related to the current through the appliance and the potential difference across it. You can also find the energy transferred per second using the equation:

power (W) = current (A) × potential difference (V)

$$P = I \times V$$

Calculating cost

The amount of energy an appliance transfers depends on how long the appliance is switched on for and its power rating. A more convenient unit is the kilowatt-hour (kWh).

To calculate the energy transferred, E, from the mains (power, P, and time, t), you use:

$$E(\text{kWh}) = P(\text{kW}) \times t(\text{h})$$

Electricity companies charge for each kWh used.

Learn the answers to the questions below then cover the answers column with a piece of paper and write as many as you can. Check and repeat.

	P16 questions	Answers
1	Why is the current provided by a cell called a direct current (dc)?	only flows in one direction
2	What is an alternating current (ac)?	current that repeatedly reverses direction
3	What kind of current is supplied by mains electricity?	alternating current
4	How do you find the frequency of the mains from a voltage–time graph?	calculate $\dfrac{1}{\text{time for one oscillation}}$
5	What colours are the live, neutral, and earth wires in a three-core cable?	live = brown, neutral = blue, earth = green and yellow stripes
6	What is the function of the live wire in a three-core cable?	carries the alternating potential difference from the supply
7	What is the function of the neutral wire in a three-core cable?	completes the circuit
8	What is the function of the earth wire in a three-core cable?	safety wire to stop current going through you if the appliance becomes live and you touch it
9	When is there a current in the earth wire?	when the live wire touches the case of an appliance
10	Why is the live wire dangerous?	provides a large pd that would cause a large current to flow through a person if they touched it
11	What does Fleming's left-hand rule show?	relative orientation of the force, current in the conductor, and magnetic field for the motor effect
12	What is the motor effect?	when a conductor placed in a magnetic field experiences a force
13	What causes the motor effect?	interaction between the magnetic field created by current in a wire and the magnetic field in which the wire is placed
14	What two things does energy transfer to an appliance depend on?	power of appliance, time it is switched on for
15	What are the units for power, current, potential difference, and resistance?	watts (W), amps (A), volts (V), ohms (Ω)
16	What unit is used for calculating the cost of the energy transferred by an appliance?	kWh

Put paper here

Now use the questions below to check your knowledge from previous chapters.

P16

Previous questions

Answers

1	What does momentum depend on?	mass and velocity
2	What is the normal (on a ray diagram)?	a construction line perpendicular to the reflecting surface at the point of incidence
3	What is the internal energy of a substance?	the total kinetic energy and potential energy of all the particles in the substance
4	What factors does the strength of the magnetic field around a straight wire depend upon?	size of current, distance from wire
5	How is the ratio of pd across the primary coil and secondary coil related to the ratio of the number of turns on each coil?	the ratios are the same: $\dfrac{V_p}{V_s} = \dfrac{N_p}{N_s}$

Maths Skills

Practise your maths skills using the worked example and practice questions below.

Plotting graphs	Worked example	Practice

Plotting graphs

When plotting a graph, draw it so that it covers at least half the graph paper.

Use a sensible scale that makes it easy to plot and read the graph. Generally, each large square on the graph paper should represent a numerical value of 1, 2, 5, or 10.

The labels on each graph axis should give the name and unit of the variable plotted.

A line of best fit is a smooth line that passes through *or near* each plotted point – this can be curved or straight.

A linear graph is any straight-line graph; if this goes through the origin the two variables are directly proportional.

The equation of all straight lines is:
$$y = mx + c$$
Where:
y = variable plotted on y-axis
m = gradient of line
x = variable plotted on x-axis
c = y-intercept

Worked example

A student measured the potential difference across a fixed resistor while varying the current.

Current in A	Potential difference in V
0.05	1
0.10	2
0.15	3
0.20	4
0.25	5
0.30	6
0.35	7
0.40	8

1 Plot a graph of the data. Draw a line of best fit, and describe the correlation the graph shows.

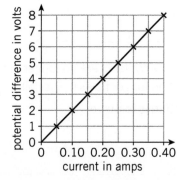

Answer: The graph is linear, and shows a perfect positive correlation.

2 Use the line of best fit to predict the potential difference if the current was 0.55 A.
Answer: 11 V

Practice

1 The table below shows how the concentration of HCl changed over the course of a reaction.

Plot a graph of the data. Draw a line of best fit.

Time in s	Concentration of HCl in mol/dm³
25	1.25
50	0.95
75	0.80
100	0.70
125	0.60
150	0.55
175	0.50
200	0.50

Exam-style questions

01 A student sets up a simple motor.

They connect the motor to a battery as shown in **Figure 1**.

Figure 1

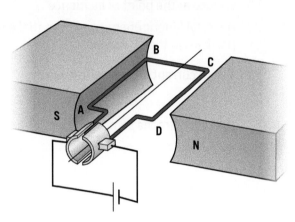

01.1 Describe the direction of the current in the coil of wire in terms of **A**, **B**, **C**, and **D**. **[1 mark]**

_____

_____

01.2 Compare the force on side **AB** with the force on side **CD**.

Use your answer to describe which way the coil spins. **[3 marks]**

_____

_____

_____

_____

01.3 Explain why there is no force on side **BC**. **[2 marks]**

_____

_____

_____

01.4 When the coil is vertical, the contacts are no longer in contact with the battery and a current no longer flows in the coil.

Explain why the coil continues to move. **[2 marks]**

_____

_____

_____

02 A student has a small electric motor.

02.1 They connect the motor in a circuit with a 6 V battery.
A current of 1.5 A flows in the circuit.
Show that the power of the motor is 9 W. **[2 marks]**

_____

_____

_____

_____

> (!) **Exam Tip**
>
> 'Show' questions are great! You already know the answer (9 W), so you just need to clearly show the examiner that you can use an equation to get this answer.

02.2 The student turns the motor on for 30 seconds.
Write down the equation that links power, energy, and time. **[1 mark]**

_____

02.3 Calculate the energy transferred by the motor. **[3 marks]**

> (!) **Exam Tip**
>
> For this question you need to use the answer from **02.1**. This is common in exams – you may have to look back at this question to get all the information you need.

_____ J

02.4 The student finds a lamp with the same power rating as the motor.
They connect the lamp to another 6 V battery.
They then turn both circuits on for 30 seconds.
Select the correct statement below. **[1 mark]**
Tick **one** box.

> (!) **Exam Tip**
>
> Only tick **one** box – if you tick two you'll get no marks.

The motor transfers more energy than the lamp. ☐

Both devices transfer the same amount of energy. ☐

The lamp transfers more energy than the motor. ☐

03 **Figure 2** shows how the motor that drives a desk fan is connected to the mains supply.

Figure 2

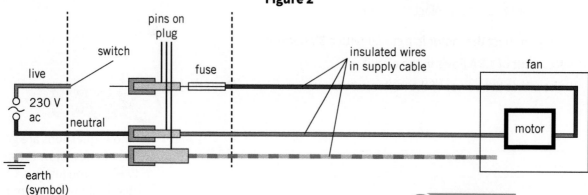

03.1 Use **Figure 2** to explain how the fuse and earth wire prevent a person being injured if there is a fault. **[5 marks]**

03.2 Suggest how to construct the fan so that an earth wire is not required. Explain your suggestion. **[2 marks]**

03.3 When the motor is working the current in the wire is 4.5 A. Calculate the power of the fan motor. Give your answer to **two** significant figures. **[2 marks]**

03.4 There is a fault and the current in the fuse reaches a value of 5.0 A. The fuse melts in a time of 0.63 seconds. The energy needed to melt the fuse is 5.4 J. Calculate the resistance of the fuse wire to an appropriate number of significant figures. **[4 marks]**

04 A student looks at the information on a hairdryer. The power of the hairdryer is 2000 W. The potential difference that the hairdryer needs to work is 230 V.

04.1 Write down what 2000 W means in terms of energy and time. **[1 mark]**

04.2 Write down what 230 V means in terms of energy and charge. **[1 mark]**

04.3 The student estimates that it takes 5 minutes to dry their hair. Write down the equation that links time, power, and energy. **[1 mark]**

04.4 Calculate the energy transferred from the mains during that time. **[2 marks]**

04.5 Write down the equation that links potential difference, charge, and energy. **[1 mark]**

04.6 Calculate the charge flowing in the hairdryer. Use your answer to **04.4** to help you. **[3 marks]**

(!) **Exam Tip**

This question may seem easy, but look at the number of marks – 5!

To get full marks on this question you must refer back to the information in the figure.

(!) **Exam Tip**

For this question you'll need to use two different equations to get the final answer. The first clue of this is the fact you're given three numbers in the question.

(!) **Exam Tip**

Remember that the standard units for time are seconds!

05 A student looks at two appliances and produces **Table 1**.

Both appliances work when connected to the mains supply.

Table 1

Appliance	Power rating
toaster	1200 W
kettle	2.0 kW

05.1 Write down the equation that links power, potential difference, and current. **[1 mark]**

05.2 Use the potential difference of the mains supply and the data in the table to calculate the current flowing in the wires in the kettle when it is turned on.

Give your answer to **two** significant figures. **[6 marks]**

05.3 Give the equation that links current, potential difference, and resistance. **[1 mark]**

05.4 Show that the resistance of the kettle is approximately 26 Ω.

Give your answer to **two** significant figures. **[4 marks]**

05.5 Write the equation to calculate energy transfer from power and time. **[1 mark]**

05.6 It takes 2 minutes to boil water in the kettle.

Calculate the length of time that the toaster would take to transfer the same amount of energy as the kettle.

Give your answer in minutes. **[6 marks]**

05.7 A student says: '*In terms of energy types and transfers, the toaster and kettle are identical.*'

Do you agree? Explain your answer. **[2 marks]**

06 A student makes a simple motor. They use a piece of wire to make a coil and connect the coil to a battery. There is a current flowing in the coil but the coil does not spin.

06.1 Describe what the student needs to do to make the coil spin. Give reasons for your answer. **[2 marks]**

06.2 The student wonders if they can make a loudspeaker using the same equipment used for the motor.

Compare the construction of a simple direct current motor with the construction of a simple loudspeaker.

Suggest and explain what would happen if the student constructed a loudspeaker with the same equipment as the motor. **[6 marks]**

> **(!) Exam Tip**
>
> Watch out for the change between W and kW in this question.

> **(!) Exam Tip**
>
> There are two ways to approach this question: rearrange the equation and then put the numbers in, or put the numbers in and then rearrange the equation.
>
> In an exam you can get marks for putting the numbers in the right places, so it's a good idea to do that bit first!

> **(!) Exam Tip**
>
> This answer needs to be given in minutes, so you don't have to convert time into seconds. Be careful if you get a decimal – remember there are 60 seconds in a minute not 100.

> **(!) Exam Tip**
>
> 'Yes' or 'no' isn't going to be enough to get full marks on this question. You must explain your reasoning.

> **(!) Exam Tip**
>
> Moving coil loudspeakers and moving coil microphones operate in a very similar manner. It is worth learning this mechanism because it can be applied to a range of different answers.

07 A student has found a box of metal rods.

The metal rods are numbered but the type of material that each rod is made of is not clear.

The student wants to put the rods in order from best to worst conductor of thermal energy.

They attach a small nail to each rod with wax.

The equipment the student uses is shown in **Figure 3**.

Figure 3

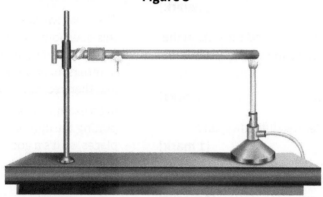

07.1 Design a results table that could be used to collect the data in this experiment. **[3 marks]**

07.2 Write down **two** control variables in the experiment. **[2 marks]**

07.3 Explain why it would be difficult to collect valid data. **[2 marks]**

07.4 Suggest an improvement to this method that would improve the quality of the data. **[1 mark]**

Exam Tip

Control variables are the ones we keep the same.

08 **Table 2** shows a survey of some electrical appliances in a student's house.

All of the devices use mains pd.

Table 2

Appliance	Power rating in W	Potential difference in V
hairdryer	2200	
iron	2800	
toaster	2000	

Exam Tip

You may think you need a calculator and equations for **08.1**, but this is *not* a maths question. The key word in the question is *mains* pd.

08.1 Write down the potential difference that should go in the third column.

Explain your answer. **[2 marks]**

08.2 Describe where some energy ends up when **all** the appliances are being used. **[1 mark]**

08.3 Put the appliances in order from largest to smallest current.

Explain your reasoning. **[2 marks]**

08.4 The current of the toaster is 8.7 A.

Calculate the resistance using the equation:

$$power = (current)^2 \times resistance$$

Give your answer to **two** significant figures. **[4 marks]**

Exam Tip

Correct use of significant figures comes up all the time. This may not be something you've been taught in your science lessons, but hopefully you've covered it in maths.

09 A student connects a long thin strip of aluminium foil in a circuit with a battery. They lay the foil on the desk and bring a very strong magnet close to the foil. The foil moves.

09.1 Suggest why the foil moves. **[1 mark]**

09.2 The student notices that as they move the magnet further away from the foil it no longer moves. Explain why. **[2 marks]**

09.3 The student also has a magnetic field sensor attached to a data logger which measures magnetic field strength. The student wants to collect data to find the relationship between the magnetic field strength around the foil and the distance from the foil.

Describe a method of collecting data to find this relationship. **[3 marks]**

09.4 Sketch the graph the student would plot with the data they collected. Explain the shape of the graph. **[2 marks]**

10 A student learns that the oven in their kitchen works on a separate circuit to that of the toaster and other small electrical appliances.

They find the following information:

- the oven has a power of 9 kW
- the toaster has a power of 2 kW
- ovens are connected to the mains with much thicker wires than other appliances.

10.1 Calculate the current flowing in the oven. **[3 marks]**

10.2 Compare the current flowing in the oven with that of the toaster. **[4 marks]**

10.3 Suggest why the oven is connected with thicker wires. **[2 marks]**

10.4 Current larger than 0.1 A is dangerous to the human body.

Explain why the student can use both appliances safely. **[2 marks]**

11 A student uses a data logger to measure the speed of rotation of a motor as they change the current through it.

Their results are shown in **Table 3**.

Table 3

Current in A	Speed in rev/s
0.00	0
0.05	45
0.10	100
0.15	183
0.17	227

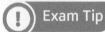

> **! Exam Tip**
>
> Data loggers are a great way to increase the resolution of results. They can take results continuously and feed them to a computer. They can also draw the graph for you!

> **! Exam Tip**
>
> **09.4** is a two-mark question. One mark will be for the correct shape of the line on the graph and the other will be for explaining why you drew it like that.

> **! Exam Tip**
>
> For **10.1** and **10.2**, you'll need to do two separate calculations and then compare them. Remember to make it very clear which calculation applies to which appliance, and then give the similarities and differences.

11.1 Plot the data in **Table 3** onto **Figure 4**. Draw a line of best fit.

[3 marks]

! Exam Tip

Always uses crosses to plot points and draw a line of best fit.

Figure 4

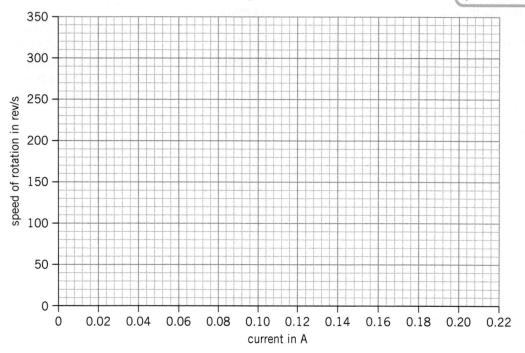

11.2 Describe the relationship between the current and the speed.

[2 marks]

11.3 There is a magnetic field around a coil of wire when a current flows through it.

Use this idea to explain the relationship you have described in **11.2**.

[5 marks]

11.4 Apart from current, suggest **one** other factor that affects the speed of rotation of the motor. **[1 mark]**

12 A teacher sets up a demonstration to show how an electric motor works. They suspend a light metal current-carrying rod in a magnetic field as shown in **Figure 5**.

Figure 5

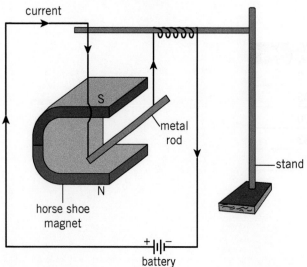

! Exam Tip

This is the same set-up as in **Figure 1**, even if it does look very different. This is seeing if you can take what you know and apply it to a new situation. You will definitely have to do this in your exam. If you think a question in your exam is asking you something that isn't on the specification, it isn't! Look for the science behind the question – this will be familiar to you.

12.1 Write down the direction that the rod will move. **[1 mark]**

12.2 Suggest what would happen to the movement of the rod if the strength of the magnet was doubled. **[1 mark]**

12.3 Magnetic field lines are like elastic bands. When they are stretched they try to return to their original shape. This produces a force.

Compare the shape of the magnetic fields between the poles of the horse shoe magnet and around the rod in **Figure 5**.

Suggest what happens to the fields when they combine and why the rod moves. **[5 marks]**

13 A student is comparing the brightness of two bulbs connected in different types of circuit.

Bulb **A** has a resistance of 5 Ω.

Bulb **B** has a resistance of 10 Ω.

The student connects the two bulbs in series with a 12 V battery.

Then they connect the same two bulbs in parallel with the same 12 V battery.

Compare the brightness of the bulbs in the series and parallel circuits.

Justify your answer with calculations. **[6 marks]**

> **! Exam Tip**
>
> Brightness is dependent on power, which is current × voltage.
>
> In a series circuit the current is the same everywhere, but not in a parallel circuit.

14 **Table 4** shows some data about the output of a solar cell. When light hits a solar cell, it produces a pd. If you connect the solar cell to a resistor, then a current will flow.

Table 4

Area of solar cell exposed in %	pd across resistor in V	Current in resistor in mA
100	0.60	38
80	0.46	34
60	0.27	33
40	0.10	28
20	0.09	18
0	0.00	0

14.1 Describe the relationship between the area of solar cell exposed and the pd output of the cell. **[1 mark]**

14.2 A student suggests that the output power of the solar cell will halve if the area that is exposed is halved. Use data from the table for 80% area exposed and 40% area exposed to test this prediction. **[6 marks]**

14.3 The student wants to set up this experiment to check the data. Suggest one control variable in that investigation. **[1 mark]**

14.4 The student decides to plot a graph of area exposed against output power. State and explain which type of graph they should plot. **[2 marks]**

⚙ Knowledge

P17 Atomic structure

Modern model of an atom

The model of the **atom** we have today was developed over time with the help of evidence from experiments.

Future experiments may change our understanding and lead us to alter or replace this model of the atom.

Dalton's model

John Dalton thought of the atom as a solid sphere that could not be divided into smaller parts. His model did not include protons, neutrons, or electrons.

Plum pudding model

Scientists' experiments resulted in the discovery of charged sub-atomic particles. The first to be discovered were **electrons** – tiny, negatively charged particles.

The discovery of electrons led to the plum pudding model of the atom – a cloud of positive charge, with negative electrons embedded in it.

Protons and neutrons had not yet been discovered.

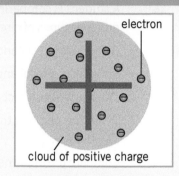

Alpha scattering experiment

1 Scientists fired small, positively charged particles (called **alpha particles**) at a piece of gold foil only a few atoms thick.
2 They expected the alpha particles to travel straight through the gold.
3 They were surprised that a few of the alpha particles bounced back and some were deflected (alpha scattering).
4 To explain why the alpha particles were repelled, the scientists suggested that the positive charge and mass of an atom must be concentrated at its centre. They called the centre the nucleus.

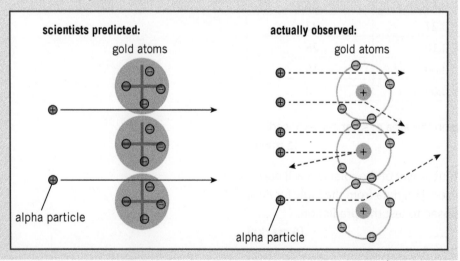

Nuclear model

Scientists replaced the plum pudding model with the **nuclear model**. They suggested that the electrons **orbit** (go around) the nucleus, but not at set distances, and the mass of the atom was concentrated in the charged nucleus.

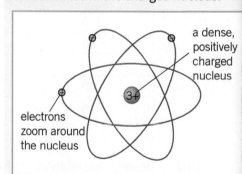

Bohr's model

Niels Bohr improved the nuclear model, and calculated that electrons must orbit the nucleus at fixed distances. These orbits are called shells or **energy levels**. Bohr's calculations agreed with experimental results.

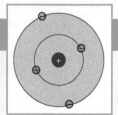

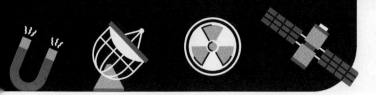

Protons, neutrons, electrons

Later experiments showed evidence that the nucleus contained positively charged particles called **protons**, and neutral particles called **neutrons**.

The relative masses of protons, neutrons and electrons are:

proton: 1   neutron: 1   electron: $\frac{1}{1836}$

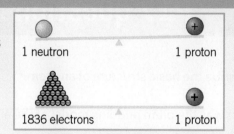

Basic structure of an atom

An atom has a radius of about 1×10^{-10} metres.

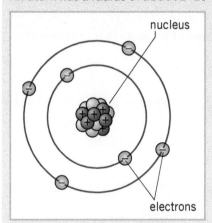

nucleus

electrons

An atom is uncharged overall, and has equal numbers of protons and electrons.

The nucleus

- Has a radius about 10 000 times smaller than the radius of an atom
- Contains protons and neutrons
- Is where most of the mass of an atom is concentrated.

Electrons

- Orbit the nucleus at different fixed distances called energy levels.
- Can gain energy by absorbing electromagnetic radiation. This causes them to move to a higher energy level.
- Can lose energy by emitting electromagnetic radiation. This causes them to move to a lower energy level.

Element symbols

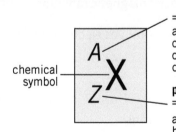

mass number
= number of protons + neutrons
atoms of the same element can have different numbers of neutrons, so they can have different mass numbers

proton number or atomic number
= number of protons
all atoms of the same element have the same number of protons in the nucleus, so they have the same atomic number

chemical symbol

$_Z^A X$

Isotopes are atoms of the same element, with the same number of protons but a different numbers of neutrons.

Ions

Atoms can become charged when they lose or gain electrons. This process is called **ionisation**.

- A positive ion is formed if an uncharged atom loses one or more electrons.
- A negative ion is formed if an uncharged atom gains one or more electrons.

 **Key Terms**

Make sure you can write a definition for these key terms.

| alpha particle | atom | atomic number | electron | energy level | ionisation |
| isotope | mass number | neutron | nuclear model | orbit | proton |

Learn the answers to the questions below then cover the answers column with a piece of paper and write as many as you can. Check and repeat.

	P17 questions	Answers
1	Describe the basic structure of an atom.	nucleus containing protons and neutrons, around which electrons orbit in fixed energy levels/shells
2	What was the plum pudding model of the atom?	positive mass with electrons embedded in it
3	Which particles were fired at gold foil in Rutherford's experiment?	alpha particles
4	What did most of the particles in the gold foil experiment do?	go through
5	What were the two main conclusions from the alpha particle scattering experiment?	• most of the mass of an atom is concentrated in the nucleus • nucleus is positively charged
6	Which model of the atom do we use in science lessons?	the Bohr model
7	What charges do protons, neutrons, and electrons carry?	protons = positive, neutrons = no charge, electrons = negative
8	Why do atoms have no overall charge?	equal numbers of positive protons and negative electrons
9	What is the radius of an atom?	around 1×10^{-10} m
10	How small is a nucleus compared to a whole atom?	around 10 000 times smaller
11	What is an energy level?	the fixed distance from the nucleus where an electron is allowed to be
12	How can an electron move up an energy level?	absorb sufficient electromagnetic radiation
13	What is ionisation?	process which adds or removes electrons from an atom
14	What is formed if an atom loses an electron?	positive ion
15	How does an atom become a negative ion?	gains one or more electrons
16	What is the atomic number of an element?	number of protons in one atom of the element
17	What is the mass number of an element?	number of protons + number of neutrons
18	Which particle do atoms of the same element always have the same number of?	protons
19	What are isotopes?	atoms of the same element (same number of protons) with different numbers of neutrons

Put paper here

Now use the questions below to check your knowledge from previous chapters.

P17

Previous questions

Answers

1	What is the function of the earth wire in a three-core cable?	safety wire to stop the appliance becoming live
2	What will two objects carrying the same type of charge do if they are brought close to each other?	repel each other
3	What is the specific latent heat of fusion of a substance?	the energy required to change 1 kg of the substance from solid to liquid at its melting point, without changing its temperature
4	How do you calculate refractive index in terms of speed?	$n = \dfrac{\text{speed of light in vacuum (air)}}{\text{speed of light in the medium}}$
5	How does a lever reduce the amount of force needed to create a particular sized moment?	by increasing the distance from the pivot

Put paper here *Put paper here* *Put paper here*

 # Maths Skills

Practise your maths skills using the worked examples and practice questions below.

Orders of magnitude	Worked examples	Practice
Orders of magnitude are useful for comparing the size of numbers. An order of magnitude is a factor of 10, so it is usually written as 10^n. For example, if one number is roughly 10 times bigger than another number, it is one order of magnitude bigger. If a number is 1000 times bigger than another number, it is three orders of magnitude bigger, because: $1000 = 10 \times 10 \times 10 = 10^3$. Two numbers are of the same order of magnitude if dividing the bigger number by the smaller number gives an answer less than 10. For example, 12 and 45 are the same order of magnitude, but 13 and 670 are not. If numbers are written in standard form, their orders of magnitude can be compared by dividing the larger power of ten by the smaller power of ten.	**1** A mouse has a mass of about 40 g, and an elephant has a mass of about 4×10^6 g. How many orders of magnitude heavier is the elephant compared to the mouse? **Answer:** Divide the larger power of ten by the smaller power of ten: $\dfrac{10^6}{10^1} = 10^5$, or five orders of magnitude. **2** The mass of the Sun is about 2.0×10^{30} kg. The mass of the Earth is 6.0×10^{24} kg. How many orders of magnitude bigger is the Sun's mass? **Answer:** Divide the larger power of ten by the smaller power of ten: $\dfrac{10^{30}}{10^{24}} = 10^6$, or six orders of magnitude.	**1** How many orders of magnitude bigger is the mass of a lorry around 44 000 kg compared to a human body around 70 kg? **2** How many orders of magnitude smaller is the diameter of an atom around 0.1 nm compared to the diameter of a marble of 1 cm? **3** How many orders of magnitude smaller is 70 J compared to 450 MJ?

Exam-style questions

01   **Table 1** shows the number of protons and neutrons in the neutral atoms of three elements.

Table 1

Element	Number of protons	Number of neutrons
A	10	10
B	10	12
C	11	12

01.1   Write down the number of electrons in an atom of element **A**.

[1 mark]

_____

01.2   Explain your answer to **01.1**.   **[2 marks]**

_____

_____

_____

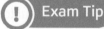

! Exam Tip

Use data from the table.

01.3   Name the two elements that are isotopes.   **[1 mark]**

_____

01.4   Explain your answer to **01.3**.   **[2 marks]**

_____

_____

_____

! Exam Tip

Isotopes have the same atomic number.

02   A student has drawn two diagrams that show the nuclei of isotopes of an element (**Figure 1**).

Figure 1

Key

⬤ particle **A**

◯ particle **B**

nucleus 1   nucleus 2

02.1   Write down which particle, **A** or **B**, is a proton. Explain your answer.

[2 marks]

_____

_____

02.2   Name the other type of particle.   **[1 mark]**

_____

Table 2

Element	Atomic number
lithium	3
beryllium	4
carbon	6
nitrogen	7

02.3 Use **Table 2** to identify the element the student drew. Explain your answer. **[2 marks]**

_____

_____

_____

02.4 Give the complete chemical symbol of each isotope. **[2 marks]**

_____

_____

02.5 Compare the charge on nucleus **1** with the charge on nucleus **2**. Justify your answer. **[2 marks]**

_____

_____

03 Atoms are very small.

03.1 Choose an approximate radius of an atom from the numbers in the box.

10^{15} m	10^{10} m	10^1 m	10^{-10} m	10^{-15} m

[1 mark]

03.2 Atoms have electrons that are arranged in different energy levels. Define an 'energy level'. **[1 mark]**

03.3 **Figure 2** shows the first three energy levels in a hydrogen atom.

Normally the electron in hydrogen is in the lowest energy level, which is level 1.

Compare what happens to the electron when an atom absorbs electromagnetic radiation with what happens when it emits electromagnetic radiation.

Use the diagram to provide examples. **[4 marks]**

Figure 2

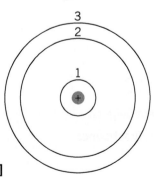

Exam Tip

Only select **one** answer – picking two will cause you to lose marks.

Exam Tip

Clearly label the lines you draw on the diagram to ensure the examiner can give you the marks for your answer.

04 A student is explaining what the symbols on the Periodic Table mean. They use the example of the element nitrogen shown in **Figure 3**.

Figure 3

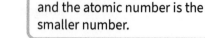

04.1 Complete the student's sentences.

You can work out the number of protons in an atom of this element by…

You can work out the number of neutrons in an atom of this element by…

You can work out the number of electrons in an atom of this element by… **[3 marks]**

> **! Exam Tip**
>
> Remember that the mass number is the larger number and the atomic number is the smaller number.

04.2 Another student says: '*The number of neutrons is always equal to the number of protons.*' Is this student correct? Explain your answer. **[2 marks]**

> **! Exam Tip**
>
> You *must* use data to back up your answer.

05 In the development of the model of the atom there have been many discoveries and different models have been developed.

- The electron was discovered in 1899 by J. J. Thompson.
- The nuclear model of the atom was proposed by Ernest Rutherford in 1911.
- The proton was named in 1920 by Rutherford.
- The neutron was discovered in 1932 by James Chadwick.

Describe how it was possible for Rutherford to develop a nuclear model before the particles that make up the nucleus had been discovered or identified. **[6 marks]**

06 A student investigates how high a ball bounces. They use a metre rule and a ball, as shown in **Figure 4**.

Figure 4

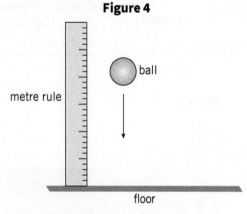

They drop the ball from different heights.

They measure the height of the first bounce.

Their results are shown in **Table 3**.

Table 3

Height of drop in cm	Height of bounce in cm
20	16
40	30
60	49
80	55
100	70

06.1 Explain in terms of energy why the ball does not bounce back to the height from which it was dropped. **[2 marks]**

06.2 Plot a graph of the results. **[5 marks]**

06.3 Identify the anomalous result. **[1 mark]**

06.4 Suggest whether the bounce height is proportional to the drop height. Explain your answer. **[2 marks]**

07 **Figure 5** shows the experimental equipment that scientists working with Rutherford used to develop the nuclear model of the atom.

Figure 5

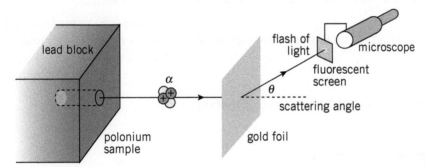

Table 4 shows the number of alpha particles deflected through different angles.

07.1 Use the data in **Table 4** to show that the percentage of alpha particles that were scattered back from the foil was approximately 0.14%. **[2 marks]**

07.2 Write down the percentage of alpha particles that went through the foil. **[1 mark]**

07.3 Suggest how the data in **Table 4** may have led Rutherford to propose the nuclear model. **[2 marks]**

07.4 The alpha particle is a helium nucleus.
Write down the charge on an alpha particle. **[1 mark]**

07.5 Suggest whether the data about the angle of deflection supports the idea that the charge on the nucleus is positive or negative.
Justify your answer. **[4 marks]**

Exam Tip

This is a brilliant question to test your practical skills with. You may not be familiar with this practical, but these are exactly the sort of questions you'll get in the exam!

Exam Tip

To go through the foil, the alpha particles must have been scattered less than 90 degrees.

Table 4

Angle of deflection in °	Experimental count
150	33
135	43
120	52
105	70
75	211
60	477
45	1435
30	7800
15	132 000
	Total = 142 141

Exam Tip

A helium nucleus has a mass of 4 and an atomic number of 2.

08   **Figure 6** shows transitions of electrons between different energy levels in an atom.

Figure 6

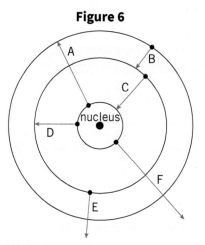

08.1   Write down the letters that show the transition of electrons when electromagnetic radiation is absorbed.   **[2 marks]**

08.2   Write down the letters that show the transition of electrons when electromagnetic radiation is emitted.   **[2 marks]**

08.3   Write down the letters that show ionisation of the atom.   **[2 marks]**

08.4   Write down the charge on the atom when the atom is ionised.   **[1 mark]**

08.5   The nucleus in **Figure 6** is not drawn to scale.

A student measures the diameter of the atom in a textbook and finds that it is 2 cm.

Estimate the diameter of the dot that would represent the nucleus if it was drawn to scale.

Explain your calculation.

Suggest a reason why your answer may not be feasible.   **[4 marks]**

09   **Figure 7** shows the plum pudding model of an atom.

Figure 7

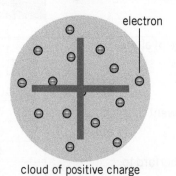

09.1   Use the diagram in **Figure 7** to describe the plum pudding model.   **[3 marks]**

09.2   Describe the model of the atom that came before the plum pudding model.   **[1 mark]**

> (!) **Exam Tip**
>
> Make sure you pick arrows that are all going in the same direction – for example, either all pointing out, or all pointing in.

> (!) **Exam Tip**
>
> There is a range of possible answers for this, so make sure you explain what you do fully.

> (!) **Exam Tip**
>
> To help you answer the next question try labelling any parts you can.

> (!) **Exam Tip**
>
> This is a great question – all the information you need to answer it is in the figure.

09.3 The plum pudding model could not explain some of the results of the alpha particle scattering experiment. Describe one of the results that the plum pudding model could **not** explain. **[2 marks]**

10 A student looks at a packet of fuse wires. They notice that the wires have different thicknesses.

10.1 Describe the action of a fuse in a circuit where an appliance is connected to the mains. **[2 marks]**

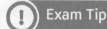

10.2 Suggest why the wires for different currents are different thicknesses. **[3 marks]**

> **! Exam Tip**
>
> Think about the symbol for a fuse and the need for a complete circuit.

10.3 **Table 5** shows some data relating to a particular fuse wire.

Table 5

Parameter	Fuse data
length	0.5 cm
cross-sectional area	$1 \times 10^{-6} \, m^2$
density	$7000 \, kg/m^3$
specific heat capacity	$230 \, J/kg \, °C$
melting point of fuse metal	$687 \, °C$
specific latent heat	$300\,000 \, J/kg$

Write down the equation that links density, mass, and volume. **[1 mark]**

10.4 Calculate the mass of the fuse wire using the data in **Table 5**. **[5 marks]**

> **! Exam Tip**
>
> This is a wire, so its going to be cylindrical in shape

10.5 Use the *Physics Equations Sheet* to calculate the energy needed to raise the temperature of the wire to its melting point, and then melt the fuse. **[5 marks]**

10.6 Write down the equation that links energy transferred, power, and time. **[1 mark]**

10.7 The resistance of the fuse wire is $1.8 \, \Omega$ and the fuse melts in about $0.5 \, s$.

Calculate the current in the wire when it melts. **[3 marks]**

Use the equation power = current^2 × resistance.

> **! Exam Tip**
>
> You also need to use the equation you wrote down in your answer to **10.6**.

11 A student finds a circuit component.

They want to make measurements to find out the relationship between the current and the potential difference for the component.

11.1 Draw a circuit diagram of the equipment that they need to make these measurements.

Label all the components in the circuit.

Use the symbol **X** for the unknown component. **[3 marks]**

> **! Exam Tip**
>
> Do not get the unknown component confused with the symbol for a bulb!

11.2 Design an experiment to find out whether or not the component is ohmic. **[4 marks]**

Exam Tip

Designing experiments is becoming more and more common in exams. Think about practicals you have done in class and base your method on one of those.

11.3 The student plots the graph shown in **Figure 8**.

Explain why you cannot use the gradient of the line to decide whether the component is ohmic. **[1 mark]**

Figure 8

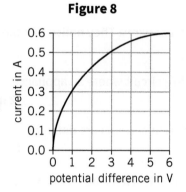

11.4 The student reverses the battery and repeats the experiment.

Sketch a graph to show what happens to the potential difference when the current is reversed. **[3 marks]**

11.5 Write down the equation that links potential difference, current, and resistance. **[1 mark]**

11.6 The resistance of the component at 2 V is 5 Ω.

Use the graph in **Figure 8** to calculate the resistance of the component at 6 V. **[2 marks]**

Exam Tip

Draw construction lines on the graph to show your working.

11.7 Determine whether the component is ohmic or non-ohmic. Explain your answer. **[2 marks]**

12 A student puts a beaker of hot water on the desk. They put a beaker of cold water next to it, as shown in **Figure 9**. The volume of water in each beaker is the same.

Figure 9

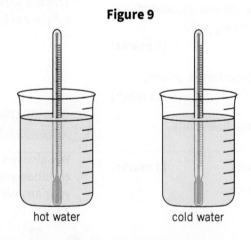

hot water   cold water

12.1 Complete the sentences below using phrases from the box.

You may need to use some phrases more than once.

| greater than   the same as   less than |

[3 marks]

The average speed of the molecules in *hot* water is _____ the average speed of molecules in *cold* water.

The total kinetic energy of the molecules in *hot* water is _____ the total kinetic energy of molecules in *cold* water.

The total potential energy of the molecules in *hot* water is _____ the total potential energy of molecules in *cold* water.

12.2 Select the correct phrase to complete this sentence.

The internal energy of the molecules in hot water is **greater than / the same as / less than** the internal energy of the molecules in cold water. **[1 mark]**

12.3 Compare the specific heat capacity of the hot water with the specific heat capacity of the cold water. **[1 mark]**

12.4 The student pours out half of the water from the beaker of hot water.

Which of the quantities (average speed, total kinetic energy, total potential energy, internal energy, or specific heat capacity) will change?

Explain your answer. **[4 marks]**

13 A liquid is heated until it boils. The temperature is measured as it is being heated.

Figure 10 shows the graph of temperature against time for the liquid.

Figure 10

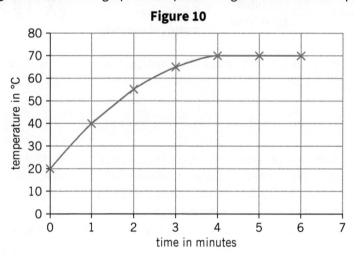

13.1 Write down the temperature of the room. **[1 mark]**

13.2 Write down the boiling point of the liquid. **[1 mark]**

13.3 Give the equation that links power, energy transferred, and time. **[1 mark]**

13.4 The power of the heater used to heat the liquid was 1 kW. The specific latent heat of vaporisation of the liquid is 365 kJ/kg. Calculate the mass of liquid that was vaporised between 4 and 6 minutes. Use an equation from the *Physics Equations Sheet*. **[5 marks]**

13.5 Suggest whether your answer to **13.4** is an overestimate or an underestimate of the actual mass of liquid that evaporated. Explain your answer. **[2 marks]**

13.6 Sketch a line on **Figure 10** to show what would happen if the power of the heater was doubled. **[3 marks]**

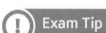

> **!** **Exam Tip**
>
> In **13.1** we can assume that the liquid started at room temperature.

> **!** **Exam Tip**
>
> You need to use more than one equation to solve **13.4**.

P18 Nuclear physics

Radioactive decay

Radioactive decay is when nuclear radiation is emitted by unstable atomic nuclei so that they become different, more stable elements. It is a *random* process in which energy is emitted by changes in the nucleus. This radiation can knock electrons out of atoms in a process called **ionisation**. Unstable nuclei can also emit neutrons.

Type of radiation	Change in the nucleus	Ionising power	Range in air	Stopped by	Decay equation
α **alpha** particle (two protons and two neutrons)	nucleus loses two protons and two neutrons	highest ionising power	travels a few centimetres in air	stopped by a sheet of paper	$^{A}_{Z}X \rightarrow ^{(A-4)}_{(Z-2)}Y + ^{4}_{2}\alpha$
β **beta** particle (fast-moving electron)	a neutron changes into a proton and an electron	high ionising power	travels $\approx 1\,m$ in air	stopped by a few millimetres of aluminium	$^{A}_{Z}X \rightarrow ^{A}_{(Z+1)}Y + ^{0}_{-1}\beta$
γ **gamma** radiation (short-wavelength, high-frequency EM radiation)	some energy is transferred away from the nucleus	low ionising power	virtually unlimited range in air	stopped by several centimetres of thick lead or metres of concrete	$^{A}_{Z}X \rightarrow ^{A}_{Z}X + ^{0}_{0}\gamma$

Chemical and physical processes, such as adding acid or heating, do not affect radioactive decay. It is impossible to predict when an atom will decay.

Activity and count rate

The **activity** of a radioactive source is the rate of decay of an unstable nucleus, measured in becquerel (Bq).

$$1\,Bq = 1\ decay\ per\ second$$

Detectors (e.g., Geiger-Muller tubes) record a **count rate** (number of decays detected per second).

$$\text{count rate after } n \text{ half-lives} = \frac{\text{initial count rate}}{2^n}$$

Half-life

With a large enough number of nuclei, it is possible to predict how many will decay in a certain amount of time. The **half-life** of a radioactive source is the average time:

- for half the number of unstable nuclei in a sample to decay
- for the count rate or activity of a source to halve.

The half-life of a source can be found from a graph of its count rate or activity against time.

To find the reduction in activity after a given number of half-lives:

1 calculate the activity after each half-life

2 subtract the final activity from the original activity.

Irradiation versus contamination

irradiation (object does not become radioactive)	when an object is exposed to nuclear radiation	cause harm through ionisation	prevented by shielding, removing, or moving away from the source of radiation
contamination (object *does* become radioactive)	when atoms of a radioactive isotope are on or in an object		object remains exposed to radiation as long as it is contaminated contamination can be very difficult to remove

Protection against irradiation and contamination

The type of radiation emitted affects the level of hazard. You can protect against irradiation and contamination by:

- maintaining a distance from the radiation source
- limiting time near the source
- shielding from the radiation.

Radiation and the human body

Living cells can be damaged or killed by ionising radiation.

The risk depends on the half-life of the source and the type of radiation.

Alpha radiation is very dangerous inside the body because it affects all of the surrounding tissue. Outside the body it only affects the skin and eyes because it cannot penetrate further.

Beta and gamma radiation are dangerous outside and inside the body because they can penetrate into tissues.

Background radiation

Background radiation is radiation that is around us all the time. It comes from:

- natural sources like rocks and cosmic rays
- devices such as X-ray machines and nuclear weapons.

Background radiation is always present but the levels are higher in some locations and in some jobs.

Uses of radioactive isotopes

Radioactive isotopes have a very wide range of half-life values.

- The most unstable nuclei have the shortest half-lives. They decay quickly and a lot of radiation is emitted in a short time.
- The least unstable nuclei have the longest half-lives. They emit little radiation each second, but emit radiation for a long time.

The use of a particular isotope will depend on the half-life and the type of radiation it emits.

- Radioactive iodine has a short half-life and is used to explore internal organs. It emits gamma radiation, which can be detected outside the body.
- Radioactive uranium has a half-life of 4500 million years and is used to find the age of igneous rocks.

Nuclear fission

Nuclear **fission** is when a large unstable nucleus absorbs an extra neutron and splits into two smaller nuclei of roughly equal size.

During nuclear fission:

- gamma radiation is emitted and energy is released
- two or three neutrons are emitted that can go on to cause a **chain reaction**
- the energy released is much greater than that released in a chemical reaction.

The chain reaction in a power station reactor is controlled by using control rods to absorb neutrons. Most reactors use uranium-235, but can also use plutonium-239.

Nuclear explosions are uncontrolled chain reactions.

Nuclear power stations produce radioactive waste that may be dangerous, and stays radioactive for a long time depending on its half-life.

The disposal of this waste has to be managed carefully. This could affect decisions about the use of nuclear power.

Nuclear fusion

Nuclear **fusion** is when two light nuclei join to make a heavier one. Very high temperatures and pressures are needed to overcome the electrostatic repulsion of the nuclei. Fusion is the process that releases energy in stars. Some of the mass is converted to energy and transferred as radiation.

 **Key Terms**

Make sure you can write a definition for these key terms.

alpha	activity	background radiation	beta	chain reaction	contamination	count rate
fission	fusion	gamma	half-life	ionisation	irradiation	radioactive decay

Learn the answers to the questions below then cover the answers column with a piece of paper and write as many as you can. Check and repeat.

P18 questions	Answers
1 What are the three types of nuclear radiation?	alpha, beta, and gamma
2 What is gamma γ radiation?	electromagnetic radiation from the nucleus
3 Which type of nuclear radiation is the most ionising?	alpha
4 What is the range in air of alpha, beta, and gamma radiation?	a few cm, 1 m, and unlimited, respectively
5 Which materials can stop alpha, beta, and gamma radiation?	sheet of paper, thin aluminium sheet, and thick lead/concrete, respectively
6 Which type of nuclear radiation does not cause a change in the structure of the nucleus when it is emitted?	gamma
7 What are the equation symbols for alpha and beta particles?	$^{4}_{2}\alpha$ and $^{0}_{-1}\beta$
8 What is radioactive activity?	the rate at which a source of unstable nuclei decays
9 What unit is used to measure the activity of a radioactive source?	becquerel (Bq)
10 What is count rate?	number of decays recorded each second (by a detector, e.g., Geiger-Muller tube)
11 What is meant by the half-life of a radioactive source?	average time taken for half the unstable nuclei to decay or the time taken for the count rate to halve
12 What is irradiation?	exposing an object to nuclear radiation
13 What is radioactive contamination?	unwanted presence of substances containing radioactive atoms on or in other materials
14 Where does background radiation come from?	rocks, cosmic rays, fallout from nuclear weapons testing, nuclear accidents
15 What is nuclear fusion?	when two light nuclei join to make a heavier one
16 How do you control a nuclear reaction?	use control rods that absorb neutrons
17 What is nuclear fission?	the splitting of a large and unstable nucleus into two smaller nuclei
18 How does nuclear fission occur?	an unstable nucleus absorbs a neutron, it splits into two smaller nuclei, and emits two or three neutrons plus gamma rays

Put paper here

Now use the questions below to check your knowledge from previous chapters.

P18

Previous questions

Answers

1	How can an object be accelerating even if it is travelling at a steady speed?		if it is changing direction
2	What is a transverse wave?		oscillations/vibrations are perpendicular (at right angles) to the direction of energy transfer
3	What is the frequency range of normal human hearing?	Put paper here	20 Hz to 20 000 Hz (20 kHz)
4	Which lens is used to correct long sight?		convex lenses
5	Describe four factors that affect the rate of evaporation of a liquid.	Put paper here	surface area, temperature difference, boiling point, air movement across surface
6	What happens to the resistance of a wire as the current increases if the temperature does not change?		it stays the same
7	How is a step-up transformer used in transmitting electricity?	Put paper here	to increase the pd from the power station to the transmission cables

Maths Skills

Practise your maths skills using the worked examples and practice questions below.

Ratios, fractions, percentages	Worked examples	Practice
A **ratio** is a way of comparing the size of two quantities. For example, a ratio of 2:4 radioactive atoms to non-radioactive atoms in a sample means for every 2 radioactive atoms, there are 4 non-radioactive atoms. A ratio can be simplified by dividing both numbers by their highest common factor. A **fraction** can be a way of expressing part of a whole number, or a way of writing one number divided by another in an equation. To find fractions from a ratio, each number in the ratio can be a numerator, and the denominator is the sum of both numbers. For example, if the ratio of apples to oranges is 2:3, the fraction of apples $= \dfrac{2}{2+3} = \dfrac{2}{5}$ A **percentage** is a number expressed as a fraction of 100. For example, $45\% = \dfrac{45}{100}$ To find one number as a percentage of another, divide the first number by the second and multiply by 100.	**1** A sample has a ratio of 8:20 radioactive atoms to non-radioactive atoms. Simplify this ratio, and find the fraction of radioactive atoms. **Answer:** Find the greatest common factor for 8 and 12 = 4. Divide both sides of the ratio by 4, which gives 2:5. Fraction of radioactive atoms: $$= \frac{2}{2+5} = \frac{2}{7}$$ **2** The resistance of a thermistor changes from 250 Ω to 175 Ω when it is heated. Calculate the percentage change in its resistance. **Answer:** Calculate the change in resistance: 250 − 175 = 75 Divide the change by the original value of the resistance and multiply by 100: $$\frac{75}{250} = 0.3 \times 100 = 30\%$$	**1** A sample has 40 radioactive atoms for every 120 non-radioactive atoms. Write this as a ratio in its simplest form. **2** In the above example, what fraction of atoms are not radioactive? **3** In the above example, what percentage of atoms are radioactive?

Practice

Exam-style questions

01 One of the uses of radioactive materials is in smoke detectors.

The isotope inside the smoke detector produces alpha radiation.

When there is smoke inside the detector, the smoke stops a current flowing in a circuit. This causes an alarm to go off.

01.1 Explain why the source needs to produce alpha radiation, and not beta or gamma radiation. **[2 marks]**

_____

_____

_____

01.2 The decay of the isotope used in the smoke detector can be shown by the equation:

$$^{241}_{95}\text{Am} \rightarrow {}^{4}_{2}\alpha + {}^{\square}_{\square}\text{Np}$$

The equation shows how an americium nucleus decays into a neptunium nucleus.

Calculate the proton or atomic number and atomic mass of the neptunium.

Show your working. **[4 marks]**

Exam Tip

The maths here may look hard but its not. Take it one line at a time.

atomic number = _____

atomic mass = _____

01.3 Explain why americium decays into a different element. **[2 marks]**

_____

_____

_____

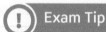
Exam Tip

Think about the one thing that all atoms and ions of an element have in common. What makes one element different from another?

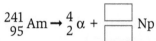
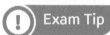
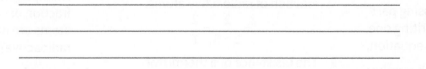

02   One atom in 10^{10} atoms of carbon is an atom of a carbon-14 isotope.

Figure 1 shows the count rate of carbon-14 against time.

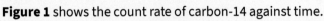

Figure 1

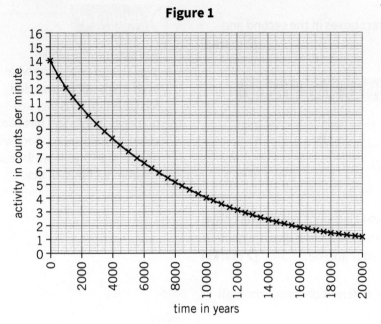

02.1   Deduce the half-life of carbon-14.   **[1 mark]**

_____

02.2   An archaeologist finds a fragment of a wooden spear. The spear contains carbon.

The fragment has an activity of 5 counts per minute.

Use **Figure 1** to deduce the age of the spear.   **[1 mark]**

_____ years

> **! Exam Tip**
>
> You can simply read the answer off **Figure 1** for both **02.1** and **02.2**.

02.3   The last ice age ended around 11 000 years ago.

Is the spear old enough to have been used during the last ice age? Give a reason for your answer.   **[2 marks]**

_____

_____

03   A teacher demonstrates how to measure the activity of a radioactive material.

03.1   Which **two** statements about activity are correct? Choose **two** answers.   **[2 marks]**

The activity of a sample is the number of particles it emits.

The activity of a sample is measured in becquerels (Bq).

The activity of a sample is the amount of radiation it emits.

The activity of a sample is the number of decays recorded per second.

> **! Exam Tip**
>
> As you read through the options
> - cross out any you know are wrong
> - put a question mark next to any you're unsure about
> - put a tick next to the ones you are confident are correct.
>
> That will only leave you a few to pick from.

03.2 Suggest a detector that the teacher could use to measure the activity. **[1 mark]**

03.3 The radiation emitted by a nucleus can

- be a particle or an electromagnetic wave
- be charged or have no charge.

Complete **Table 1** by ticking the correct boxes in the second and third columns. **[2 marks]**

Table 1

Type of radiation	Is a particle	Has no charge
alpha		
beta		
gamma		
neutron		

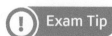

Exam Tip

You can use the marks available to determine what each mark will be awarded for. Question **03.3** has two marks available and has two columns to fill in, so there will be one mark available for each column not for each tick.

03.4 A teacher uses dice to demonstrate what happens when radioactive material decays. Suggest **one** reason why throwing dice is a good model for radioactive decay. Explain your answer. **[2 marks]**

04 Different types of radiation can travel different distances through the air.

04.1 Complete **Table 2** with the words alpha, beta, and gamma. **[2 marks]**

Table 2

Type	Range in air
	>3 m
	1 m
	<10 cm

04.2 A student says: '*There is a link between the ionising power of radiation and how far they go in air. If they do not go as far, that means that they are not as ionising.*'

Do you agree with the student? Explain your answer. **[3 marks]**

04.3 A teacher has a source that emits all three types of radiation. The activity of the source is 35 Bq. The teacher puts a sheet of aluminium between the source and the detector. The activity recorded is lower. Explain why the activity is lower, but radiation can still be detected. **[2 marks]**

05 Caesium-137, $^{137}_{55}$Cs, has a half-life of 30 years.

05.1 Determine the mass of caesium-137 that remains in a 24 g sample after 90 years. **[3 marks]**

05.2 Complete the equation for the decay of caesium-137 when it emits a beta particle. **[2 marks]**

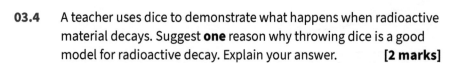

$$^{137}_{55}\text{Cs} \rightarrow ^{137}_{\square}\text{Ba} + \square$$

05.3 Another isotope is caesium-134. Caesium-134 was emitted during an explosion at the Chernobyl nuclear reactor in Ukraine. Following the explosion, caesium-134 isotopes were found in fields in Wales. Sheep were farmed in these fields. Explain why the presence of radioactive material on the grass produces a hazard for sheep.

[2 marks]

06 A teacher is modelling a chain reaction. The teacher uses long matches in a tray of sand. They arrange the matches so that when they light the first match the other matches are ignited.

> **(!) Exam Tip**
>
> Clearly indicate which points you give are the strengths and which are the limitations.

06.1 Describe how this demonstration is a model for a fission chain reaction. **[3 marks]**

06.2 Suggest **two** strengths and **two** limitations of the model. **[4 marks]**

07 **Table 3** shows the average percentage of background radiation that a person gets from different sources of background radiation.

Table 3

Source	Percentage
radon gas	48.0
rocks and soil	15.0
inside our bodies	13.0
medical X-rays and γ-rays	12.0
cosmic rays	10.0
nuclear fallout	0.8
air travel	0.4
nuclear waste	0.2
industry	0.2
luminous watches	0.1

07.1 Suggest what 'inside our bodies' might mean in terms of a source of radiation. **[1 mark]**

07.2 Describe where cosmic rays come from. **[1 mark]**

07.3 Radon emits alpha particles. Explain why the hazard from alpha particles is greater than the hazard from beta particles. **[1 mark]**

07.4 Suggest whether there is a greater risk of contamination or irradiation with radon gas. Explain your answer. **[2 marks]**

07.5 Suggest the type of graph or chart a student could plot to show the data in **Table 3**. Give reasons for your answer. **[2 marks]**

08 When a nucleus decays, the mass of the nucleus might, or might not, change.

08.1 Write down a type of radiation that does **not** change the mass of the nucleus when it is emitted. **[1 mark]**

08.2 An equation that shows the decay of bismuth-214 is

$$^{214}_{83}\text{Bi} \rightarrow ^{214}_{84}\text{Po} + \mathbf{X}$$

Name particle **X**. Give a description of this particle. **[2 marks]**

08.3 Explain why the mass of the nucleus does not change. **[2 marks]**

08.4 Describe how the decay equation shows what happens to the charge on the nucleus when particle **X** is emitted. Explain your answer. **[2 marks]**

09 Technetium isotopes are used for medical imaging. Doctors inject a patient with a very small amount of the technetium isotope, which is taken up by an organ of the body. The doctor looks at the emitted radiation on a gamma camera. **Table 4** shows three isotopes of technetium, the radiation that they emit, and their half-lives.

! **Exam Tip**

You need to consider a few things for this question.

• Which one will be safest for the patient?

• Which one will last long enough for the doctors to be able to record the results?

• Which one will not cause long-term damage?

Table 4

Name	Type of emitter	Half-life
technetium-95	gamma	61 days
technetium-99	beta	2.1×10^5 years
technetium-99m	gamma	6 hours

Suggest which isotope should be used as a tracer. Justify your answer. Suggest the consequences of using one of the other isotopes listed in **Table 4**. **[6 marks]**

10 A student collects data on the activity of a sample of radioactive material. The data is shown in **Table 5** and **Figure 2**.

Table 5

Time in s	Count rate in Bq
0	42.6
20	35.2
40	24.9
60	20.9
80	17.7
100	15.2
120	10.7
140	8.7
160	4.5
180	6.1
200	4.3
220	3.7

Figure 2

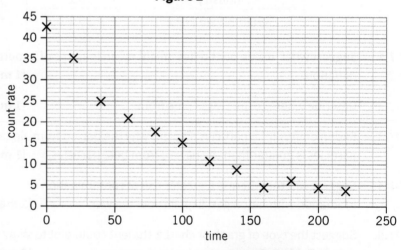

10.1 Draw a line of best fit on **Figure 2**. **[1 mark]**

10.2 Use **Figure 2** to find the half-life of the isotope. **[3 marks]**

10.3 A student says that the data is wrong because there are some points that are not on the line of best fit. Do you agree? Justify your answer. **[2 marks]**

! **Exam Tip**

A line of best fit is *not* a dot-to-dot. You do not have to include every point in your line. It should show the trend of the data. Use a ruler to see if all the points will fit on a straight line. If they don't, draw a curved line.

10.4 Identify **one** thing that the student has done incorrectly when producing **Figure 2**. Assume that all the data points are correct. **[1 mark]**

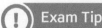

11 Strawberry fruits have microorganisms on them that cause the strawberries to decay. If the strawberries are irradiated, the radiation kills the microorganisms. Some people do not like to eat irradiated strawberries because they think that they themselves will become contaminated.

11.1 Describe the difference between contamination and irradiation in this context. **[2 marks]**

11.2 Explain why the hazard due to radiation is low when eating irradiated strawberries. **[1 mark]**

11.3 There are regulations that cover processes involving radioactive materials. The data that is used to produce the regulations comes from reports published in peer-reviewed journals. Describe the process of peer review. Explain why it is very important for regulations covering these processes to be based on peer-reviewed articles. **[3 marks]**

12 A student uses a heater to find the specific heat capacity of a liquid. The student connects the heater to an energy meter connected to a data logger. They put a temperature probe into a beaker of liquid and use the data logger to record the temperature of the liquid over time. **Table 6** shows the student's data.

Table 6

Time in s	Temperature in °C
0	25.0
16	32.5
32	39.0
48	45.5
64	54.5
80	61.0
96	69.5
112	75.0
128	84.0
144	90.5
160	97.0
176	98.5
192	98.5
208	98.5

12.1 Explain the trend shown by **Table 6** in terms of energy. **[4 marks]**

12.2 The student looks up a graph of energy transferred to the liquid against temperature of the liquid in a textbook (**Figure 3**).

Figure 3

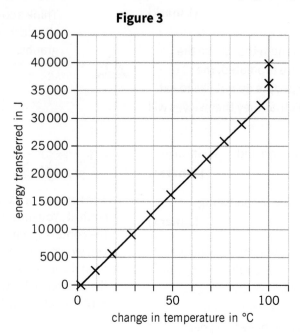

Describe the trend shown by **Figure 3**. **[2 marks]**

12.3 Use **Figure 3** to calculate the specific heat capacity of the liquid. Give your answer to **two** significant figures. Assume the mass of the liquid is 100 g. Use the correct equation from the *Physics Equations Sheet*. **[4 marks]**

> **Exam Tip**
>
> If you are unsure what equation to use, find the equation that includes what you've been asked to calculate. If you are still unsure, read through the whole question and write down all the variables you know. Remember to include any you may have calculated in an earlier question. Then look for the equation that includes these.

> **Exam Tip**
>
> Watch out for units in **12.3**.

12.4 Suggest why it is better to calculate the specific heat capacity at a change in temperature of 80 °C instead of at 50 °C. **[1 mark]**

13 A student sets up an experiment to compare the potential difference across components in series and parallel circuits. The circuit diagrams are shown in **Figure 4**.

Figure 4

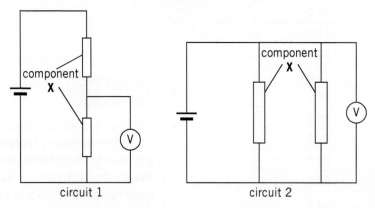

13.1 Identify component **X**. **[1 mark]**

13.2 The cell in each circuit has a potential difference of 6 V. Compare the readings on the voltmeters in the two circuits.

Explain your answer. **[4 marks]**

> **Exam Tip**
>
> You need to identify the circuit symbol.

13.3 The student replaces all of the components labelled **X** with bulbs. The bulbs are identical. Suggest what happens to the readings on the voltmeters. Explain your answer. **[2 marks]**

14 In some parts of the world there are many hours of sunshine every day. People use photovoltaic (PV) cells on their houses to generate electricity.

Figure 5 shows the PV output of 20 homes over one day and the amount of electricity used in the homes. The homes are also connected to a transmission system.

Figure 5

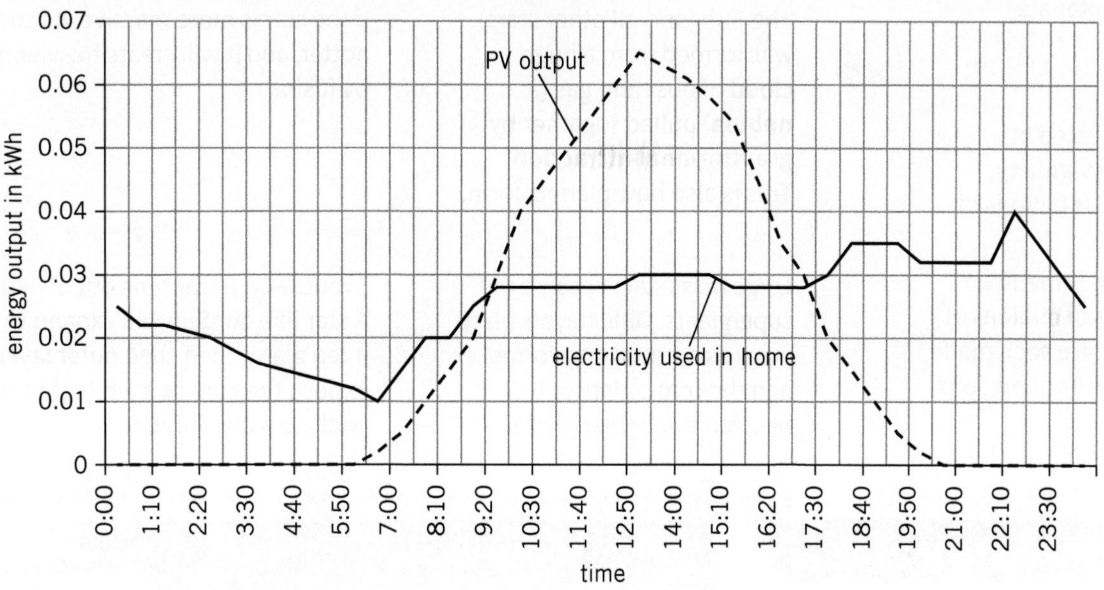

(graph: y-axis "energy output in kWh" from 0 to 0.07; x-axis "time" from 0:00 to 23:30. Dashed curve labelled "PV output"; solid curve labelled "electricity used in home")

14.1 Explain why photovoltaic cells use a renewable energy resource. **[2 marks]**

14.2 There is a difference between the output of the PV cells and the energy that is needed in the home. If the output of the PV cells is greater than needed, the homeowner can sell the electricity back to the supplier.

Identify the time period during the day when the output of the PV cells is greater than is needed by the houses. **[1 mark]**

14.3 Describe what happens when the output of the PV cells is less than the energy needed in the home. **[1 mark]**

14.4 If it is cloudy, the output of the PV cells drops below that needed to power a house.

Suggest **two** other reasons why a person might choose *not* to have PV cells on their house. **[2 marks]**

P19 Space

Our Solar System

Our **Solar System** is made up of the Sun (a star) and all the objects that orbit it, including:

- eight planets
- dwarf planets
- moons (natural **satellites**) that orbit planets
- asteroids
- comets

The Sun is located in the **Milky Way galaxy**, which contains billions of other stars.

Our **universe** is made up of thousands of millions of galaxies that are each made up of thousands of millions of stars.

Formation of stars

When the core temperature and density are high enough, fusion will start. The core is where most fusion takes place.

During the 'main sequence' period of a star's life cycle, fusion happens in the core, and energy is released as heat and light. A main sequence star is stable because the forces within it are balanced.

The Sun (and all other stars) was formed from a huge cloud of dust and gas (a **nebula**) pulled together by **gravitational attraction**. This is also how planets form.

If the star is more massive, its core will be hotter, and it will create heavier nuclei by fusion.

Large mass stars become red supergiants. Outer layers blast away as a **supernova** forms, and the core collapses to a neutron star or black hole.

Eventually, a star runs out of hydrogen. A star like our Sun will expand to become a red giant, then shed outer layers to expose the core as a white dwarf, which cools to a black dwarf.

Life cycles of stars

All stars go through changes as part of a life cycle. The life cycle of a particular star is determined by its mass.

Starting as a nebula, stars with the same mass as the Sun, and more massive than the Sun, follow specific life cycles.

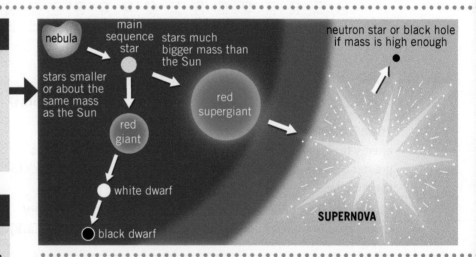

Formation of the elements

The nuclei for all the naturally occurring elements are produced by nuclear fusion in stars:

- Hydrogen nuclei are fused together to form helium nuclei.
- Other small nuclei are formed in stars with large masses.
- When a star becomes a red giant or red supergiant, helium, lithium, and other small nuclei are fused to form larger nuclei.

Elements heavier than iron require more energy to be produced, so are only produced when a massive star explodes (a supernova).

The elements produced in stars are distributed throughout the universe by massive stars going supernova.

Orbital motion and satellites

The Earth and other planets in the Solar System **orbit** the Sun.

The Moon is a natural satellite that orbits the Earth, while other planets have other moons orbiting them.

The Earth also has artificial satellites orbiting it in **geostationary** or low **polar orbits**.

When one object orbits another, the less massive (smaller) object orbits the more massive (bigger) one.

Circular orbits

The Moon and the artificial satellites around the Earth move in circular orbits, while the orbits of the planets around the Sun are almost circular.

An object moving in a circle is constantly changing direction, meaning it is constantly changing velocity (though not speed).

The object must therefore be constantly accelerating, and so have a resultant force acting on it.

This resultant force is called the **centripetal force** and is always directed towards the centre of the circular orbit, so the acceleration of the object is always directed towards the centre.

For planets and satellites, gravity provides the resultant force that maintains their circular orbits.

At any instant in time, the direction of the velocity of an object in a circular orbit is at right angles (perpendicular) to the direction of the resultant force acting on it.

Since the resultant force is at right angles to the velocity, it does not cause the object to speed up but only changes its direction.

Stable orbits

To stay in a stable orbit at a fixed distance from a larger object, the smaller object must move at a particular speed.

If the speed of an object in a stable orbit changes, the radius of the orbit must also change.

The slower the speed of an orbiting object, the bigger the radius of the circle it moves in. This is because the centripetal force due to gravity decreases as the separation of the orbiting objects increases.

Doppler effect and red shift

When a wave source (e.g., of light, sound, or microwaves) moves relative to the observer, there is a change of frequency and wavelength called the **Doppler effect**.

If the source moves:

- towards the observer, the wavelength decreases
- away from the observer, the wavelength increases.

Red shift is the name given to the effect that makes the wavelengths of light *longer* if the light source is moving away from the observer.

Scientists have observed that the wavelengths of light from most distant galaxies are longer than expected – they are red-shifted.

This suggests that these galaxies are moving away from the Earth.

The further away galaxies are, the more their light is red-shifted, suggesting distant galaxies are moving away from Earth more quickly than close galaxies.

These observations suggest that the universe (space itself) is expanding.

Since 1998, scientists have observed light from supernovae that suggests distant galaxies are moving away more and more quickly.

This indicates that the speed at which the universe is expanding is increasing.

Big Bang theory

Scientists used these observations to propose the **Big Bang theory** for the start of the universe about 14 thousand million years ago.

The Big Bang theory suggests that the universe began as an extremely small, hot, and dense object that exploded.

As well as the red shift of light from galaxies, there is other evidence to support the Big Bang theory, like the existence of cosmic microwave background radiation (CMBR) that was produced just after the Big Bang.

Key Terms

Make sure you can write a definition for these key terms.

Big Bang theory	centripetal force	Doppler effect	geostationary orbit
gravitational attraction	Milky Way galaxy	nebula	orbit	polar orbit
red shift	satellite	Solar System	supernova	universe

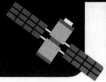
Learn the answers to the questions below then cover the answers column with a piece of paper and write as many as you can. Check and repeat.

P19 questions	Answers
1. What are the main objects in our Solar System?	Sun, (eight) planets, dwarf planets, moons, asteroids, comets
2. What kind of object is the Sun?	star
3. Which galaxy is the Solar System in?	the Milky Way
4. What do all stars start off as?	huge cloud of gas and dust
5. Which force is responsible for forming stars and planets?	gravity
6. What kind of reaction causes the expansion of a star?	nuclear fusion
7. How does a main sequence star remain stable?	fusion reactions produce outwards forces which balance the gravitational forces pulling it inwards
8. What determines the life cycle of a star?	mass
9. What is the life cycle of a star with about the same mass as the Sun?	dust and gas → main sequence star → red giant → white dwarf → black dwarf
10. What is the life cycle of a star with much more mass than the Sun?	dust and gas → main sequence star → red supergiant → supernova → neutron star or black hole (if mass is big enough)
11. How are naturally occurring elements formed?	from nuclear fusion during the life cycle of stars
12. Which elements are only produced in a supernova?	elements heavier than iron
13. How are the elements distributed throughout the universe?	massive stars going supernova (exploding)
14. How does the force of gravity make objects in orbit change their velocity but not their speed?	gravity provides a centripetal force which keeps orbiting objects moving in a circle – they are constantly changing direction
15. To change the speed of an object in stable orbit, what factor must change?	radius of the orbit
16. What is red shift?	wavelengths of light get longer if the light source is moving away from the observer
17. What evidence suggests that the universe is expanding?	light from more distant galaxies is more red-shifted, so more distant galaxies are moving away more quickly
18. What is the name of the scientific theory for the origin of the universe that suggests it started off as an extremely small, hot, and dense region?	the Big Bang theory

(Put paper here)

Now use the questions below to check your knowledge from previous chapters.

P19

Previous questions | Answers

	Previous questions	Answers
1	What is happening to an object if it has a negative acceleration?	it is slowing down
2	Which distance is proportional to the speed of the vehicle?	thinking distance
3	When is diffraction noticeable?	when the wavelength is about the same size as the gap size
4	Describe three factors that affect the rate of transfer of energy.	surface to volume ratio, type of material, type of surface
5	What are the main features of a parallel circuit?	pd across each branch is the same; current splits between branches; total resistance of all resistors is less than the resistance of the smallest individual resistor

Put paper here

 Maths Skills

Practise your maths skills using the worked examples and practice questions below.

Standard form	Worked examples	Practice
Standard form is a convenient way of writing very large or very small numbers. Numbers written in standard form must take the form: $A \times 10^n$ 'A' is a decimal number between 1 and 10 (but not including 10). 'n' is a whole number and can be positive or negative. If n is positive, the number is greater than one. If n is negative, the number is less than one. For large numbers, the n is positive, and the decimal point is shifted to the left: $48\,000\,000 = 4.8 \times 10^7$ For small numbers, the n is negative, and the decimal point is shifted to the right: $0.000\,000\,48 = 4.8 \times 10^{-7}$ To convert numbers *from* standard form, move the decimal point back to the right for a positive n, and back to the left for a negative n.	1 The diameter of an atom is $0.000\,000\,000\,1$ m. Express this in standard form. **Answer:** As this is a small number, move the decimal point 10 places to the right to give a number between 1 and 10. 1.0×10^{-10} m 2 The frequency of some radio waves is $2\,750\,000\,000$ Hz. Express this in standard form. **Answer:** This is a big number, so move the decimal point 9 places to the left. 2.75×10^9 m	1 The wavelength of red light is around 7.0×10^{-7} m. Write this as a decimal number. 2 The distance from the Earth to the Sun is $150\,000\,000\,000$ m. Write this in standard form. 3 The estimated age of the universe is 4.32×10^{17} seconds. Write this as a decimal number.

Exam-style questions

01   In August 2006, the International Astronomical Society changed the status of Pluto from planet to dwarf planet.

01.1   Complete the following statements using the words below. You may need to use the words once, more than once, or not at all.   **[6 marks]**

Milky Way	moons	Sun	satellite
gravity	planets	Andromeda	centripetal

Both planets and dwarf planets orbit the _____.

Natural satellites, which are called _____, and

artificial satellites orbit planets.

All _____ and _____ are in

orbit because of the force of _____.

This force is an example of a _____ force.

> **Exam Tip**
>
> Read the instructions carefully: 'You may need to use the words once, more than once, or not at all.' Don't panic if there is a word you haven't used.

01.2   Give **one** similarity and **one** difference between a planet and a moon.   **[2 marks]**

Similarity: _____

_____

Difference: _____

_____

> **Exam Tip**
>
> There are lots of different types of planet, so be careful with your answer. Your answer must refer to all planets.

01.3   Give **two** similarities between an artificial and a natural satellite.   **[2 marks]**

1 _____

_____

2 _____

_____

01.4   Give the name of the galaxy that the Sun and Earth are part of.   **[1 mark]**

_____

02   An astronomer makes an observation of the spectrum of light from a distant galaxy.

The galaxy is moving away from the Earth.

They compare the lines in the spectrum with the lines due to the same element produced in the Sun.

The line spectra are shown in **Figure 1**.

Figure 1

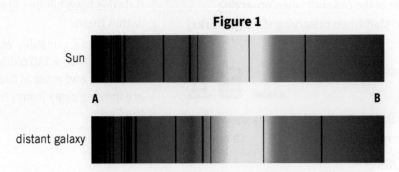

Sun

A   B

distant galaxy

02.1 Write down which end of the spectrum, **A** or **B**, has the longer wavelength.

Explain your reasoning. **[2 marks]**

_____

_____

_____

02.2 Describe the link between the position of the lines in the spectra and the speed of the galaxy. **[1 mark]**

_____

_____

02.3 Describe what the astronomer would observe if the galaxy was moving away at a smaller speed. **[1 mark]**

_____

_____

02.4 The astronomer observes that a star is inside our galaxy. The star is moving towards our Solar System.

Describe what the astronomer would observe in terms of the spectrum. **[1 mark]**

_____

_____

03 A teacher is explaining how astronomers work out the speed at which galaxies are moving away from our galaxy. The students watch a video showing how the pitch of a sound changes as the source of the sound moves away. The sound gets lower in pitch. The teacher explains how this is analogous to light being red-shifted.

03.1 Name the effect that produces the change in pitch. **[1 mark]**

03.2 Explain the link between the change in pitch and the change in colour. **[2 marks]**

> ⓘ **Exam Tip**
>
> You can still use data from the figure, even though there are no numbers given.

> ⓘ **Exam Tip**
>
> Stars that are moving towards us are blue-shifted. This is similar to red shift but in the other direction.

03.3 Scientists have worked out that most galaxies are red-shifted, but stars within our galaxy can be red or blue-shifted. Suggest why there is a difference between the origin of the red shift when observing galaxies and the origin of the red shift when observing stars. **[2 marks]**

04 A bar in a ripple tank makes ripples on the surface of the water.

04.1 Describe the motion of the bar that produces the ripples shown in **Figure 2**. Explain why the wave is transverse. **[2 marks]**

Figure 2

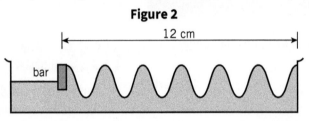

04.2 Write down the number of waves in the 12 cm shown in **Figure 2**. Use your answer to calculate the wavelength of the waves. **[2 marks]**

04.3 Write down the other quantity that a student needs to measure in order to use the wave equation to calculate the speed of the waves. **[1 mark]**

04.4 Suggest how you could make a precise measurement of this quantity. **[2 marks]**

05 Every star, including the Sun, has a life cycle. Here is the life cycle of Betelgeuse, a red supergiant.

dust and gas → main sequence → red supergiant → **X**

05.1 Circle the correct word or phrase in bold in the sentences below. **[2 marks]**

Betelgeuse is **about the same mass as / bigger than** the Sun
The word for **X** should be **star / supernova**.

05.2 Give the name of the process that produces the energy to make a star shine. **[1 mark]**

05.3 The human body is made up of many different elements. Some people say: '*Everyone is made of stardust*'. Suggest how the elements that were formed in supernovae ended up on Earth. **[2 marks]**

06 Astronomers have discovered thousands of exoplanets. An exoplanet orbits a star that is not the Sun. One system of exoplanets is the Upsilon Andromedae system.

06.1 The planet Saffar has an orbit that is a circle. Describe the direction of the force on Saffar in relation to its motion. **[1 mark]**

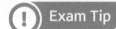

Exam Tip

Galaxies have billions of stars within them.

For example, our Milky Way has 250 billion ± 150 billion stars in it, and most of them are moving away from the Earth.

 Exam Tip

Instead of measuring the wavelength of one wave, it is better to count the waves in a set distance and divide this distance by the number of waves.

This reduces errors from any variability in the waves.

Exam Tip

The size of a star determines which life cycle it will follow – small and giant stars have different life cycles.

06.2 The data for the Solar System is shown in **Table 1**.

Table 1

Name of planet	Distance from star to planet in million km	Time for one orbit in days
Saffar	8.91	4.62
Samh	124.35	241.00
Majriti	379.50	1276.00
Planet E	787.50	3848.00

Plot a graph of the time for one orbit against distance on **Figure 3**.

[2 marks]

Figure 3

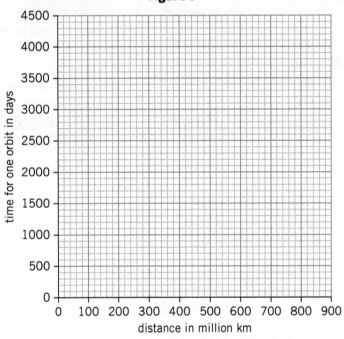

06.3 Astronomers discover a new exoplanet that is at a distance of 200 million km from the star. Use **Figure 3** to estimate the expected time for one orbit of this exoplanet. Give the unit with your answer.

[2 marks]

06.4 All the planets are in stable orbits. The radius of the orbit of Planet E is approximately twice that of Majriti. Use ratios, and the equation that links speed, distance, and time, to show that the speed of Planet E is about $\frac{2}{3}$ that of Majriti. **[3 marks]**

07 Scientists use the Big Bang theory to explain why the universe is expanding.

07.1 Describe what the Big Bang theory says about the beginning of the universe. **[3 marks]**

07.2 Hubble found that galaxies that were further away had a larger recessional speed (the speed at which they were moving away). Explain how this provided evidence for the Big Bang theory. **[1 mark]**

> ! **Exam Tip**
>
> Don't worry if you've never heard of these stars before.
> This is testing if you can apply what you've learnt in class to a new context.

> ! **Exam Tip**
>
> Always plot graph points as crosses, and include a line of best fit.

> ! **Exam Tip**
>
> Draw construction lines on your graph to show your working.

07.3 Hubble also predicted that the recessional speed was proportional to their distance. Astronomers have now found that very distant galaxies are moving faster than expected. Sketch a graph to show how the speed of galaxies varies with distance if the speed of recession is proportional to the distance (label the line **P**). The gradient of the graph of velocity against distance is known as the Hubble constant. Explain why the units of the Hubble constant are 1/time. Add a line to your graph to show what happens if the speed of recession is increasing with distance (label the line **I**). **[6 marks]**

08 Our Sun is in a phase of its life cycle that will last for another 5 billion years.

08.1 Explain how the Sun formed and why it is now in a state of equilibrium. **[6 marks]**

08.2 A black hole is an object so dense that to escape from it requires a velocity greater than the velocity of light. Our Sun will not become a black hole. Compare the end of the life cycle of a star with a similar mass to the Sun with that of a larger mass star.

[6 marks]

09 The Earth is made of a mixture of elements. The atmosphere is 78% nitrogen and the crust is 62% oxygen. Until the 1920s, astronomers thought the chemical composition of stars was the same as that of the Earth. In 1925, an astronomer called Cecilia Payne concluded from her research into the atmosphere of stars that stars were mainly composed of hydrogen with some helium.

09.1 Her conclusion was not accepted at the time. Suggest a reason why. **[1 mark]**

09.2 Some years later, her conclusion was accepted. Suggest a reason for this change. **[1 mark]**

09.3 The process of fusion happens in stars. Complete the equation for the fusion of hydrogen. **[2 marks]**

$$^{3}_{1}\text{H} + {}^{2}_{1}\text{H} \rightarrow {}^{\square}_{\square}\text{He} + {}^{1}_{0}\text{n}$$

09.4 The following elements are also produced by the process of fusion in stars:

$$^{4}_{8}\text{Be} \qquad\qquad {}^{12}_{8}\text{C}$$

Use the reaction in **09.3** to suggest how $^{8}_{4}\text{Be}$ and $^{12}_{6}\text{C}$ are formed in stars. **[2 marks]**

09.5 It becomes increasingly difficult to fuse elements as they get more massive. Suggest why this is. **[3 marks]**

09.6 Name the element with the largest mass that is produced by the fusion process in stars. **[1 mark]**

10   A student models a satellite in an orbit by swinging a rubber bung in a horizontal circle, as shown in **Figure 4**. A piece of string connects the bung to some small slotted masses.

Figure 4

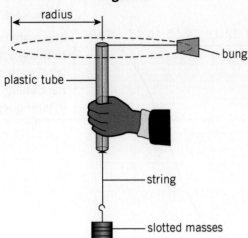

10.1   Write down the object in **Figure 4** that is analogous to the satellite.
[1 mark]

10.2   Write down what is analogous to the force of gravity acting on the satellite.
[1 mark]

10.3   The student measures the speed of the bung at different lengths of string for the same number of slotted masses. Describe **two** sources of uncertainty in the measurements.
[2 marks]

10.4   Describe the relationship between the radius of the circular path and the speed of the bung.
[1 mark]

10.5   Suggest another force that may act on a satellite to alter the speed of its orbit.
[1 mark]

11   Astronomers measure the red shift of two galaxies. Galaxy **A** is further away than galaxy **B**.

11.1   Write down the letters of the true statements.   [2 marks]
   W: The red shift of galaxies is evidence for the Big Bang theory.
   X: Galaxy **A** has a bigger red shift than galaxy **B**.
   Y: Galaxy **B** is moving faster than galaxy **A**.
   Z: The space between the galaxies is expanding.

11.2   A student is modelling red shift. The student draws a wave on a piece of elastic. Suggest how they can use the elastic to show how light is red-shifted. Explain what the model shows.
[2 marks]

11.3   The model described in **11.2** is an example of a physical model. Give **two** reasons why scientists use models.
[2 marks]

> **Exam Tip**
>
> This is asking which part of the model in **Figure 4** is acting as the satellite.

> **Exam Tip**
>
> Think of all the different things that need to be controlled and how difficult it would be to control them.

> **Exam Tip**
>
> The number of marks can give you a clue to the number of true statements.

12 A student uses an application on their phone to measure displacement while they are using a lift. The phone detects the upwards direction as a positive value. The graph produced by the phone is shown in **Figure 5.**

Exam Tip

There are three main sections to this graph. Divide it up and label each section with what is happening – this will help you in later questions.

Figure 5

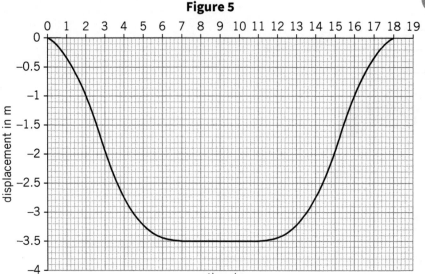

12.1 Describe the motion of the lift between 0 s and 4 s. **[3 marks]**

12.2 Describe the motion of the lift between 7 s and 10 s. **[1 mark]**

12.3 Calculate the velocity of the lift at 5 s. Show how you worked out your answer. **[3 marks]**

12.4 Sketch a velocity–time graph for the lift. **[4 marks]**

Exam Tip

Draw lines on your graph to help with the working out, and write down which equation you use.

13 A trampoline is made of a rubber sheet attached to a frame by springs.

Each spring stretches by 0.01 m when a person stands on the trampoline.

The spring constant of each spring is 500 N/m.

13.1 Calculate the energy stored in the spring. Use the correct equation from the *Physics Equations Sheet*. **[2 marks]**

13.2 A student bounces on the trampoline.

On the first bounce they reach a height of 2 m above the trampoline.

On the second bounce they reach a height of 1.5 m.

Describe the energy types at the top of the first bounce and at the top of the second bounce.

Use your description to explain why the second bounce is lower than the first. **[3 marks]**

Exam Tip

Think about wasted energy when answering this question.

13.3 Describe **two** processes by which the energy is transferred in **13.2**. **[2 marks]**

14 A student is investigating what happens when a moving trolley collides with a stationary trolley and they stick together. They change the mass of the moving trolley and measure the velocity of the combined trolleys after the collision.

14.1 Identify the independent and dependent variables in this investigation. **[2 marks]**

14.2 Identify **two** control variables. **[2 marks]**

14.3 The student collects the data shown in **Table 2**.

Table 2

Mass of moving trolley in g	Combined final velocity in m/s			
	Repeat 1	Repeat 2	Repeat 3	Mean
100	0.50	0.80	0.60	0.63
200	0.90	1.10	1.20	1.07
300	1.20	1.30	1.30	1.27
400	1.34	1.35	1.34	1.34
500	1.41	1.43	1.43	1.42

Use **Table 2** to determine the uncertainty in the measurements of combined final velocity. Explain your method. **[2 marks]**

14.4 Plot a graph of the data on the axes in **Figure 6**. Suggest whether or not the line of best fit should go through (0, 0). Explain your answer. **[4 marks]**

Figure 6

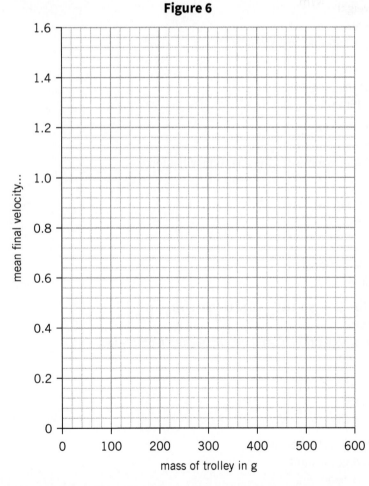

14.5 The mass of a stationary trolley is 200 g. The initial velocity of the moving trolley is 2.0 m/s. Use the principle of conservation of momentum to calculate the predicted final velocity for the combined trolleys if the moving trolley has a mass of 100 g. Calculate the percentage error between the predicted and the measured value. Give your answer to an appropriate number of significant figures. **[6 marks]**

You will be provided with a *Physics Equations Sheet* that contains the following equations.
You should be able to select and apply the correct equation to answer the question.

$v = \dfrac{s}{t}$	v	velocity
	s	displacement
	t	time
$a = \dfrac{\Delta v}{t}$	a	acceleration
	Δv	change in velocity
	t	time taken
$F = m \times a$	F	force
	m	mass
	a	acceleration
$p = m \times v$	p	momentum
	m	mass
	v	velocity
$F = \dfrac{\Delta p}{t}$	F	force
	Δp	change in momentum
	t	time
$W = m \times g$	W	weight
	m	mass
	g	gravitational field strength
$F = k \times e$	F	force
	k	spring constant
	e	extension
$W = F \times d$	W	work done
	F	force
	d	distance moved in the direction of the force
$P = \dfrac{W}{t}$	P	power
	W	work done
	t	time
$P = \dfrac{E}{t}$	P	power
	E	energy transferred
	t	time
$E_p = m \times g \times h$	E_p	change in gravitational potential energy
	m	mass
	g	gravitational field strength (acceleration of free fall)
	h	height
$E_k = \dfrac{1}{2} \times m \times v^2$	E_k	kinetic energy
	m	mass
	v	velocity
$E_e = \dfrac{1}{2} \times k \times e^2$	E_e	elastic potential energy
	k	spring constant
	e	extension
$M = F \times d$	M	moment of the force
	F	force
	d	perpendicular distance from the line of action of the force to the pivot

$v = f \times \lambda$	v	speed
	f	frequency
	λ	wavelength
$n = \dfrac{\sin i}{\sin r}$	n	refractive index
	i	angle of incidence
	r	angle of refraction
$n = \dfrac{1}{\sin c}$	n	refractive index
	c	critical angle
$\text{magnification} = \dfrac{\text{image height}}{\text{object height}}$		
$E = m \times c \times \Delta\theta$	E	energy
	m	mass
	c	specific heat capacity
	$\Delta\theta$	temperature change
$E = m \times L_V$	E	energy
	m	mass
	L_V	specific latent heat of vaporisation
$E = m \times L_F$	E	energy
	m	mass
	L_F	specific latent heat of fusion
$\text{efficiency} = \dfrac{\text{useful energy out}}{\text{total energy in}} \; (\times 100\%)$		
$\text{efficiency} = \dfrac{\text{useful power out}}{\text{total power in}} \; (\times 100\%)$		
$I = \dfrac{Q}{t}$	I	current
	Q	charge flow
	t	time
$V = \dfrac{E}{Q}$	V	potential difference
	E	energy transferred
	Q	charge
$V = I \times R$	V	potential difference
	I	current
	R	resistance
$P = I \times V$	P	power
	I	current
	V	potential difference
$E(\text{kWh}) = P(\text{kW}) \times t(\text{h})$	E	energy transferred
	P	power
	t	time
$\dfrac{V_p}{V_s} = \dfrac{n_p}{n_s}$	V_p	potential difference across the primary coil
	V_s	potential difference across the secondary coil
	n_p	number of turns on the primary coil
	n_s	number of turns on the secondary coil
$V_p \times I_p = V_s \times I_s$	V_p	potential difference across the primary coil
	I_p	current in the primary coil
	V_s	potential difference across the secondary coil
	I_s	current in the secondary coil

Great Clarendon Street, Oxford, OX2 6DP, United Kingdom

Oxford University Press is a department of the University of Oxford.
It furthers the University's objective of excellence in research, scholarship, and education by publishing worldwide. Oxford is a registered trade mark of Oxford University Press in the UK and in certain other countries.

British Library Cataloguing in Publication Data

Data available

978-1-38-203384-8

10 9 8 7 6 5 4

Paper used in the production of this book is a natural, recyclable product made from wood grown in sustainable forests.

The manufacturing process conforms to the environmental regulations of the country of origin.

Printed and bound by CPI Group (UK) Ltd, Croydon, CR0 4YY

Acknowledgements

The publisher and authors would like to thank the following for permission to use photographs and other copyright material:

Cover: David Parker / Science Photo Library

Photos: Photos: p44(l): Eline Oostingh/Shutterstock; p44(r): LaNataly/Shutterstock; p55: Charlesimage/Shutterstock; p110(t): MXW Stock/Shutterstock; p110(b): Sansanorth/Shutterstock; p129: Jerry Lin/Shutterstock.

Artwork by Q2A Media, Edward Fullick, Tech-Set Ltd, GreenGate Publishing Services, IFA Design, Clive Goodyer, Jeff Bowles, Roger Courthold, Mike Ogden, Jeff Edwards, Russell Walker, Jamie Sneddon, Tech Graphics, Integra Software Services, Erwin Haya, Phoenix Photosetting, Six Red Marbles, Oxford Designers and Illustrators Ltd, Wearset Ltd, HL Studios, Peter Bull Art Studio, James Stayte, Trystan Mitchell, Thomson Digital, Pantek Arts Ltd, David Russell Illustration, and Oxford University Press.

Every effort has been made to contact copyright holders of material reproduced in this book. Any omissions will be rectified in subsequent printings if notice is given to the publisher.